Young People's Literature in Series:

Publishers' and Non-Fiction Series

Young People's Literature in Series: Publishers' and Non-Fiction Series

An Annotated Bibliographical Guide

JUDITH K. ROSENBERG

&

KENYON C. ROSENBERG

1973

Libraries Unlimited, Inc.

Littleton, Colo.

Library of Congress Card Number 73-75237
International Standard Book Number 0-87287-058-8

LIBRARIES UNLIMITED, INC.
P.O. Box 263
Littleton, Colorado 80120

TABLE OF CONTENTS

INTRODUCTION

Young People's Literature in Series is designed to help identify the various titles published in series for young people and to provide descriptive and evaluative information about each series. The first volume of this bibliography, *Young People's Literature in Series: Fiction* (1972), listed and described books published in fiction series. This second volume covers publishers' and non-fiction series.

No other work specifically lists, let alone evaluates, juvenile series titles. Gardner's *Sequels* (London, Library Association, Association of Assistant Librarians, 1955 and 1967) restricts itself to fiction series published in England and provides no annotations at all. The *Children's Catalog* only evaluates individual titles of a series, but does not attempt to list (in an associative manner) series, fiction or non-fiction, in their entirety. Baer's *Titles in Series* (Scarecrow, 1964 and 1971) lists only adult non-fiction titles and does not annotate them.

In her review of the *Fiction* volume of this bibliography (*School Library Journal*, April 15, 1973, p. 1366), Lillian N. Gerhardt expressed the hope that the authors would "go to work in the same way on the maddening, always multiplying nonfiction juvenile titles in series." It is rare that a reviewer's wishes coincide so well with the authors' plans.

For the purposes of this bibliography, a publisher's series is a series of books (either fiction or non-fiction) prepared by more than one author, but having a common format and a basic theme. The Macmillan Classics and the Putnam Sports Shelf are examples of publishers' series. The volumes of non-fiction series also have a common theme and format, but they are authored by a single person. Clarence Hylander's Young Naturalist series and Shirley Glubok's The Art of . . . series are typical non-fiction series. Coverage in this volume is intended to include all in-print series designed for grades 3 to 12 published through 1972. Although out-of-print titles from fiction series will often be periodically resurrected, non-fiction generally remains unavailable when out of print, because the material becomes dated. Series with appeal to reluctant readers—regardless of their reading level—have been included, with appropriate mention of their special interest in the annotation.

The bibliography aims to list all individual volumes of a given series, thus providing substantial assistance to anyone who attempts to locate the sometimes elusive companion volumes to books of proven worth or popularity. In addition, the bibliography will be useful as an aid in book selection because of the extensive listing of titles in each series and because of the annotations for each series. The annotations are based primarily on format, durability, reading level, and the inclusion of illustrations, indices, and bibliographies. Overall writing style of the series is noted, when possible, but the number of authors and titles involved in each publisher's series makes it difficult to assess the quality of individual books in the space available for annotations.

Arrangement is alphabetical by series title or, in the case of untitled author series, by author. Individual titles within each series are arranged first by author, then by title. Entries are numbered consecutively through the two volumes: *Fiction* contains 1,428 entries, and the present volume lists a total of 6,023 non-fiction and publishers' series (7,451 numbered entries in the two volumes).

In several instances there are books that are common to both fiction and publishers' series; these books are provided with "See" references to the *Fiction* volume. All entries are indexed by author and by title.

An attempt was made to include all existing material, but in view of the proliferation of series today, omissions are unavoidable. The authors would greatly appreciate notice of any omission or error for correction in future editions.

The authors wish to thank most heartily Betty Campbell, Roberta Fannin, Anna Myers, Linda Bordenkircher, Irene Radabaugh, Marge Furrer, Janet Stavole, and Kathy Wallis for their hard-working assistance. Finally, the aid and encouragement of Lorna S. Rosenberg, Victoria L. Rosenberg, and John A. Campbell, Jr., were invaluable in the preparation of this work.

J. K. R.

K. C. R.

ABELARD SPORTS BOOKS
  Rydell, Wendell
    1429. Baseball (1971)
    1430. Basketball (1971)
    1431. Football (1971)
    1432. Hockey (1971)
The first part of these books deals with the rules of the game, with some pointers as
to how it is played, and some vocabulary. The second half deals with the history of
the sport including biographies of some outstanding players. There are plenty of photographs, but this series seems to be a repetition of many others of the same genre.

ABOUT . . . —Childrens Press
  Allison, Dorothy
    1433. About Helpful Helicopters (1954)
  Baker, Eugene
    1434. About a Bicycle for Linda (1968)
  Carlisle, Madelyn
    1435. About Satellites (1971)
  Carlisle, Madelyn, and Norman Carlisle
    1436. About Roads (1965)
    1437. About Submarines (1969)
  Chace, Haile
    1438. About the Captain of a Ship (1959)
    1439. About the Pilot of a Plane (1959)
  Dean, Anabel
    1440. About Paper (1968)
  Dickey, Albert
    1441. About Rivers (1959)
  Dickson, Naida
    1442. About Doctors of Long Ago (1972)
  Dillon, Ina
    1443. About Policemen (1957)
  Dobrin, Norma
    1444. About Foresters (1962)
  Eggleston, Joyce
    1445. About Things That Grow (1958)
  Friskey, Margaret
    1446. About Measurement (1965)
  Gibson, Gertrude
    1447. About Garden Dwellers (1958)
    1448. About Insects That Help Plants (1963)
    1449. About Our Weather (1960)
  Harmer, Mabel
    1450. About Penguins and Other Arctic Animals (1964)
  Hastings, Evelyn
    1451. About All Kinds of Days (1955)
    1452. About Postmen (1967)
  Hoffman, Elaine, and Jane Hefflinger
    1453. About Family Helpers (1967)
    1454. About Firemen (1957)
    1455. About Friendly Helpers Around Town (1967)
    1456. About Friendly Helpers for Health and Safety (1967)
    1457. About Helpers Who Work at Night (1963)
    1458. About School Helpers (1955)

ABOUT ... —Childrens Press (cont'd)
      Hudson, Selma
          1459. About Spices (1971)
      Johnson, Irma
          1460. About Truck Farming (1962)
      Johnson, Siddie
          1461. About the Engineer of a Train (1959)
      Jubelier, Ruth
          1462. About Jack's Dental Checkup (1959)
          1463. About Jill's Checkup (1957)
      Kramer, Bettina
          1464. About Cavemen of the Old Stone Age (1955)
      Landin, Les
          1465. About Atoms for Junior (1961)
          1466. About Cowboys Around the World (1963)
          1467. About Policemen Around the World (1964)
      McGrath, Thomas
          1468. About Clouds (1959)
      Marx, Richard
          1469. About Mexico's Children (1959)
      Newman, Shirlee
          1470. About the People Who Run Your City (1963)
      Payton, Evelyn
          1471. About Farm Helpers (1967)
      Radlauer, Ruth
          1472. About Four Seasons and Five Senses (1960)
          1473. About Men at Work (1958)
      Reck, Alma, and Helen Fichter
          1474. About Some Holidays and Special Days (1968)
      Roberts, Hortense
          1475. About Insects—Indoors and Out (1957)
      Russell, Solveig
          1476. About Bananas (1968)
          1477. About Cheese (1972)
          1478. About Fruit (1962)
          1479. About Nuts (1963)
          1480. About Saving Wild Life for Tomorrow (1960)
      Shannon, Terry
          1481. About Caves (1960)
          1482. About Food and Where It Comes From (1961)
          1483. About Ready-to-Wear Clothes (1961)
          1484. About the Land, the Rain and Us (1963)
      Sherman, Diane, and Shirlee Newman
          1485. About Canals (1969)
      Simpson, Wilma
          1486. About News and How It Travels (1960)
      Simpson, Wilma, and John Simpson
          1487. About Pioneers: Yesterday, Today and Tomorrow (1963)
      Telfer, Dorothy
          1488. About Salt (1965)
          1489. About That Amazing Portland Cement (1971)
      Thompson, Frances
          1490. About Jerry and Jimmy and the Pharmacist (1964)
          1491. About Miss Sue, the Nurse (1961)

ABOUT . . . —Childrens Press (cont'd)
>   Uhl, Melvin
>   1492. About Cargo Ships (1962)
>   1493. About Eggs and the Creatures That Hatch from Them (1966)
>   Wormser, Sophie
>   1494. About Silkworms and Silk (1961)
>   Ziner, Feenie
>   1495. About Wonderful Wheels (1959)
This series on a large variety of subjects is an introduction to various aspects of life for
the child beginning to read. The print is large, the books are small; thus, while the
appeal would be to the primary reader, these books could also be used with reluctant readers. A good bet for those in grades 2 to 4 who need basic material.

ADRIAN NATURE MYSTERIES —Hastings House
>   Adrian, Mary
>   1496. Fox Hollow Mystery (1963)
>   1497. Ghost Town Mystery (1970)
>   1498. Indian Horse Mystery (1966)
>   1499. Kite Mystery (1968)
>   1500. Lightship Mystery (1969)
>   1501. Mystery of the Dinosaur Bones (1965)
>   1502. Mystery of the Night Explorers (1962)
>   1503. Rare Stamp Mystery (1960)
>   1504. Skin Diving Mystery (1964)
Strictly speaking, this is a fiction series, but because there are no continuing characters from book to book, it has been included with publishers' and non-fiction series.
The Adrian Mysteries have an easy-to-read format with line drawings. Plots are fast-
moving and have the added attraction of considerable information on various aspects
of natural history. Very good for reluctant readers. For grades 3 to 5.

ADVENTURES IN EYEWITNESS HISTORY —Walck
>   Hoff, Rhona
>   1505. Africa: Adventures in Eyewitness History (1963)
>   1506. America: Adventures in Eyewitness History (1962)
>   1507. America's Immigrants: Adventures in Eyewitness History (1967)
>   1508. China: Adventures in Eyewitness History (1965)
>   1509. Russia: Adventures in Eyewitness History (1964)
These books contain excerpts from letters and documents written by people during
the times portrayed. The documents have been chosen to give varying opinions on
the historical events covered. First-rate supplementary material for any history or
social science course. There is a bibliography, but no index, which may prove to be
a handicap to some. However, the table of contents may be sufficient.

ADVENTURES IN NATURE AND SCIENCE —Childrens Press
>   Anderson, William
>   1510. The Atomic Submarine (1968)
>   Bonstell, Chesley
>   1511. Rocket to the Moon (1968)
>   1512. Solar System (1968)
>   Colbert, Edwin
>   1513. Digging for Dinosaurs (1967)
>   Klots, Alexander
>   1514. Tropical Butterflies (1968)

ADVENTURES IN NATURE AND SCIENCE   —Childrens Press   (cont'd)
    Larson, Peggy
       1515. Life in the Desert (1967)
    Ross, Edward
       1516. Ants (1967)
       1517. Camouflage in Nature (1968)
    Saunders, John
       1518. Young Animals (1967)
    Sloan, Tay
       1519. Under the Microscope (1968)
       1520. Wonders of the Pacific Shore (1968)
    Teale, Edwin
       1521. Bees (1967)
    Verite, Marcelle
       1522. Animals of the Sea (1968)
This series may serve to increase children's interest in nature. There are plenty of illustrations, most of which are in color. The drawings are true-to-life and the text, while not terribly detailed, is accurate. There is generally a bibliography, always an index, and sometimes a list of places to visit where the reader can see some of the things discussed.

ALL ABOUT . . .   —Random House
    Andrews, Roy Chapman
       1523. All About Dinosaurs (1953)
       1524. All About Strange Beasts of the Past (1956)
       1525. All About Whales (1954)
    Brindze, Ruth
       1526. All About Courts and Law (1964)
       1527. All About Sailing the Seven Seas (1962)
       1528. All About Undersea Exploration (1960)
    Burger, Carl
       1529. All About Cats (1966)
       1530. All About Dogs (1962)
       1531. All About Elephants (1965)
       1532. All About Fish (1960)
    Castillo, Edmund
       1533. All About the U.S. Navy (1961)
    Commins, Dorothy
       1534. All About the Symphony Orchestra (1961)
    Dietz, David
       1535. All About Great Medical Discoveries (1960)
       1536. All About Satellites and Space Ships (1958)
       1537. All About the Universe (1965)
    Epstein, Samuel, and Beryl Epstein
       1538. All About Engines and Power (1962)
       1539. All About Prehistoric Cave Men (1959)
       1540. All About the Desert (1957)
    Freeman, Ira
       1541. All About Electricity (1957)
       1542. All About Light and Radiation (1965)
       1543. All About the Atom (1955)
       1544. All About the Wonders of Chemistry (1954)
    Glemser, Bernard
       1545. All About Biology (1964)

ALL ABOUT . . . —Random House (cont'd)
    1546. All About the Human Body (1958)
Goldenson, Robert
    1547. All About the Human Mind (1963)
Goodwin, Harold
    1548. All About Rockets and Space Flight (1968)
Gould, Jack
    1549. All About Radio and Television (1960)
Henry, Marguerite
    1550. All About Horses (1962)
Holden, Raymond
    1551. All About Famous Scientific Expeditions (1955)
    1552. All About Fire (1964)
Lane, Ferdinand
    1553. All About the Flowering World (1956)
    1554. All About the Sea (1953)
Lauber, Patricia
    1555. All About the Ice Age (1959)
    1556. All About the Planet Earth (1962)
Lemmon, Robert
    1557. All About Birds (1955)
    1558. All About Moths and Butterflies (1956)
    1559. All About Strange Beasts of the Present (1957)
Loomis, Robert
    1560. All About Aviation (1964)
McClung, Robert
    1561. All About Animals and Their Young (1958)
Marsh, Susan
    1562. All About Maps and Mapmaking (1963)
Pough, Frederick
    1563. All About Volcanoes and Earthquakes (1953)
Pratt, Fletcher
    1564. All About Famous Inventors and Their Inventions (1955)
Randal, Judith
    1565. All About Heredity (1963)
Ronan, Margaret
    1566. All About Our Fifty States (1962)
Sperry, Armstrong
    1567. All About the Arctic and Antarctic (1957)
    1568. All About the Insect World (1954)
    1569. All About the Jungle (1959)
Tannehill, Ivan
    1570. All About the Weather (1953)
White, Anne Terry
    1571. All About Archaeology (1959)
    1572. All About Great Rivers of the World (1957)
    1573. All About Mountains and Mountaineering (1962)
    1574. All About Rocks and Minerals (1955)
    1575. All About the Stars (1954)
The quality of this series is not as impressive as its range of material. The binding
is often poor, the paper is of low quality, and the illustrations—not very many—
are merely average.

ALL AROUND SERIES —McGraw-Hill
Pine, Tillie, and Joseph Levine
1576. Air All Around (1960)
1577. Friction All Around (1960)
1578. Gravity All Around (1963)
1579. Heat All Around (1963)
1580. Light All Around (1961)
1581. Magnets and How to Use Them (1958)
1582. Rocks and How We Use Them (1967)
1583. Simple Machines and How We Use Them (1965)
1584. Sounds All Around (1959)
1585. Trees and How We Use Them (1969)
1586. Water All Around (1959)
1587. Weather All Around (1966)

In these basic beginning books for easy reading, subjects are simply handled, and the reader learns how to pronounce all strange words. Unfortunately, there is no index. For grades 3 and 4.

ALL-STAR SPORTS BOOKS —Follett
Archibald, Joseph
1588. Baseball (1972)
1589. Bowling for Boys and Girls (1963)
Cromie, Robert
1590. Golf for Boys and Girls (1965)
Gillelan, G. Howard
1591. Archery for Boys and Girls (1965)
Jordan, Payton
1592. Track and Field for Boys (1960)
Kirby, George, and George Sullivan
1593. Soccer (1971)
Kramp, Harry, and George Sullivan
1594. Swimming (1971)
Larson, Finn, and George Sullivan
1595. Skiing for Boys and Girls (1966)
McNally, Tom
1596. Camping (1972)
1597. Fishing (1972)
Mahan, Beverly
1598. Horseback Riding for Boys and Girls (1963)
Mahan, Beverly, and Margaret Steinberg
1599. Riding: A Guide to Horsemanship (1971)

This is a first-rate series of how-to's for various sports. The photos used to illustrate each step are quite clear, as are the descriptions of the various rules and techniques for each sport. There are also sections on equipment and safety. No index, but a glossary of terms is included.

AMERICA IN THE MAKING —Crowell
Buckmaster, Henrietta
1600. The Seminole Wars (1966)
1601. Women Who Shaped History (1966)
Clarke, Fred
1602. John Quincy Adams (1966)
Feuerlicht, Roberta
1603. Andrews' Raiders (1967)

AMERICA IN THE MAKING   —Crowell   (cont'd)
> 1604. The Legends of Paul Bunyan (1966)

Gordon, Edwin
> 1605. Mark Twain (1966)

Hebb, David
> 1606. Wheels on the Road (1966)

Manber, David
> 1607. The Wizard of Tuskegee (1967)

Meyer, Howard
> 1608. Let Us Have Peace (1966)

Reinfeld, Fred
> 1609. The Pony Express (1966)

Reit, Seymour
> 1610. America Laughs (1966)

Rennert, Vincent
> 1611. The Cowboy (1966)

Roland, Albert
> 1612. Great Indian Chiefs (1966)

Rublowsky, John
> 1613. Music in America (1967)

Rushmore, Robert
> 1614. The Life of George Gershwin (1966)

Wade, William
> 1615. From Barter to Banking (1967)

This highly readable series attempts to include biography, history, inventions, and some social character of the American people. Generally readable, some of the book depend too much on fictionalized conversations, which detracts from their value for school use. Although there is no index, there are photos, a glossary, and a bibliography. For supplementary use.

AMERICAN BATTLES AND CAMPAIGNS   —Putnam
Braun, Saul
> 1616. The Struggle for Guadalcanal (1969)

Brown, Dee
> 1617. Andrew Jackson and the Battle of New Orleans (1972)

Norman, James
> 1618. Kearny Rode West (1971)
> 1619. The Young Generals (1968)

This series is intended not so much to recreate famous battles, like the Macmillan series, but to relive momentous campaigns. They are written in on-the-spot technique devised to make the reader feel as though he is participating. The publisher claims this series is not intended to glorify war, but the books must be judged independently to decide whether this is true or not. For grades 6 through 10.

AMERICAN BIRTHRIGHTS   —Random House
Lavine, David
> 1620. The Mayor and the Changing City (1966)

Lewis, Anthony
> 1621. The Supreme Court and How It Works (1966)

Although nothing has been added to this series recently, these two offerings help to further a better understanding of American government. The Supreme Court book uses the Gideon case to show how the Court operates. This type of treatment can be much more valuable than an overview. The books have a glossary and an index. For ages 11 to 15.

17

AMERICAN CHARACTER SERIES —Putnam
    Epstein, Samuel, and Beryl Epstein
        1622. Who Says You Can't? (1969)
    Goldhurst, Richard
        1623. American Is Also Jewish (1972)
    Malmberg, Carl
        1624. American Is Also Scandinavian (1970)
    Mangione, Jerre
        1625. America Is Also Italian (1969)
This series is better done than Messner's on the various ethnic and racial heritages
that make up our country. There is no fictionalized character to follow in this series—
merely facts and figures, which are fascinating enough in themselves. Very well-
written, told with humor and interspersed with real-life anecdotes, these books
emphasize the differences in a particular ethnic group, as well as what members of
the group have contributed to American life. An outstanding series.

AMERICAN DEMOCRACY SERIES —Garrard
    Blassingame, Wyatt
        1626. The Story of the Boy Scouts (1968)
        1627. The Story of the U.S. Flag (1969)
    DeLeeuw, Adele
        1628. The Girl Scout Story (1965)
    Kraske, Robert
        1629. America the Beautiful: Stories of Patriotic Songs (1972)
        1630. The Statue of Liberty Comes to America (1972)
    Peterson, Helen
        1631. Electing Our Presidents (1970)
This series does not emphasize the working of government, as the title might
indicate. Rather, it examines the various institutions and symbols of America. The
books on scouting do emphasize the importance of democratic procedures in running
these organizations.

AMERICAN FOLK TALES —Garrard
    Blassingame, Wyatt
        1632. How Davy Crockett Got a Bearskin Coat (1972)
        1633. John Henry and Paul Bunyan Play Baseball (1972)
    Calhoun, Mary
        1634. Three Kinds of Stubborn (1972)
    Coatsworth, Elizabeth
        1635. Bob Bodden and the Good Ship "Rover" (1968)
        1636. Bob Bodden and the Seagoing Farm (1970)
        1637. Daniel Webster's Horses (1971)
    DeLeeuw, Adele
        1638. Casey Jones Drives an Ice Cream Train (1971)
        1639. John Henry: Steel Drivin' Man (1966)
        1640. Old Stormalong: Hero of the Seven Seas (1967)
        1641. Paul Bunyan and His Blue Ox (1968)
        1642. Paul Bunyan Finds a Wife (1969)
        1643. Uncle Davy Lane: Mighty Hunter (1970)
    Felton, Harold
        1644. Big Mose: Hero Fireman (1969)
    Justus, May
        1645. Eben and the Rattlesnake (1969)
        1646. Jumping Johnny Outwits Skedaddle (1971)

AMERICAN FOLK TALES —Garrard (cont'd)
      1647. Holidays in No-End Hollow (1970)
      1648. It Happened in No-End Hollow (1968)
      1649. Tales from Near-Side and Far (1970)
   Lauber, Patricia
      1650. Curious Critters (1969)
   Rushmore, Helen
      1651. Bigfoot Wallace and the Hickory Nut Battle (1970)
      1652. Ghost Dance on Coyote Butte (1971)
      1653. Gib Morgan: Fantastic Driller (1970)
      1654. Look Out for Hogan's Goat (1969)
      1655. The Magnificent House of Man Alone (1968)
   Shapiro, Edna
      1656. Windwagon Smith (1969)
   Shapiro, Irwin
      1657. Sam Patch: Champion Jumper (1972)
   Simon, Charlie May
      1658. Razorbacks Are Really Hogs (1972)
   Steele, William O.
      1659. Hound Dog Zip to the Rescue (1970)
   Voight, Virginia
      1660. The Adventures of Hiawatha (1969)
      1661. Close to the Rising Sun: Algonquian Indian Legends (1972)
Aimed at grades 2 to 5 and reluctant readers, this series retells some old folk tales
in jaunty style, as well as inventing some new tales about favorite heroes. The format
and tall tale humor should appeal to readers.

AMERICAN GIRL LIBRARY —Random House
   American Girl Magazine, Editors
      1662. The American Girl Beauty Book (1964)
      1663. The American Girl Book of Dog Stories (1965)
      1664. The American Girl Book of First Date Stories (1963)
      1665. The American Girl Book of Horse Stories (1963)
      1667. The American Girl Book of Mystery and Suspense Stories (1964)
      1668. The American Girl Book of Pat Downing Stories (1963)
      1669. The American Girl Book of Sport Stories (1966)
      1670. The American Girl Book of Teenage Questions (1963)
   Turngren, Annette
      1671. When Girls Meet Boys (1965)
These collections of various types of stories, recipes, and articles that have appeared
in *American Girl Magazine* are gathered in a moderately attractive format. The illustrations are acceptable, but the quality of paper and binding, unless bought in
prebound format, is not sturdy. For grades 6 through 9.

AMERICAN HERITAGE JUNIOR LIBRARY
   Andrist, Ralph
      1672. Andrew Jackson: Soldier and Statesman (1963)
      1673. California Gold Rush (1961)
      1674. Steamboats of the Mississippi (1962)
      1675. The Erie Canal (1964)
      1676. To the Pacific with Lewis and Clark (1967)
   Berger, Josef
      1677. Discoverers of the New World (1960)

Blow, Michael
   1678. Men of American Science and Invention (1960)
   1679. The History of the Atomic Bomb (1968)
Catton, Bruce
   1680. The Battle of Gettysburg (1963)
Cochran, Hamilton
   1681. Pirates of the Spanish Main (1961)
Cross, Wilbur
   1682. Naval Battles and Heroes (1960)
Cunliffe, Marcus
   1683. George Washington and the Making of a Nation (1966)
Dille, John
   1684. Americans in Space (1965)
Donovan, Frank
   1685. Ironclads of the Civil War (1964)
   1686. The Many Worlds of Benjamin Franklin (1963)
Downey, Fairfax
   1687. Texas and the War with Mexico (1961)
Fishwick, Marshall
   1688. Jamestown and the Virginia Colony (1965)
Fleming, Thomas
   1689. The Battle of Yorktown (1968)
Gardner, Joseph
   1690. Labor on the March (1969)
Garraty, John
   1691. Theodore Roosevelt and the Strenuous Life (1967)
Hine, Al
   1692. D-Day, the Invasion of Europe (1962)
Hubbard, Freeman
   1693. Great Days of the Circus (1962)
Jones, Evan
   1694. Trappers and Mountain Men (1961)
Lyon, Jane
   1695. Clipper Ships and Captains (1962)
McCready, Albert
   1696. Railroads in the Days of Steam (1960)
Miers, Earl Schenck
   1697. Abraham Lincoln in Peace and War (1964)
Moscow, Henry
   1698. Thomas Jefferson and His World (1960)
Place, Marian
   1699. Westward on the Oregon Trail (1962)
Platt, Rutherford
   1700. Adventures in the Wilderness (1963)
Rachlis, Eugene
   1701. Indians of the Plains (1960)
Reynolds, Robert
   1702. Commodore Perry in Japan (1963)
Russell, Francis
   1703. Lexington, Concord and Bunker Hill (1963)
   1704. The French and Indian Wars (1962)
Sears, Stephen
   1705. The Air War Against Hitler's Germany (1964)

AMERICAN HERITAGE JUNIOR LIBRARY (cont'd)
>1706. The Battle of the Bulge (1969)
>1707. The Carrier War in the Pacific (1966)

Shapiro, Irwin
>1708. The Story of Yankee Whaling (1959)

Spinar, Z. V.
>1709. Life Before Man (1972)

Sullivan, Wilson
>1710. Franklin Delano Roosevelt (1970)

Ward, Don
>1711. Cowboys and Cattle Country (1961)

Weisberger, Bernard
>1712. Captains of Industry (1966)

Ziner, Feenie
>1713. The Pilgrims and the Plymouth Colony (1961)

This first-rate series combines highly readable text with beautiful visual material. Many of the reproduced prints and paintings are in color and add considerable interest to the books. All are indexed, and most have bibliographies. Grades 5 and up.

AMERICAN HERO BIOGRAPHIES —Putnam
Andrews, Peter
>1714. Sergeant York, Reluctant Hero (1969)

Cook, Fred
>1715. Franklin D. Roosevelt, Valiant Leader (1969)

Haughey, Betty
>1716. William Penn: American Pioneer (1968)

Miller, Helen Markley
>1717. George Rogers Clark: Frontier Fighter (1968)
>1718. Jedediah Smith on the Far Frontier (1971)

Rikhoff, Jean
>1719. Robert E. Lee: Soldier of the South (1968)

Rink, Paul
>1720. John Paul Jones: Conquer or Die (1968)

Rouverol, Jean
>1721. Harriet Beecher Stowe: Woman Crusader (1968)

Steiner, Stan
>1722. George Washington: The Indian Influence (1970)

Thomas, Henry
>1723. Dwight D. Eisenhower: General, President (1969)

Wise, William
>1724. Charles A. Lindbergh (1970)

Intended for use by grades 3 to 5. The style of writing is generally easy to comprehend, the drawings are quite good, and the text is not as simplistic as that found in many works intended for this age group. The books are also indexed.

AMERICAN INDIANS THEN AND NOW —Putnam
Baldwin, Gordon
>1725. Indians of the Southwest (1970)

Haines, Francis
>1726. Indians of the Great Basin and Plateau (1970)

Powers, William
>1727. Indians of the Northern Plains (1969)
>1728. Indians of the Southern Plains (1971)

Covers the American Indian first geographically and then historically by subject—

AMERICAN INDIANS THEN AND NOW —Putnam (cont'd)
that is, arts and crafts, hunting, homes, etc. The use of photographs is quite good,
there are generally bibliographies, always indices, and many quotes from people of
the time and from documents, which add interest. Another interesting aspect: there
is no attempt to cover up the role of the white man in the destruction of Indian
culture. For grades 5 on up.

AMERICAN INSTITUTIONS —Viking
      Schwartz, Alvin
          1729. The Unions (1972)
          1730. The University (1969)
A survey of important institutional concepts. The institutions are also treated
historically, covering important events in their development, outstanding personalities
involved with them, the successes and failures they have encountered, and the possibilities that the future has in store. An ambitious undertaking, and one that will
supplement very well courses in civics and social sciences. There are both glossaries
and indices. For grades 7 on up.

AMERICANS ALL SERIES —Garrard
      Anderson, LaVere
          1731. Allan Pinkerton: First Private Eye (1972)
          1732. Quanah Parker: Indian Warrior for Peace (1970)
      Blassingame, Wyatt
          1733. Jake Gaither: Winning Coach (1969)
      Clark, Margaret
          1734. Benjamin Banneker: Astronomer and Scientist (1971)
      Epstein, Samuel, and Beryl Epstein
          1735. Enrico Fermi: Father of Atomic Power (1970)
          1736. Harriet Tubman: Guide to Freedom (1968)
      Fuller, Miriam
          1737. Phillis Wheatley: America's First Black Poetess (1971)
      Graves, Charles
          1738. Father Flanagan: Founder of Boys Town (1972)
          1739. Grandma Moses: Favorite Painter (1969)
          1740. Nellie Bly: Reporter of the World (1971)
          1741. Robert F. Kennedy: Man Who Dared to Dream (1970)
      Groh, Lynn
          1742. Walter Reed: Pioneer in Medicine (1971)
      Luce, Willard, and Celia Luce
          1743. Lou Gehrig: Iron Man of Baseball (1970)
      Malone, Mary
          1744. Andrew Carnegie: Giant of Industry (1969)
          1745. Milton Hershey: Chocolate King (1971)
      Montgomery, Elizabeth
          1746. Duke Ellington: King of Jazz (1972)
          1747. Henry Ford: Automotive Pioneer (1969)
          1748. Walt Disney: Master of Make-Believe (1971)
          1749. Will Rogers: Cowboy Philosopher (1970)
          1750. William C. Handy: Father of the Blues (1968)
      Patterson, Lillie
          1751. Martin Luther King, Jr.: Man of Peace (1969)
      Peterson, Helen
          1752. Sojourner Truth: Fearless Crusader (1972)
          1753. Susan B. Anthony: Pioneer in Women's Rights (1971)

AMERICANS ALL SERIES —Garrard (cont'd)
     Sullivan, George
         1754. Jim Thorpe: All-Around Athlete (1971)
         1755. Knute Rockne: Notre Dame's Football Great (1970)
This series is intended by the publisher to emphasize the importance of character and
personal determination in these success stories. Unfortunately, the books lean too
much on presenting things in a story form, which tends to detract from factual
acceptability. For grades 3 and up.

ANIMALS —Abelard
     Bothwell, Jean
         1756. Vanishing Wildlife of East Africa (1967)
     Burton, Maurice
         1757. Animals of Australia (1969)
     Burton, Robert
         1758. Animals of the Antarctic (1970)
     Malkus, Alida
         1759. Animals of the High Andes (1966)
     Matschat, Cecile
         1760. Animals of the Valley of the Amazon (1965)
     May, Charles
         1761. Animals of the Far North (1964)
     Osmond, Edward
         1762. Animals of Central Asia (1968)
These are excellent books on the wildlife of various areas of the world. In addition to
maps of the areas, there are full-page detailed drawings of the animals under discussion.
The information is detailed and both common and scientific names of the animals are
supplied. There are bibliographies and indices. For grades 5 on up.

ART FOR CHILDREN —Doubleday
     Raboff, Ernest
         1763. DaVinci (1971)
         1764. Durer (1970)
         1765. Henri de Toulouse-Lautrec (1970)
         1766. Henri Rousseau (1970)
         1767. Marc Chagall (1968)
         1768. Michelangelo (1971)
         1769. Pablo Picasso (1968)
         1770. Paul Klee (1968)
         1771. Pierre-Auguste Renoir (1970)
         1772. Raphael (1971)
         1773. Rembrandt (1970)
         1774. Velasquez (1970)
These slim volumes are first-rate introductions for young people into the art of
various masters. The hand-lettered text is simple but does not talk down to the
reader. Important words in the text are emphasized in color. There is a brief explanation of the artist's life and his philosophy, then a discussion of some of his individual
works which are reprinted in color in the text. For grades 4 on up.

ART TELLS A STORY —Parents
     Alden, Carella
         1775. From Early American Paintbrushes: Colony to New Nation (1971)
         1776. Sunrise Island: A Story of Japan and Its Arts (1971)
These texts are intended as introductions to various periods and styles of art. Un-

ART TELLS A STORY —Parents (cont'd)
fortunately, the text is often oversimplified, lacking specific dating of various
artists and works of art. In the book on Japanese art, no attempt is made to tie in
its influence on Western art. Not as good as Shirley Glubok's series.

ASK ME A QUESTION ABOUT . . . —Harvey
     Rosenfeld, Sam
          1777. Ask Me a Question about Rockets, Satellites and Space
             Stations (1971)
          1778. Ask Me a Question about the Atom (1969)
          1779. Ask Me a Question about the Earth (1966)
          1780. Ask Me a Question about the Heavens (1966)
          1781. Ask Me a Question about the Weather (1966)
These books are set up in a question-and-answer format. The answers to each question cover several paragraphs. Photos and drawings are interspersed throughout and
there is an index for easier location of specifics. The author is well-qualified, being
a former research scientist. Good supplementary material for science students.

AT WORK —Harvey
     Elting, Mary
          1782. Aircraft at Work (1964)
          1783. Helicopters at Work (1972)
          1784. Machines at Work (1962)
          1785. Ships at Work (1962)
          1786. Spacecraft at Work (1965)
          1787. Trains at Work (1962)
          1788. Trucks at Work (1965)
Although portions of these works are fictionalized, there is still much unusual information presented. Each book covers all aspects of its subject: the stages of the job,
different types of equipment, and history. There is both a glossary and an index, and
most of the illustrations are in color. For grades 3 to 6.

BACKGROUND BOOKS FOR YOUNG PEOPLE —Parents
     Dareff, Hal
          1789. From Vietnam to Cambodia (1971)
     Jacker, Corinne
          1790. The Biological Revolution: On the Making of a New World (1971)
     Liston, Robert
          1791. The Democratic Process (1972)
     Trupin, James
          1792. West Africa: From Ancient Kingdoms to Modern Times (1971)
     Walton, Richard
          1793. Canada and the U.S.A. (1972)
     Williams, Byron
          1794. Continent in Turmoil (1971)
This series, intended for young adults, examines in depth some of the major
problems in the present-day world. Some of the aspects covered are the right of
this government to move into Cambodia, the shape the democratic process has taken
today, and some of the problems between Canada and this country. Very good
material for social studies and civics classes.

BALANCE OF NATURE —Hastings House
     Adrian, Mary
          1795. A Day and a Night in a Forest (1967)

BALANCE OF NATURE   —Hastings House (cont'd)
>   1796. A Day and a Night in a Tide Pool (1972)
>   1797. A Day and a Night in the Arctic (1970)

These books are intended partly as studies in ecology and partly to show readers just how much is going on around them. The author, therefore, studies just a small segment of the world—e.g., a tide pool and a forest—and shows all the various creatures and stages of life occurring there. For ages 7 to 11.

BAUER, HELEN   —Doubleday
>   1798. California Indian Days (1968)
>   1799. California Mission Days (1951)
>   1800. California Rancho Days (1953)

Ms. Bauer's series on California history is quite outstanding. She gives complete coverage not only to social customs of the day, but also to economic, political, educational, and religious happenings. She furnishes maps and indices, plus excellent photographs and illustrations and occasionally addenda of interest.

BEGINNER'S GUIDE TO NATURE   —Putnam
>   Hausman, Ethel
>   1801. Beginner's Guide to Seashore Life (1949)
>   1802. Beginner's Guide to Wildflowers (1948)
>   Hausman, Leon
>   1803. Beginner's Guide to Fresh-Water Life (1950)
>   Mayall, R., and Margaret Mayall
>   1804. Beginner's Guide to the Skies (1960)

These books are intended for use as tools of identification of the various natural phenomena. The books feature full-page drawings of several creatures and on the opposite page a brief paragraph of information. The books have bibliographies and indices. The only problem with using these for identification is that only the common name and not the scientific name for the animal or plant is given.

BEGINNING KNOWLEDGE SERIES   —Macmillan
>   Epple, Anne
>   1805. The Beginning Knowledge Book of Ants (1969)
>   1806. The Beginning Knowledge Book of Fossils (1969)
>   Ivins, Ann
>   1807. The Beginning Knowledge Book of Stars and Constellations (1969)
>   Posell, Elsa
>   1808. The Beginning Knowledge Book of Seashells (1969)

These texts feature simple vocabulary and plentiful color illustrations as well as basic information. Very good introduction to these various fields of natural science.

BEGINNING SCIENCE SERIES   —Follett
>   Asimov, Isaac
>   1809. Light (1971)
>   1810. Mars (1967)
>   1811. Stars (1968)
>   1812. The Moon (1966)
>   Brouillette, Jean
>   1813. Butterflies (1961)
>   1814. Moths (1966)
>   Carona, Philip
>   1815. Crystals (1971)
>   1816. Water (1966)

Cromer, Richard
  1817. Soil (1967)
Dillon, Wallace
  1818. Salmon (1962)
Feilen, John
  1819. Squirrels (1967)
Follett, Robert
  1820. Your Wonderful Body (1961)
Gendron, Val, and David McGill
  1821. Whales (1965)
John, Betty
  1822. Hummingbirds (1960)
Keeney, Mary
  1823. Your Wonderful Brain (1971)
Luce, Willard
  1824. Birds That Hunt (1971)
May, Julian
  1825. Rockets (1967)
  1826. Weather (1966)
Neal, Charles
  1827. Sound (1962)
Page, Lou
  1828. Rocks and Minerals (1962)
Preston, Edna
  1829. Air (1965)
Schoenknecht, Charles
  1830. Ants (1961)
  1831. Frogs and Toads (1960)
Sullivan, George
  1832. Plants to Grow Indoors (1969)
  1833. Trees (1971)
Tellander, Marian
  1834. Space (1960)
Victor, Edward
  1835. Airplanes (1966)
  1836. Friction (1961)
  1837. Machines (1962)
  1838. Magnets (1962)
  1839. Planes and Rockets (1965)
Waters, John
  1840. Turtles (1971)
Wood, Dorothy
  1841. Beavers (1961)
Woods, Loren
  1842. Fishes (1969)
  1843. Tropical Fish (1971)

Another series of introductory books to various phases of natural science. These are rather small books, but they do have color illustrations and a vocabulary list, as well as suggestions for further study with which the student or reader can experiment. For grades 2 to 4.

BEHIND THE SCENES AT . . . —Dodd
>Busby, Edith
>>1844. Behind the Scenes at the Library (1960)
>Cooke, David C.
>>1845. Behind the Scenes at an Airport (1968)
>>1846. Behind the Scenes in Television (1967)
>Lewis, Alfred
>>1847. Behind the Scenes at the Post Office (1965)

The format of these books finds the text on one page alternating with full-page photos on the next. This is to give the reader a better idea of how the process he is reading about really looks. Unfortunately, not all of these books are indexed, so finding specific items may prove troublesome, even with the use of the table of contents.

BEING TOGETHER SERIES —Lerner
>Lipke, Jean
>>1848. Birth (1971)
>>1849. Conception and Contraception (1971)
>>1850. Dating (1971)
>>1851. Heredity (1971)
>>1852. Loving (1971)
>>1853. Marriage (1971)
>>1854. Pregnancy (1971)
>>1855. Puberty and Adolescence (1971)
>>1856. Sex Outside of Marriage (1971)

Here is an excellent series of books on sex education. Although some of the texts overlap, each one has some additional information, so that purchase of the whole set is desirable. The books are indexed, although there are no tables of contents. The only problem here is that the format makes the books look as though they were intended for a younger audience than the writing would indicate. The illustrations are acceptable but not superior. For grades 6 on up.

THE BEST BOOKS SERIES —Doubleday
>Evans, Pauline
>>1857. The Best Book of Adventure Stories (1964)
>>1858. The Best Book of Bedtime Stories (1966)
>>1859. The Best Book of Horse Stories (1964)
>>1860. The Best Book of Mystery Stories (1963)
>>1861. The Best Book of Read Aloud Stories (1965)
>Rosenbaum, Robert
>>1862. The Best Book of Sports Stories (1966)
>>1863. The Best Book of True Aviation Stories (1966)
>>1864. The Best Book of True Sea Stories (1966)

This series is a combination of short stories and excerpts from longer books. They will suit the reader who is looking for stories along a specific line, and may lead him to longer books in his field of interest.

BETTER SPORTS BOOKS —Dodd
>Claus, Marshall
>>1865. Better Gymnastics for Boys (1971)
>Cook, Joseph, and William Romeika
>>1866. Better Surfing for Boys (1967)
>Cooke, David C.
>>1867. Better Baseball for Boys (1959)

BETTER SPORTS BOOKS —Dodd (cont'd)
    1868. Better Basketball for Boys (1960)
    1869. Better Bowling for Boys (1963)
    1870. Better Football for Boys (1958)
    1871. Better Physical Fitness for Boys (1961)
Docherty, Tommy
    1872. Better Soccer for Boys (1968)
Golf Digest, Editors
    1873. Better Golf for Boys (1965)
Hopman, Harry
    1874. Better Tennis for Boys and Girls (1972)
Horner, Dave
    1875. Better Scuba Diving for Boys (1966)
Jacobs, Helen Hull
    1876. Better Physical Fitness for Girls (1964)
Joseph, James
    1877. Better Water Skiing for Boys (1964)
Kenealy, James
    1878. Better Camping for Boys (1971)
    1879. Better Fishing for Boys (1968)
Robinson, Bill
    1880. Better Sailing for Boys and Girls (1968)
Sullivan, George
    1881. Better Archery for Boys and Girls (1970)
    1882. Better Boxing for Boys (1966)
    1883. Better Horseback Riding for Boys and Girls (1969)
    1884. Better Ice Hockey for Boys (1965)
    1885. Better Swimming and Diving for Boys and Girls (1967)
    1886. Better Swimming for Boys and Girls (1968)
    1887. Better Table Tennis for Boys and Girls (1972)
    1888. Better Track and Field Events for Boys (1967)
In this how-to series, the authors show how to select equipment, go over the rules of the games, show how to keep score, and provide a glossary of terms. The photos are excellent indications on how the sports are played. One could only wish that more emphasis had been placed on girls' participation in the same sports.

BIG CITIES OF AMERICA —McGraw-Hill
Borreson, Mary Jo
    1889. Washington, D.C.: Government City (1970)
Kohn, Marion, and Walter Kohn
    1890. Chicago: Midwestern Giant (1969)
Williams, Barbara
    1891. Boston: Seat of American History (1969)
In an attempt to show major cities as they are today, the authors discuss the history of each city, the heritage, the various ethnic and racial minorities that make them up and what these groups have contributed to the cities, in addition to providing information on politics, industry, and economics. The authors also try to discuss some of the problems the cities face today. This series is more up to date than the Key to the City series. For ages 10 and up.

BIOGRAPHY OF AN ANIMAL —Putnam
Hopf, Alice
    1892. Biography of an Octopus (1971)

BIOGRAPHY OF AN ANIMAL —Putnam (cont'd)
    Smith, Harry
        1893. Biography of a Bee (1970)
    Trost, Lucille
        1894. Biography of a Cottontail (1971)
These books are just what their titles indicate: the story of an individual animal,
his physical development, his way of life, and his mating. Factual information on
each species is interspersed in the story form. Unfortunately, the story form makes
it difficult to use this series to complete school assignments. There are no indices.

BLACK AUTOBIOGRAPHIES SERIES —Dutton
    Kennerly, Karen
        1895. The Slave Who Bought His Freedom: Equiano's Story (1971)
    Knight, Michael
        1896. In Chains to Louisiana: Solomon Northrup's Story (1971)
These books are adapted from first-person accounts by various Blacks. The adaptations prove quite readable and even, in their authenticity, haunting. Excellent
supplements to Black history courses.

BLACK LEGACY —McGraw-Hill
    Booker, Simeon
        1897. Susie King Taylor: Civil War Nurse (1969)
    Fenderson, Lewis
        1898. Daniel Hale Williams: Open Heart Doctor (1972)
        1899. Thurgood Marshall: Fighter for Justice (1969)
    Lewis, Claude
        1900. Benjamin Banneker: The Man Who Saved Washington (1970)
Another first-rate series of biographies on outstanding Blacks and what they contribu
to American life. It is to be hoped that, as the series develops, more attention will be
paid to some of the less well-known Blacks who have yet to be written about.

BLEEKER, SONJA —Morrow
        1901. The Apache Indians (1951)
        1902. The Ashanti of Ghana (1966)
        1903. The Aztec, Indians of Mexico (1963)
        1904. The Cherokee (1952)
        1905. The Chippewa Indians (1955)
        1906. The Crow Indians (1953)
        1907. The Delaware Indians (1953)
        1908. The Eskimo (1959)
        1909. The Horsemen of the Western Plateaus (1957)
        1910. The Ibo of Biafra (1969)
        1911. The Inca (1960)
        1912. The Indians of the Longhouse (1950)
        1913. The Masai, Herders of East Africa (1963)
        1914. The Maya, Indians of Central America (1961)
        1915. The Mission Indians of California (1956)
        1916. The Navajo (1958)
        1917. The Pueblo Indians (1955)
        1918. The Pygmies (1968)
        1919. The Sea Hunters (1951)
        1920. The Seminole Indians (1954)
        1921. The Sioux Indians (1962)
        1922. The Tuareg (1964)

29

BLEEKER, SONJA —Morrow (cont'd)
       1923. The Zulu of South Africa, Cattlemen, Farmers, and Warriors (1970)
This is an outstanding series on various Indian tribes and African minorities. Although there are few illustrations, the books are clear and concise. Some of the earlier publications begin in a story form, then move on to factual information. The later volumes, however, do not suffer from this difficulty. In them, the author sticks strictly to facts. One desirable feature is the information on some fast-disappearing African tribes—the Pygmies, the Masai, and the Ibo—all of whom are being decimated in racial wars.

BOARDMAN, FON W. —Walck
       1924. Canals (1959)
       1925. Castles (1957)
       1926. Roads (1958)
       1927. Tunnels (1960)
In this outstanding series on various engineering feats of mankind, the author discusses some of the famous examples in each field, and the differences to be found in castles, canals, etc., geographically. He also discusses basic characteristics, and the principles involved in construction. The books are indexed with many photos, maps, and illustrations.

BOYS LIFE LIBRARY —Random House
       Boys Life, Editors
       1928. The Boys Life Book of Baseball Stories (1964)
       1929. The Boys Life Book of Basketball Stories (1966)
       1930. The Boys Life Book of Flying Stories (1964)
       1931. The Boys Life Book of Football Stories (1963)
       1932. The Boys Life Book of Horse Stories (1963)
       1933. The Boys Life Book of Mystery Stories (1963)
       1934. The Boys Life Book of Outer Space Stories (1964)
       1935. The Boys Life Book of Sports Stories (1965)
       1936. The Boys Life Book of Wild Animal Stories (1965)
       1937. The Boys Life Book of World War Two Stories (1965)
       Keith, Donald
       1938. Mutiny in the Time Machine (1963)
Rather like the American Girl series, this one includes excerpts from *Boys Life Magazine*. There are both stories and jokes included. The collections here are not of the quality of the Best Books series along the same lines.

BRANLEY, FRANKLYN —Crowell
       1939. A Book of Astronauts for You (1963)
       1940. A Book of Mars for You (1968)
       1941. A Book of Moon Rockets for You (1970)
       1942. A Book of Outer Space for You (1970)
       1943. A Book of Planets for You (1966)
       1944. A Book of Satellites for You (1971)
       1945. A Book of Stars for You (1967)
       1946. A Book of the Milky Way Galaxy for You (1965)
       1947. A Book of Venus for You (1969)
An introduction to the space sciences for young readers. Unfortunately, the drawings are cartoon-like rather than representational, there is no index, there is no guide to pronunciation, and some terms that beginning readers might have trouble with are not explained.

BREAKTHROUGH BOOKS SERIES —Harper
  Davis, Burke
    1948. Appomattox: Closing Struggle of the Civil War (1963)
    1949. Yorktown: The Winning of American Independence (1969)
  Lord, Walter
    1950. Peary to the Pole (1963)
  Mirsky, Jeannette
    1951. Balboa: Discoverer of the Pacific (1964)
  Putnam, Peter
    1952. Triumph of the Seeing Eye (1963)
  Renault, Mary
    1953. Lion in the Gateway: Heroic Battles of the Greeks and the
           Persians (1964)
  Robinson, Jackie, and Alfred Duckett
    1954. Breakthrough to the Big League: The Story of Jackie Robinson
           (1965)
  Ungermann, Kenneth
    1955. Race to Nome (1963)
These are very well-done examinations of some unusual breakthroughs: the first
Negro in big league baseball, the use of seeing eye dogs in helping the blind, along
with other more historical breakthroughs. The use of paintings and drawings of the
time is a good idea. Where necessary, maps of the battlegrounds are given. There are
both bibliographies and indices.

BUILDING AMERICA —Putnam
  Borreson, Mary Jo
    1956. Let's Go to Colonial Williamsburg (1962)
    1957. Let's Go to Mount Vernon (1962)
    1958. Let's Go to Plymouth with the Pilgrims (1963)
  Buchheimer, Naomi
    1959. Let's Go down the Mississippi with LaSalle (1962)
  Granberg, W. J.
    1960. Let's Go Exploring with Magellan (1965)
  Polking, Kirk
    1961. Let's Go on the "Half Moon" with Henry Hudson (1964)
    1962. Let's Go with Lewis and Clark (1963)
  Rosenfield, Bernard
    1963. Let's Go to Build the First Transcontinental Railroad (1963)
  Ruffo, Vinnie
    1964. Let's Go to the New World with Christopher Columbus (1969)
  Spiegelman, Judith
    1965. Let's Go to the Battle of Gettysburg (1965)
    1966. Let's Go with George Washington at Valley Forge (1967)
  Wolfe, Louis
    1967. Drake Drills for Oil (1966)
    1968. Let's Go to the Klondike Gold Rush (1964)
    1969. Let's Go to the Louisiana Purchase (1963)
Intended for a younger reader than the We-Were-There series. Not only do the
books describe the happenings of the title, but they also discuss what life was like
at that time: chores, holidays, school, and other activities that children could expect
to experience. Although there is a glossary, there is no index.

BUILDINGS —Scott
  Leacroft, Helen, and Richard Leacroft
    1970. The Buildings of Ancient Egypt (1963)
    1971. The Buildings of Ancient Greece (1966)
    1972. The Buildings of Ancient Rome (1969)
These are excellent books which can be used in conjunction with courses on ancient history and architecture. The drawings showing homes, public buildings, and famous buildings of each time are very precise. Often floor plans are included. The authors are qualified in their field. Many of the illustrations are in color.

BYWAYS LIBRARY —Walck
  Hornby, John
    1973. Clowns through the Ages (1965)
  Jenkins, Alan
    1974. Pirates and Highwaymen (1965)
  Pilkington, Roger
    1975. The River (1965)
  Wilkins, Frances
    1976. Wizards and Witches (1965)
  Willson, Robina
    1977. Musical Instruments (1966)
This is a non-fiction series that is "designed to lead the reader off the main roads into the byways of the curious, the little-known, and seldom explored." The books present both factual history and stories and legends associated with each subject. For example, among witches discussed is the one in Hansel and Gretel. A most enjoyable series to have around.

CAREERS FOR TOMORROW —Walck
  Ashworth, John
    1978. Careers in Accounting (1963)
  Barnett, Leo, and Lou Ellen Davis
    1979. Careers in Computer Programming (1967)
  Boylan, James
    1980. School Teaching as a Career (1962)
  Chamberlin, Jo
    1981. Careers in the Protective Services (1963)
  Cohn, Angelo
    1982. Careers in Public Planning and Administration (1966)
    1983. Careers with Foreign Languages (1963)
  Ducas, Dorothy
    1984. Modern Nursing (1962)
  Fox, William
    1985. Careers in the Biological Sciences (1963)
  Friedberg, Robert, and Gene Hawes
    1986. Careers in College Teaching (1965)
  Herbert, Fred
    1987. Careers in Natural Resource Conservation (1965)
  Kaplan, Albert, and Margaret DeMille
    1988. Careers in Department Store Merchandising (1962)
  Kasper, Sydney
    1989. Careers in the Building Trades (1969)
  Koestler, Frances
    1990. Careers in Social Work (1965)

CAREERS FOR TOMORROW —Walck (cont'd)
>Lattin, Gerald
>>1991. Careers in Hotels and Restaurants (1967)
>Lobsenz, Norman
>>1992. Writing as a Career (1963)
>Logsdon, Irene, and Richard Logsdon
>>1993. Library Careers (1963)
>Mann, Roland
>>1994. Careers in Business Management (1963)
>Nathan, Raymond
>>1995. Careers in Airline Operations (1964)
>Roth, Claire, and Lillian Weiner
>>1996. Hospital Health Services (1964)
>Splaver, Sarah
>>1997. Careers in Personnel Administration (1962)
>Sullivan, Mary
>>1998. Careers in Government (1964)
>Wachs, Theodore
>>1999. Careers in Engineering (1964)
>>2000. Careers in Research Science (1961)
>Ward, John
>>2001. Careers in Music (1968)

Many of the volumes of this basic career series are now outdated, particularly the ones on teaching and engineering. There are some photos and some information on different areas these careers could be practiced in, but there is no indication as to where an individual might obtain training.

CASE BOOK MYSTERY SERIES —Dial
>Touster, Irwin, and Richard Curtis
>>2002. The Perez Arson Mystery (1972)
>>2003. The Runaway Bus Mystery (1972)

This new series attempts to give readers some indication of how our modern legal system works. Each book contains a fictionalized mystery and the legal solution thereof. Each volume has been authenticated by a practicing attorney. Good for enjoyment reading as well as for supplementing social studies courses.

CAVALCADE . . . —Walck
>Brown, Michael
>>2004. A Cavalcade of Sea Legends (1972)
>Farjeon, Eleanor, and William Mayne
>>2005. A Cavalcade of Kings (1965)
>>2006. A Cavalcade of Queens (1965)
>Garner, Alan
>>2007. A Cavalcade of Goblins (1969)
>Green, Roger Lancelyn
>>2008. A Cavalcade of Dragons (1971)
>Hope-Simpson, Jacynth
>>2009. A Cavalcade of Witches (1966)

A first-rate series of collections of stories, poems, legends, and folk and fairy tales. Several of the authors also include excerpts from novels. The black-and-white illustrations are effective, and the format is enticing. A welcome addition for any collection.

CENTURY —Garrard

    Blassingame, Wyatt

        2010. Joseph Stalin and Communist Russia (1971)

    Epstein, Samuel, and Beryl Epstein

        2011. Winston Churchill: Lion of Britain (1971)

    Glendinning, Sally

        2012. Queen Victoria: English Empress (1970)

    Montgomery, Elizabeth

        2013. Gandhi: Peaceful Fighter (1970)

    Zagoren, Ruby

        2014. Chaim Weizmann: First President of Israel (1972)

The authors not only present biographies of important leaders of this century, but also try to place the individual in his time, showing related events occurring at the same time. Some mention is made of other world movements, the history of each country, as well as religious, governmental, and scientific developments that happened during each lifetime. For grades 4 to 6.

CHALLENGE BOOKS —Coward

    Archer, Sellers

        2015. Rain, Rivers and Reservoirs: The Challenge of Running Water (1969)

    Berry, Erick

        2016. Men, Moss and Reindeer: The Challenge of Lapland (1959)

    Brown, Bill

        2017. People of the Many Islands: The Challenge of the Polynesians (1958)

    Buckley, Peter

        2018. Spanish Plateau: The Challenge of a Dry Land (1959)

    Cary, Sturges

        2019. Volcanoes and Glaciers: The Challenge of Iceland (1959)

    Duckett, Alfred

        2020. Changing of the Guard: The New Black Political Breed (1972)

    Francis, Henry, and Philip Smith

        2021. Defrosting Antarctic Secrets: The Challenge of the Frozen
                Frontier (1962)

    Gallant, Kathryn

        2022. Mountains in the Sea: The Challenge of Crowded Japan (1957)

    Goldman, Peter

        2023. Civil Rights: The Challenge of the Fourteenth Amendment (1965)

    Greene, Wade

        2024. Disarmament: The Challenge of Civilisation (1966)

    Griffin, Ella

        2025. The Challenge of a Continent in a Hurry: Africa Today (1962)

    Harris, Miles

        2026. Man against Storm: The Challenge of Weather (1962)

    Haverstock, Nathan

        2027. The Organization of American States: The Challenge of the
                Americas (1966)

    Holbrook, Sabra

        2028. Capital without a Country: The Challenge of Berlin (1961)

        2029. Taming the Columbia River: The Challenge of American-Canadian
                Co-operation (1964)

    Ingraham, Joseph

        2030. Friendship Road: The Challenge of the Pan-American Highway
                (1961)

CHALLENGE BOOKS —Coward (cont'd)
    Joy, Charles R.
        2031. Desert Caravans: The Challenge of the Changing Sahara (1960)
        2032. Island in the Desert: The Challenge of the Nile (1959)
        2033. The Race Between Food and People: The Challenge of a Hungry
            World (1961)
    Joyce, James Avery
        2034. Decade of Development: The Challenge of the Underdeveloped
            Nations (1966)
    Lauber, Patricia
        2035. Battle against the Sea: How the Dutch Made Holland (1956)
        2036. Changing Face of North America: The Challenge of the St. Law-
            rence Seaway (1968)
        2037. Dust Bowl: The Story of Man on the Great Plains (1958)
    Lawrence, Mortimer
        2038. The Rockets Red Glare: The Challenge of Outer Space (1960)
    Martin, Lealon
        2039. Conquest of Disease: The Challenge of Your Life (1961)
    Noshpitz, Joseph
        2040. Understanding Ourselves: The Challenge of the Human Mind (1963)
    O'Daniel, John
        2041. Vietnam Today: The Challenge of a Divided Nation (1966)
    Partridge, Ben, and Cora Cheney
        2042. Underseas: The Challenge of the Deep Frontier (1961)
    Seegers, Kathleen
        2043. Alliance for Progress: The Challenge of the Western Hemisphere
            (1964)
    Seldin, Joel
        2044. Automation: The Challenge of Men and Machines (1965)
    Straus, Richard
        2045. Coal, Steel, Atoms and Trade: The Challenge of Uniting
            Europe (1962)
    Tolbloom, Wanda
        2046. People of the Snow: The Challenge of Eskimo Canada (1957)
    Weaver, Warren
        2047. Making Our Government Work: The Challenge of American
            Citizenship (1964)
    West, Fred
        2048. Breaking the Language Barrier: The Challenge of World Com-
            munications (1961)
    Whittlesey, Susan
        2049. U.S. Peace Corps: The Challenge of Goodwill (1963)
        2050. VISTA: The Challenge to Poverty (1970)
The authors of these books are unusually well qualified to write on their individual
subjects. There are good photos, usually glossaries, and always indices. Unfortunately,
many of these books are outdated by recent developments—e.g., the book on civil
rights does not mention American Indians or women. For grades 5 to 7.

CHAMPION BOOKS —Coward
    Brown, Michael
        2051. Shackleton's Epic Voyage (1969)
    Carter, Bruce
        2052. Jimmy Murphy and the White Duesenberg (1968)
        2053. Nuoolari and the Alfa Romeo (1968)

CHAMPION BOOKS —Coward (cont'd)
        Fisk, Nicholas
            2054. Lindbergh, the Lone Flyer (1968)
            2055. Richthofen, the Red Baron (1968)
        Styles, Showell
            2056. First up Everest (1969)
These are easy-to-read adventures with a historical base. There are both color and
black-and-white illustrations, but photographs might have been both more realistic
and more exciting than what has been presented. The adventures are written in
story format, which also tends to detract from their value as source material. Good
for reluctant readers, however. Grades 2 to 4.

CHANGING WORLD SERIES —Holt
        Anderson, John
            2057. The Changing World of Birds (1972)
        Behnke, Frances
            2058. The Changing World of Living Things (1972)
        Gray, William
            2059. The Changing World of Decomposers (announced)
        Oliver, John
            2060. The Changing World of Weather (announced)
This is a reworking of the typical books on natural science from an ecological standpoint. Much of this information is already available; only the ecological aspects
are of value here.

CHILDHOOD OF FAMOUS AMERICANS SERIES —Bobbs-Merrill
        Aird, Hazel, and Catherine Ruddiman
            2061. Henry Ford: Boy with Ideas (1960)
        Anderson, Dorothy
            2062. John Jacob Astor: Young Trader (1961)
        Anderson, LaVere
            2063. Robert Todd Lincoln: President's Boy (1967)
        Bare, Margaret
            2064. John Deere: Blacksmith Boy (1964)
        Barton, Thomas
            2065. John Smith: Jamestown Boy (1966)
            2066. Patrick Henry: Young Spokesman (1960)
        Bebenroth, Charlotta
            2067. Meriwether Lewis: Boy Explorer (1962)
        Borland, Kathryn, and Helen Speicher
            2068. Allan Pinkerton: Young Detective (1962)
            2069. Eugene Field: Young Poet (1964)
            2070. Harry Houdini: Boy Magician (1969)
            2071. Phillis Wheatley: Young Colonial Poet (1968)
        Brabham, Janet
            2072. Bret Harte: Young Storyteller (1969)
        Bryant, Bernice
            2073. Dan Morgan: Wilderness Boy (1952)
            2074. George Gershwin: Young Composer (1965)
        Burnett, Constance
            2075. Cecil B. DeMille: Young Dramatist (1963)
            2076. Lucretia Mott: Girl of Old Nantucket (1963)
        Burt, Olive
            2077. Chief Joseph: Boy of the Nez Perce (1967)

2078. Jed Smith: Young Western Explorer (1954)
2079. John Alden: Young Puritan (1964)
2080. John Wanamaker: Boy Merchant (1962)
2081. Luther Burbank: Boy Wizard (1962)
2082. Mary McLeod Bethune: Girl Devoted to Her People (1970)
2083. Ringling Brothers: Circus Boys (1962)

Chappell, Carl
2084. Virgil I. Grissom: Boy Astronaut (1971)

Clark, Electa
2085. Osceola: Young Seminole Indian (1965)
2086. Robert Peary: Boy of the North Pole (1962)

Cleven, Cathrine
2087. Black Hawk: Young Sauk Warrior (1966)
2088. John Hancock: New England Boy (1963)

Comfort, Mildred
2089. Herbert Hoover: Boy Engineer (1965)
2090. James J. Hill: Young Empire Builder (1968)

Corcoran, Jean
2091. Elias Howe: Inventive Boy (1962)

DeGrummond, Lena
2092. Babe Didrikson, Girl Athlete (1963)
2093. Jean Felix Piccard: Boy Balloonist (1968)

DeGrummond, Lena, and Lynn Delaune
2094. Jeff Davis: Confederate Boy (1960)

Dobler, Lavinia
2095. Cyrus McCormick: Farmer Boy (1961)
2096. Lee DeForest: Electronics Boy (1956)

Dunham, Montrew
2097. Abner Doubleday: First Baseball Boy (1965)
2098. Anne Bradstreet: Young Puritan Poet (1969)
2099. George Westinghouse: Young Inventor (1963)
2100. Langston Hughes: Young Black Poet (1972)
2101. Oliver Wendell Holmes, Jr.: Boy of Justice (1961)

Frisbee, Lucy
2102. John Burroughs: Boy of Field and Stream (1964)
2103. John F. Kennedy: Young Statesman (1964)

Govan, Christine
2104. Rachel Jackson: Tennessee Girl (1955)

Guthridge, Sue
2105. Tom Edison: Boy Inventor (1959)

Hammontree, Marie
2106. A. P. Giannini: Boy of San Francisco (1962)
2107. Albert Einstein: Young Thinker (1961)
2108. Walt Disney: Young Movie Maker (1969)
2109. Will and Charlie Mayo: Boy Doctors (1962)

Harley, Ruth
2110. Glenn L. Martin: Boy Conqueror of the Air (1967)

Henry, Joanne
2111. Andrew Carnegie: Young Steelmaker (1966)
2112. Bernard Baruch: Boy from South Carolina (1971)
2113. Elizabeth Blackwell: Girl Doctor (1961)
2114. George Eastman: Young Photographer (1959)
2115. Robert Fulton: Boy Craftsman (1962)

Higgins, Helen
    2116. Alec Hamilton: Little Lion (1962)
    2117. Juliette Low: Girl Scout (1959)
    2118. Noah Webster: Boy of Words (1961)
    2119. Stephen Foster: Boy Minstrel (1963)
    2120. Walter Reed: Boy Who Wanted to Know (1961)
Howe, Jane
    2121. Amelia Earhart: Kansas Girl (1961)
Hudson, Wilma
    2122. Dwight D. Eisenhower: Young Military Leader (1970)
    2123. J. C. Penney: Golden Rule Boy (1972)
Jordan, Polly, and Lucy Frisbee
    2124. Brigham Young: Covered Wagon Boy (1962)
Korson, George
    2125. John L. Lewis: Young Militant Labor Leader (1970)
Long, Laura
    2126. David Farragut: Boy Midshipman (1962)
    2127. Douglas MacArthur: Young Protector (1965)
    2128. George Dewey: Vermont Boy (1963)
    2129. John Peter Zenger: Young Defender of a Free Press (1966)
    2130. Oliver Hazard Perry: Boy of the Sea (1962)
Mason, Miriam
    2131. Dan Beard: Boy Scout (1953)
    2132. Frances Willard: Girl Crusader (1961)
    2133. John Audubon: Boy Naturalist (1962)
    2134. Kate Douglas Wiggin: Little Schoolteacher (1962)
    2135. Mark Twain: Boy of Old Missouri (1962)
    2136. Mary Mapes Dodge: Jolly Girl (1962)
    2137. William Penn: Friendly Boy (1962)
Melin, Grace
    2138. Dorothea Dix: Girl Reformer (1963)
    2139. Henry Wadsworth Longfellow: Gifted Young Poet (1968)
    2140. Maria Mitchell: Girl Astronomer (1960)
Millender, Dharathula
    2141. Crispus Attucks: Boy of Valor (1965)
    2142. Louis Armstrong: Young Music Maker (1972)
    2143. Martin Luther King, Jr.: Boy with a Dream (1969)
Mitchell, Minnie
    2144. James Whitcomb Riley: Hoosier Boy (1962)
Monsell, Helen
    2145. Dolly Madison: Quaker Girl (1961)
    2146. Henry Clay: Young Kentucky Orator (1963)
    2147. John Marshall: Boy of Young America (1962)
    2148. Robert E. Lee: Boy of Old Virginia (1960)
    2149. Susan Anthony: Girl Who Dared (1960)
    2150. Tom Jackson: Young Stonewall (1961)
    2151. Tom Jefferson: Boy of Colonial Days (1962)
    2152. Woodrow Wilson: Boy President (1959)
Moore, Clyde
    2153. Frederic Remington: Young Artist (1971)
    2154. J. Sterling Morton: Arbor Day Boy (1962)
    2155. Robert Goddard: Pioneer Rocket Boy (1966)

Myers, Elisabeth
 2156. David Sarnoff: Radio and T.V. Boy (1972)
 2157. Edward Bok: Young Editor (1967)
 2158. F. W. Woolworth: 5 and 10 Boy (1962)
 2159. Frederick Douglass: Boy Champion of Human Rights (1970)
 2160. George Pullman: Young Sleeping Car Builder (1963)
 2161. Katharine Lee Bates: Girl Poet (1961)
Myers, Hortense, and Ruth Barnett
 2162. Carl Ben Eilson: Young Alaskan Pilot (1960)
 2163. Edward R. Murrow: Young Newscaster (1969)
 2164. Vilhjalmur Stefansson: Young Arctic Explorer (1966)
 2165. Vincent Lombardi: Young Football Coach (1971)
Newman, Shirlee
 2166. Ethel Barrymore: Girl Actress (1966)
 2167. Liliuokalani: Young Hawaiian Queen (1960)
Paradis, Adrian
 2168. Gail Borden, Resourceful Boy (1964)
 2169. Harvey S. Firestone: Young Rubber Pioneer (1968)
Parks, Aileen
 2170. Bedford Forrest: Horseback Boy (1952)
 2171. Davy Crockett: Young Rifleman (1962)
 2172. James Oglethorpe: Young Defender (1960)
 2173. Teddy Roosevelt: All Round Boy (1961)
Peckham, Howard
 2174. Nathanael Greene: Independent Boy (1963)
 2175. Pontiac: Young Ottawa Leader (1963)
 2176. William Henry Harrison: Young Tippecanoe (1962)
Place, Marion
 2177. Lotta Crabtree: Gold Rush Girl (1962)
Schaaf, Martha
 2178. Lew Wallace: Boy Writer (1961)
Scharbach, Alexander
 2179. Matthew Calbraith Perry: Boy Sailor (1963)
Seymour, Flora
 2180. Pocahontas: Brave Girl (1961)
 2181. Sacajawea: Bird Girl (1959)
Smith, Bradford
 2182. Dan Webster: Union Boy (1962)
 2183. Stephen Decatur: Gallant Boy (1962)
 2184. William Bradford: Pilgrim Boy (1963)
Snow, Dorothea
 2185. Benjamin West: Gifted Young Painter (1967)
 2186. Eli Whitney: Boy Mechanic (1962)
 2187. John Paul Jones: Salt Water Boy (1962)
 2188. Raphael Semmes: Tidewater Boy (1952)
 2189. Samuel Morse: Inquisitive Boy (1960)
 2190. Sequoyah: Young Cherokee Guide (1960)
Steele, William O.
 2191. Francis Marion: Young Swamp Fox (1962)
 2192. John Sevier: Pioneer Boy (1953)
Stevenson, Augusta
 2193. Abe Lincoln: Frontier Boy (1959)
 2194. Andy Jackson: Boy Soldier (1962)

2195. Anthony Wayne: Daring Boy (1962)
2196. Ben Franklin: Boy Printer (1962)
2197. Booker T. Washington: Ambitious Boy (1960)
2198. Buffalo Bill: Boy of the Plains (1959)
2199. Clara Barton: Girl Nurse (1962)
2200. Daniel Boone: Boy Hunter (1961)
2201. Francis Scott Key: Maryland Boy (1960)
2202. George Armstrong Custer: Boy of Action (1963)
2203. George Carver: Boy Scientist (1959)
2204. George Washington: Boy Leader (1959)
2205. Israel Putnam: Fearless Boy (1959)
2206. John Fitch: Steamboat Boy (1966)
2207. Kit Carson: Boy Trapper (1962)
2208. Miles Standish: Adventurous Boy (1962)
2209. Molly Pitcher: Girl Patriot (1960)
2210. Nancy Hanks: Kentucky Girl (1962)
2211. Nathan Hale: Puritan Boy (1959)
2212. P. T. Barnum: Circus Boy (1964)
2213. Paul Revere: Boy of Old Boston (1962)
2214. Sam Houston: Boy Chieftain (1962)
2215. Sitting Bull: Dakota Boy (1962)
2216. Squanto: Young Indian Hunter (1962)
2217. Tecumseh: Shawnee Boy (1962)
2218. U. S. Grant: Young Horseman (1947)
2219. Virginia Dare: Mystery Girl (1959)
2220. Wilbur and Orville Wright: Boys with Wings (1959)
2221. Zeb Pike: Boy Traveler (1963)

VanRiper, Guernsey
2222. Babe Ruth: Baseball Boy (1959)
2223. Jim Thorpe: Indian Athlete (1961)
2224. Knute Rockne: Young Athlete (1959)
2225. Lou Gehrig: Boy of the Sand Lots (1959)
2226. Richard Byrd: Boy of the South Pole (1958)
2227. Will Rogers: Young Cowboy (1962)

Wagoner, Jean
2228. Abigail Adams: Girl of Colonial Days (1962)
2229. Jane Addams: Little Lame Girl (1962)
2230. Jessie Fremont: Girl of Capitol Hill (1960)
2231. Julia Ward Howe: Girl of Old New York (1962)
2232. Louisa Alcott: Girl of Old Boston (1962)
2233. Martha Washington: Girl of Old Virginia (1959)

Ward, Martha
2234. Adlai Stevenson: Young Ambassador (1967)

Warner, Ann
2235. Narcissa Whitman: Pioneer Girl (1959)

Weddle, Ethel
2236. Alvin C. York: Young Marksman (1967)
2237. Joel Chandler Harris: Young Storyteller (1946)
2238. Walter Chrysler: Boy Machinist (1960)

Weil, Ann
2239. Betsy Ross: Girl of Old Philadelphia (1961)
2240. Eleanor Roosevelt: Charitable Girl (1965)
2241. John Philip Sousa: Marching Boy (1959)

CHILDHOOD OF FAMOUS AMERICANS SERIES —Bobbs-Merrill (cont'd)
    2242. John Quincy Adams: Boy Patriot (1963)
Widdemer, Mabel
    2243. Aleck Bell: Ingenious Boy (1962)
    2244. DeWitt Clinton: Boy Builder (1961)
    2245. Harriet Beecher Stowe: Connecticut Girl (1962)
    2246. James Monroe: Good Neighbor Boy (1959)
    2247. Peter Stuyvesant: Boy with Wooden Shoes (1962)
    2248. Washington Irving: Boy of Old New York (1963)
Wilkie, Katharine
    2249. Clyde Beatty: Boy Animal Trainer (1968)
    2250. George Rogers Clark: Boy of Old Northwest (1960)
    2251. Helen Keller: Handicapped Girl (1969)
    2252. Mary Todd Lincoln: Girl of the Bluegrass (1960)
    2253. Simon Kenton: Young Trailblazer (1960)
    2254. Will Clark: Boy in Buckskins (1963)
    2255. William Fargo: Young Mail Carrier (1962)
    2256. Zack Taylor: Boy Traveler (1962)
Wilson, Ellen
    2257. Annie Oakley: Little Sureshot (1962)
    2258. Ernie Pyle: Boy from Back Home (1962)
    2259. Robert Frost: Boy with Promises to Keep (1967)
Winders, Gertrude
    2260. Ethan Allen: Green Mountain Boy (1962)
    2261. George M. Cohan: Boy Theater Genius (1968)
    2263. Harriet Tubman: Freedom Girl (1969)
    2264. James Fenimore Cooper: Leatherstocking Boy (1951)
    2265. Jeb Stuart: Boy in the Saddle (1959)
    2266. Jim Bowie: Boy with a Hunting Knife (1957)
    2267. Jim Bridger: Mountain Boy (1962)
A series of overwhelming magnitude and of generally good quality. In describing
the childhood of biographees, many of the authors use a story-like style. This style
may serve to attract some readers, but other readers may wonder how such intimate
information was obtained. Some of the books list related projects at the end of
the book. For grades 4 through 6.

CHILDREN EVERYWHERE —Hastings House
DeJaeger, Charles
    2268. Paul Is a Maltese Boy (1968)
Jessel, Camilla
    2269. Manuela Lives in Portugal (1969)
Lawson, Pat, and Dennis Hodgson
    2270. Kuma Is a Maori Girl (1967)
Levin, Deana, and Dmitri Baltermants
    2271. Nikolai Lives in Moscow (1968)
MacMahon, Bryan, and Wolfgang Suschitzky
    2272. Brendan of Ireland (1967)
Marks, Stan
    2273. Graham Is an Aboriginal Boy (1968)
Mauthner, Maria, and Charles DeJaeger
    2274. Christiane Lives in the Alps (1967)
Silverstone, Marilyn, and Luree Miller
    2275. Bala: Child of India (1968)
Each volume of this series follows the daily activities of a child in a foreign

country. The books are easy to read, with only one small paragraph of information on each page and many large photos. Some volumes of the series are in ITA. Supplemental for social studies courses.

CHILDREN OF . . . —Sterling
>Acquaye, Alfred
>>2276. Children of West Africa (1968)
>Andrlova, Marcela
>>2277. Children of Czechoslovakia (1969)
>Shirakigawa, Tomiko
>>2278. Children of Japan (1967)

This series does not deal with individual children *per se*, but rather portrays what life is like in these countries through the eyes of children. There is much more factual information here than is often found in series of this type: information on social customs, education, clothing, etc. Grades 4 through 6.

CHILDREN OF THE WORLD —Follett
>Darbois, Dominique
>>2279. Achouna, Boy of the Arctic (1962)
>>2280. Agossou, Boy of Africa (1962)
>>2281. Aslak, Boy of Lapland (1967)
>>2282. Hassan, Boy of the Desert (1961)
>>2283. Kai Ming, Boy of Hong Kong (1960)
>>2284. Lakhmi, Girl of India (1964)
>>2285. Noriko, Girl of Japan (1964)
>>2286. Rikka and Rindji, Children of Bali (1959)
>>2287. Tacho, Boy of Mexico (1961)
>>2288. Yanis, Boy of Greece (1967)
>Malois, Claude
>>2289. Giuliano, Boy of Sicily (1969)
>Maziere, Francis
>>2290. Parana, Boy of the Amazon (1959)
>>2291. Teiva, Boy of Tahiti (1960)

The best use of this series would be to arouse interest in young or reluctant readers. There is little information besides that presented in the photographs, so the volumes would not be very useful for fulfilling school assignments.

CHILDREN'S ILLUSTRATED CLASSICS —Dutton
>Alcott, Louisa May
>>2292. Good Wives (1953)
>>2293. Jo's Boys (1959)
>>2294. Little Men (1957)
>>2295. Little Women (1948)
>Andersen, Hans Christian
>>2296. Hans Andersen's Fairy Tales (1958)
>Ballantyne, Robert
>>2297. Dog Crusoe (1966)
>Blackmore, Richard
>>2298. Lorna Doone (1959)
>Browne, Frances
>>2299. Granny's Wonderful Chair (1963)
>Buchan, John
>>2300. The Thirty-Nine Steps (1964)

Bunyan, John
    2301. Pilgrim's Progress (1961)
Burnett, Frances Hodgson
    2302. Little Lord Fauntleroy (1954)
Carey, M. C.
    2303. Fairy Tales of Long Ago (1952)
Carroll, Lewis
    2304. Alice's Adventures in Wonderland and Through the Looking
        Glass (1954)
Cervantes, Miguel
    2305. Don Quixote (1954)
Childers, Erskin
    2306. Riddle of the Sands (1970)
Collodi, Carlo
    2307. Pinocchio (1960)
Coolidge, Susan
    2308. What Katy Did (1968)
Defoe, Daniel
    2309. Robinson Crusoe (1954)
Dickens, Charles
    2310. A Christmas Carol and the Cricket on the Hearth (1963)
Dodge, Mary Mapes
    2311. Hans Brinker (1956)
Ewing, Mrs.
    2312. The Brownies (1954)
Green, Roger Lancelyn
    2313. Book of Myths (1957)
    2314. Book of Nonsense (1956)
    2315. Modern Fairy Stories (1956)
    2316. Tales of Make-Believe (1960)
    2317. Ten Tales of Detection (1967)
    2318. The Tale of Ancient Israel (1969)
    2319. Thirteen Uncanny Tales (1970)
Hadfield, A. M.
    2320. King Arthur and the Round Table (1962)
Haggard, H. Rider
    2321. King Solomon's Mines (1960)
Hawthorne, Nathaniel
    2322. Tanglewood Tales (1952)
    2323. Wonder Book (1954)
Hope, Anthony
    2324. Rupert of Hentzau (1963)
    2325. The Prisoner of Zenda (1955)
Hughes, Thomas
    2326. Tom Brown's School Days (1952)
Ingelow, Jean
    2327. Mopsa the Fairy (1964)
Kingsley, Charles
    2328. Heroes (1963)
    2329. Water Babies (1959)
Lamb, Charles, and Mary Lamb
    2330. Tales from Shakespeare (1956)

Lang, Andrew
    2331. Prince Prigio and Prince Ricardo (1961)
    2332. The Adventures of Odysseus (1959)
London, Jack
    2333. Call of the Wild (1968)
    2334. White Fang (1967)
Longfellow, Henry Wadsworth
    2335. The Song of Hiawatha (1959)
MacDonald, George
    2336. At the Back of the North Wind (1948)
    2337. The Lost Princess (1950)
    2338. The Princess and the Curdie (1948)
    2339. The Princess and the Goblin (1949)
Merriman, Henry
    2340. Barlasch of the Guard (1971)
Molesworth, Mrs.
    2341. Carved Lions (1964)
    2342. The Cuckoo Clock (1954)
Nesbit, Mrs.
    2343. The Enchanted Castle (1964)
    2344. The House of Arden (1968)
Oman, Carola
    2345. Robin Hood (1951)
Poe, Edgar Allan
    2346. Tales of Terror and Fantasy (1972)
Raspe, R. E.
    2347. Baron Munchausen and Other Comic Tales from Germany (1971)
Seton, Ernest
    2348. The Trail of the Sandhill Stag (1959)
Sewell, Anna
    2349. Black Beauty
Spyri, Johanna
    2350. Heidi (1957)
Stevenson, Robert Louis
    2351. A Child's Garden of Verses (1956)
    2352. Kidnapped (1959)
    2353. The Black Arrow (1958)
    2354. Treasure Island (1959)
Swift, Jonathan
    2355. Gulliver's Travels (1952)
Twain, Mark
    2356. Huckleberry Finn (1955)
    2357. The Prince and the Pauper (1968)
    2358. Tom Sawyer (1960)
Verne, Jules
    2359. Around the World in Eighty Days (1968)
    2360. From the Earth to the Moon (1970)
    2361. Journey to the Center of the Earth (1970)
    2362. Twenty Thousand Leagues under the Sea (1969)
Warrington, John
    2363. Aesop's Fables (1959)
Wilde, Oscar
    2364. The Happy Prince and Other Stories (1968)

CHILDREN'S ILLUSTRATED CLASSICS —Dutton (cont'd)
>   Wyss, Johann
>   2365. Swiss Family Robinson (1962)
There are many series of classics for young people. This one features black-and-white illustrations, some by the original artist. The typeface used is rather small.

CITIES OF THE WORLD —Rand
>   Fritz, Jean
>   2366. San Francisco (1962)
>   Hall, Elvajean
>   2367. Hong Kong (1967)
>   Rosenbaum, Maurice
>   2368. London (1963)
>   Smith, Irene
>   2369. Paris (1961)
>   2370. Washington, D.C. (1964)
Like the Key to the City series and Big Cities series, this one covers the history, sites, and memories that make up each city. This series may be somewhat outdated by now.

CITY SCIENCE —Hastings House
>   Adrian, Mary
>   2371. Secret Neighbors: Wildlife in a City Lot (1971)
Another addition to the fictionalized life-of-an-animal genre. This one is slightly different in that it presents wildlife that can be found in the urban environment. The drawings are excellent and may help to make city children aware of all the life that is going on around them.

CLUSTERS BIOGRAPHIES —McGraw-Hill
>   Cuneo, John
>   2372. Benjamin Franklin: Ingenious Diplomat (1969)
>   Ellis, David
>   2373. The Saratoga Campaign (1969)
>   McKown, Robin
>   2374. Horatio Gates and Benedict Arnold (1969)
>   O'Connor, Richard
>   2375. John Burgoyne: Gentleman and General (1969)
This series is unusual in that it examines certain pivotal events and the individuals involved in them from four different points of view. This first cluster of four books covers the Revolutionary War. Excellent material for the 8 to 12 age group.

COLBY, CARROLL B. —Coward
>   First Books
>   2376. First Boat: How to Pick It and Use It for Fun Afloat (1956)
>   2377. First Bow and Arrow: How to Use It Skillfully for Outdoor Fun (1955)
>   2378. First Fish: What You Should Do to Catch Him (1953)
>   2379. First Hunt: With Success and Safety (1957)
>   2380. First Rifle: How to Shoot It Straight and Use It Safely (1954)
Mr. Colby examines various of the outdoor sports in depth. He not only shows readers how to do a particular sport, but continually emphasizes safety measures and rules. Very good beginning books.
>   2381. Air Drop (1953)
>   2382. Air Force Academy (1962)

COLBY, CARROLL B.   —Coward   (cont'd)
2383. Aircraft of World War I (1962)
2384. America's Natural Wonders (1956)
2385. Annapolis (1964)
2386. Arms of Our Fighting Men   (1972)
2387. Astronauts in Training (1969)
2388. Atomic Energy at Work (1968)
2389. Beyond the Moon (1971)
2390. Big Game (1967)
2391. Bomber Parade (1960)
2392. Chute! Air Drop for Defense and Sport (1972)
2393. Civil War Weapons (1962)
2394. Cliff Dwellings (1965)
2395. Coast Guard Academy (1965)
2396. Communications (1964)
2397. Count Down (1970)
2398. Danger Fighters (1953)
2399. Early American Crafts (1967)
2400. F.B.I. (1970)
2401. Fighter Parade (1960)
2402   Fighting Gear of World War I (1961)
2403. Fighting Gear of World War II (1961)
2404. Firearms by Winchester (1957)
2405. Fish and Wildlife (1955)
2406. Frogmen (1954)
2407. Historic American Forts (1963)
2408. Historic American Landmarks (1968)
2409. Jets of the World (1966)
2410. Leatherneck (1957)
2411. Modern Light (1967)
2412. Moon Exploration (1970)
2413. Musket to M-14 (1960)
2414. National Guard (1968)
2415. Night People (1969)
2416. North American Air Defense Command (1969)
2417. Our Space Age Army (1961)
2418. Our Space Age Jets (1959)
2419. Our Space Age Navy (1962)
2420. Park Rangers (1955)
2421. Plastic Magic (1959)
2422. Police (1971)
2423. Railroads, U.S.A. (1970)
2424. Revolutionary War Weapons (1963)
2425. S.A.C. (1961)
2426. Sailing Ships (1970)
2427. Secret Service (1966)
2428. Ships of Commerce (1963)
2429. Ships of Our Navy (1963)
2430. Signal Corps Today (1966)
2431. Small Game (1968)
2432. Smoke Eaters (1954)
2433. Soil Savers (1957)
2434. Space Age Spinoffs (1972)
2435. Special Forces (1964)

46

COLBY, CARROLL B. —Coward (cont'd)
        2436. Submarine (1953)
        2437. Submarine Warfare (1967)
        2438. Survival (1965)
        2439. Today's Camping (1972)
        2440. Trucks of the Highway (1964)
        2441. Underwater World (1966)
        2442. West Point (1963)
        2443. Wildlife in Our National Parks (1965)

The volumes of this series are made up primarily of photographs. Text is limited to one paragraph of explanation under each photo. The series provides good supplemental material, but there is not much detailed information. The books are not indexed.

COLLECT, PRINT AND PAINT   Whitman
     Hawkinson, John
        2444. Collect, Print and Paint from Nature (1963)
        2445. More to Collect, Print and Paint from Nature (1964)
        2446. Our Wonderful Wayside (1966)
        2447. Paint a Rainbow (1970)
        2448. Pastels Are Great! (1968)

Various aspects of drawing are covered step-by-step in these how-to books. The directions are very clear, as are the illustrations. These are basic, introductory books; they are better beginning books than the How to Draw series. For grades 3 on up.

COLONIAL AMERICANS   —Watts
     Fisher, Leonard
        2449. The Architects (1970)
        2450. The Cabinetmakers (1966)
        2451. The Doctors (1968)
        2452. The Glassmakers (1964)
        2453. The Hatters (1965)
        2454. The Limners: America's Earliest Portrait Painters (1969)
        2455. The Papermakers (1965)
        2456. The Peddlers (1968)
        2457. The Potters (1969)
        2458. The Printers (1965)
        2459. The Schoolmasters (1967)
        2460. The Shipbuilders (1971)
        2461. The Shoemakers (1967)
        2462. The Silversmiths (1965)
        2463. The Tanners (1966)
        2464. The Weavers (1966)
        2465. The Wigmakers (1965)

Each of the slim volumes contains plenty of information on a trade of colonial America. There are some photos, many drawings, and an index. This series would be helpful for school assignments and would make a fine addition to any collection.

COLONIAL HISTORY BOOKS   —Nelson
     Beals, Carleton
        2466. Colonial Rhode Island (1970)
     Burney, Eugenia
        2467. Colonial South Carolina (1970)

COLONIAL HISTORY BOOKS —Nelson
    Capps, Lucille, and Eugenia Burney
      2468. Colonial Georgia (1972)
    Christensen, Gardell
      2469. Colonial New York (1969)
    Cunningham, John T.
      2470. Colonial New Jersey (1971)
    Wallower, Lucille
      2471. Colonial Pennsylvania (1969)
    Wood, James
      2472. Colonial Massachusetts (1969)
The volumes of this excellent series cover both history and the way of life in individual colonies, although the emphasis varies from book to book. There are bibliographies, indices, maps, letters, and lists of important dates. The photos and facsimiles of etchings and paintings are excellent. In addition, some of the books mention historical sites that the reader could visit. The only similar series is the Forge of Freedom series. Grades 5 and up.

COLONIAL WILLIAMSBURG —Holt
    Cooney, Barbara
      2473. A Garland of Games and Other Diversions (1969)
    Davis, Burke
      2474. America's First Army (1962)
    Dwight, Allan
      2475. To the Walls of Cartagena (1967)
    Faulkner, Nancy
      2476. Second Son (1970)
    Havighurst, Walter
      2477. Proud Prisoner (1964)
    Hays, Wilma Pitchford
      2478. Mary's Star (1968)
      2479. The French Are Coming (1965)
      2480. The Scarlet Badge (1963)
    Miers, Earl Schenck
      2481. Pirate Chase (1965)
    Steele, William O.
      2482. Tomahawk Border (1966)
      2483. Wayah of the Real People (1964)
    Vance, Marguerite
      2484. The Beloved Friend (1963)
    Wellman, Manly Wade
      2485. Brave Horse: The Story of Janus (1968)
The works in this series, set in the Williamsburg area, are both fiction and non-fiction. The illustrations are superior—by Cooney, Burchard, and Weisgard, among others. For ages 9 to 11.

COLONY LEADERS —Garrard
    DeLeeuw, Adele
      2486. Colony Leader: Peter Stuyvesant (1970)
    Faber, Doris
      2487. Colony Leader: Anne Hutchinson (1970)
    Graves, Charles
      2488. Colony Leader: William Bradford (1969)

COLONY LEADERS —Garrard (cont'd)
    Peterson, Helen
        2489. Colony Leader: Roger Williams (1968)
    Radford, Ruby
        2490. Colony Leader: James Edward Oglethorpe (1968)
In addition to being biographies of various leaders and settlers in the early colonies, these books are also histories of the colonies themselves. Each book deals with the events leading up to the founding of the colony, then with the settlement and growth of the colony. The books are easy to read and should be good supplementary material for history and social studies courses. For grades 3 to 6.

COMPOSERS AND THEIR TIMES —Walck
    Westcott, Frederic
        2491. Bach (1967)
    Woodford, Peggy
        2492. Mozart (1966)
        2493. Schubert (1969)
Although the series purports to place the artist in relation to his art, society, and time, there are no samples of his music nor any listening suggestions for readers. There is a bibliography, but no index, and no photos or illustrations. Only when nothing else is available.

CORNERSTONES OF FREEDOM —Childrens Press
    Mayer, A. I.
        2494. The Story of Old Glory (1970)
    Miller, Natalie
        2495. The Story of Mount Vernon (1965)
        2496. The Story of the Liberty Bell (1965)
        2497. The Story of the Lincoln Memorial (1966)
        2498. The Story of the Star Spangled Banner (1965)
        2499. The Story of the Statue of Liberty (1965)
        2500. The Story of the White House (1966)
    Prolman, Marilyn
        2501. The Story of Jamestown (1969)
        2502. The Story of Mount Rushmore (1969)
        2503. The Story of the Capitol (1969)
        2504. The Story of the Constitution (1969)
    Richards, Kenneth
        2505. The Story of the Alamo (1970)
        2506. The Story of the "Bonhomme Richard" (1969)
        2507. The Story of the Conestoga Wagon (1970)
    Richards, Norman
        2508. The Story of Monticello (1970)
        2509. The Story of Old Ironsides (1967)
        2510. The Story of the Gettysburg Address (1969)
        2511. The Story of the Mayflower Compact (1967)
        2512. The Story of the Supreme Court (1970)
In these introductions to various historical places, symbols, and happenings, the treatment is very simple and not in depth, but the color illustrations enhance the text. The volumes are not indexed. For grades 3 to 5.

COUNTRY PROFILE —Praeger
    Alba, Victor
        2513. Peru: A Profile (1972)

COUNTRY PROFILE —Praeger (cont'd)
    Hatch, John
        2514. Tanzania: A Profile (1972)
    Matley, Ian
        2515. Romania: A Profile (1970)
    Naamani, Israel
        2516. Israel: A Profile (1972)
    Petrov, Victor
        2517. Mongolia: A Profile (1970)
    Wagenheim, Kal
        2518. Puerto Rico: A Profile (1971)
This is an excellent series on various countries of the world. The books cover not only the history, culture, economy, geography, and politics of these nations, but the effects of socio-economic changes on each nation. One benefit of the series is its study of some of the lesser-known countries. For grades 7 on up.

CREATIVE ACTIVITY BOOKS —Crowell
    Seidelman, Joseph, and Grace Mintoyne
        2519. Creating with Clay (1967)
        2520. Creating with Mosaics (1967)
        2521. Creating with Paint (1967)
        2522. Creating with Paper (1967)
        2523. Creating with Papier-Mache (1971)
        2524. Creating with Wood (1969)
        2525. Shopping Cart Art (1970)
The instructions in these simply illustrated craft books are easy to follow, and the projects are indexed. The materials also are generally available in the home. For grades 3 on up.

CREATIVE PEOPLE IN THE ARTS AND SCIENCES SERIES —Garrard
    Anderson, LaVere
        2526. Frederic Remington: Artist on Horseback (1971)
    Bishop, Claire
        2527. Johann Sebastian Bach: Music Giant (1972)
        2528. Mozart: Music Magician (1968)
    Colver, Anne
        2529. Louisa May Alcott: Author of "Little Women" (1969)
    DeLeeuw, Adele
        2530. Maria Tallchief: American Ballerina (1971)
        2531. Marie Curie: Woman of Genius (1970)
    Douty, Esther
        2532. Charlotte Forten: Free Black Teacher (1971)
    Epstein, Samuel, and Beryl Epstein
        2533. Michael Faraday: Apprentice to Science (1971)
    Franchere, Ruth
        2534. Carl Sandburg: Voice of the People (1970)
    Glendinning, Sally
        2535. Thomas Gainsborough: Artist of England (1969)
    Montgomery, Elizabeth
        2536. Albert Schweitzer: Great Humanitarian (1971)
        2537. Hans Christian Andersen: Immortal Storyteller (1968)
    Myers, Elisabeth
        2538. Jenny Lind: Songbird from Sweden (1968)
        2539. Langston Hughes: Poet of His People (1970)

CREATIVE PEOPLE IN THE ARTS AND SCIENCES SERIES   —Garrard (cont'd)
    Schultz, Pearle
        2540. Isaac Newton: Scientific Genius (1972)
The volumes of this good biographic series relate true incidents in the lives of the
individuals, with no attempt to fictionalize. There are photos plus, where applicable,
selections for listening and viewing. There is also a glossary of terms. For grades
4 through 7.

CROSSROADS OF AMERICA —Putnam
    Dangerfield, George
        2541. Defiance to the Old World (1970)
    DeConde, Alexander
        2542. Decisions for Peace: The Federalist Era (1970)
    McDonald, Forrest
        2543. Enough Wise Men: The Story of Our Constitution (1970)
    Wright, Esmond
        2544. A Time for Courage: The Story of the Declaration of Indepen-
            dence (1971)
These books deal in detail with the history of a single event: what led up to it, what
happened during it, and what the repercussions were. There are no illustrations, but
there is an index. For grades 6 through 12.

CROWELL BIOGRAPHIES
    Adoff, Arnold
        2545. Malcolm X (1970)
    Bertol, Roland
        2546. Charles Drew (1970)
    Cone, Molly
        2547. Leonard Bernstein (1970)
        2548. The Ringling Brothers (1971)
    Daugherty, Charles
        2549. Samuel Clemens (1970)
    Fall, Thomas
        2550. Jim Thorpe (1970)
    Franchere, Ruth
        2551. Cesar Chavez (1970)
        2552. The Wright Brothers (1972)
    Goodsell, Jane
        2553. Eleanor Roosevelt (1970)
        2554. The Mayo Brothers (1972)
    Graves, Charles
        2555. John Muir (1972)
    Jordan, June
        2556. Fannie Lou Hamer (1972)
    Kaufman, Mervyn
        2557. Fiorello LaGuardia (1972)
    Keeler, Gail
        2558. Jane Addams (1971)
    Phelan, Mary Kay
        2559. Martha Berry (1972)
    Rudeen, Kenneth
        2560. Jackie Robinson (1971)
        2561. Wilt Chamberlain (1970)

CROWELL BIOGRAPHIES (cont'd)
>   Tobias, Tobi
>   2562. Maria Tallchief (1970)
>   2563. Marian Anderson (1972)
>   Turk, Midge
>   2564. Gordon Parks (1971)

An excellent beginning-to-read biography series. The text is simple, the print is large, and the appearance of the books is improved by the pastel drawings. Some of the books are not well written and have a sing-song tone; however, the subjects of these volumes are not covered even in older biographies. For grades 2 through 4, and also for reluctant readers.

CROWELL HERO TALES
>   McGovern, Ann
>   2565. Robin Hood of Sherwood Forest (1968)
>   Newman, Robert
>   2566. The Twelve Labors of Hercules (1972)
>   Walker, Barbara
>   2567. Korolu, the Singing Bandit (1970)
>   White, Anne Terry
>   2568. David the Giantkiller (1970)
>   2569. Odysseus Comes Home from the Sea (1968)
>   Williams, Jay
>   2570. The Horn of Roland (1968)
>   2571. The Sword of King Arthur (1968)

These are retellings of various hero tales from England, Greece, Turkey, and France. Although generally well done, their appeal may be limited. For ages 9 through 12.

CROWELL POETS
>   Adams, J. Donald
>   2572. Poems of Ralph Waldo Emerson (1965)
>   Cole, William
>   2573. Poems of Thomas Hood (1968)
>   2574. Poems of W. S. Gilbert (1967)
>   Deutsch, Babette
>   2575. Poems of Samuel Taylor Coleridge (1967)
>   Frankenberg, Lloyd
>   2576. Poems of Robert Burns (1967)
>   2577. Poems of William Shakespeare (1966)
>   Fuller, Edmund
>   2578. Poems of Henry Wadsworth Longfellow (1967)
>   Gregory, Horace
>   2579. Poems of George Gordon, Lord Byron (1969)
>   Gurko, Leo
>   2580. Poems of Percy Bysshe Shelley (1968)
>   Kunitz, Stanley
>   2581. Poems of John Keats (1964)
>   Livingston, Myra
>   2582. Poems of Lewis Carroll (announced)
>   Macdonald, Dwight
>   2583. Poems of Edgar Allan Poe (1965)
>   McDonald, Gerald
>   2584. Poems of Stephen Crane (1965)
>   Munson, Amelia
>   2585. Poems of William Blake (1964)

CROWELL POETS (cont'd)
    Parker, Elinor
        2586. Poems of William Wordsworth   (1964)
    Plotz, Helen
        2587. Poems of Emily Dickinson (1964)
        2588. Poems of Robert Louis Stevenson (announced)
    Powell, Lawrence
        2589. Poems of Walt Whitman (1964)
    Rausen, Ruth
        2590. Poems of Alfred, Lord Tennyson (1964)
    Scott, Winfield Townley
        2591. Poems of Robert Herrick (1967)
    Sprague, Rosemary
        2592. Poems of Robert Browning (1964)
Aimed at the junior high and high school audience, these are collections of some
of the best-known poetry of the poets represented. The editors present some biographical and critical information in the introductions, and there are both title and
first-line indices.

CURRICULUM-RELATED BOOKS —Harcourt Brace Jovanovich
    Austell, Jan
        2593. What's in a Play? (1968)
    Avery, Curtis, and Theodore Johannis
        2594. Love and Marriage: A Guide for Young People (1971)
    Barr, Donald
        2595. Arithmetic for Billy Goats (1966)
    Callan, Eileen
        2596. A Hardy Race of Man: America's Early Indians (1970)
    Cheney, T. A.
        2597. Land of the Hibernating Rivers: Life in the Arctic (1968)
    Englebert, Victor
        2598. Camera on Africa: The World of an Ethiopian Boy (1970)
        2599. Camera on Ghana: The World of a Young Fisherman (1971)
        2600. Camera on the Sahara: The World of Three Young Nomads (1971)
    Forman, Brenda
        2601. America's Place in the World Economy (1969)
    Goldberg, George
        2602. East Meets West: The Story of the Chinese and Japanese in
                California (1970)
    Gorodetsky, Charles, and Samuel Christian
        2603. What You Should Know about Drugs (1970)
    Haber, Louis
        2604. Black Pioneers of Science and Invention (1970)
    Hayden, Robert
        2605. Kaleidoscope: Poems by American Negro Poets (1968)
    Holland, John
        2606. The Way It Is (1969)
    James, Leonard
        2607. Following the Frontier: American Transportation in the Nine-
                teenth Century (1968)
    Kastner, Jonathan, and Marianna Kastner
        2608. Sleep: The Mysterious Third of Your Life (1968)
    Krementz, Jill
        2609. Sweet Pea: A Black Girl Growing Up in the Rural South (1969)

53

CURRICULUM-RELATED BOOKS —Harcourt Brace Jovanovich (cont'd)
>   Morsbach, Mabel
>   2610. The Negro in American Life (1968)
>   Morse, Flo
>   2611. Yankee Communes: Another American Way (1971)
>   Place, Marian
>   2612. Comanches and Other Indians of Texas (1970)
>   Roberts, Eric
>   2613. From Football to Finance: The Story of Brady Keys, Jr. (1971)
>   Ruchlis, Hy
>   2614. Bathtub Physics (1967)
>   Smith, Howard E.
>   2615. From Under the Earth: America's Metals, Fuels and Minerals (1967)
>   Terrell, John
>   2616. The Discovery of California (1970)
>   2617. The Search for the Seven Cities: The Opening of the American
>   Southwest (1970)
>   Tripp, Eleanor
>   2618. To America (1969)
>   Uroff, Margaret
>   2619. Becoming a City: From Fishing Village to Manufacturing
>   Center (1968)
>   Young, A. S.
>   2620. Black Champions of the Gridiron: O. J. Simpson and
>   Leroy Keyes (1969)
>   2621. The Mets from Mobile: Cleon Jones and Tommie Agee (1970)

These good books are tangential to the school curriculum. The authors are qualified, and the books themselves, with clearly arranged chapters, have many illustrations and photographs, as well as glossaries and indices.

CURTAIN-RAISER BOOKS —Watts
>   Bizet, George
>   2622. Carmen (1969)
>   Blashfield, Jean
>   2623. The Pirates of Penzance (1966)
>   Hoffman, E. T. A.
>   2624. Coppelia (1971)
>   2625. The Nutcracker (1969)
>   Kudlacek, Jan
>   2626. Petrushka (1971)
>   Manasek, Ludek
>   2627. The Firebird (1970)
>   Mearns, Martha
>   2628. "H.M.S. Pinafore" (1967)
>   2629. Yeomen of the Guard (1967)
>   Wagner, Richard
>   2630. The Flying Dutchman (1969)

These colorful versions of the stories of various ballets and light operas are presented in picture-book format. Some of the music is interspersed with the plot, and there is a brief biography of the composer. Excellent supplementary material for music classes as well as enjoyable for the casual reader. For ages 9 to 11.

DAILY LIFE —Praeger
>   Andrieux, Maurice (Translated by Mary Fitton)
>   2631. Daily Life in Venice at the Time of Casanova (1972)
>   Defourneaux, Marcelin
>   2632. Daily Life in Spain in the Golden Age (1971)
>   Frederic, Louis (Translated by Eileen Lowe)
>   2633. Daily Life in Japan at the Time of the Samurai 1185-1603 (1972)
>   Letheve, Jacques (Translated by Hilary Paddon)
>   2634. Daily Life of French Artists in the Nineteenth Century (1972)

This foreign series is quite well done. It covers the life and customs of all the social classes of each country of the specified time. Such things as wars, religion, and theaters are discussed. The authors are unusually well qualified, and the illustrations are excellent. For grades 7 and up.

DEFENDERS OF FREEDOM   —Garrard
>   Blassingame, Wyatt
>   2635. William F. Halsey: Five-Star Admiral (1970)
>   Foster, John
>   2636. John J. Pershing: World War I Hero (1970)
>   Graves, Charles
>   2637. William Tecumseh Sherman: Champion of the Union (1968)
>   Reeder, Red
>   2638. Dwight David Eisenhower: Fighter for Peace (1968)
>   2639. Omar Nelson Bradley: The Soldier's General (1969)

According to the publisher, the aim of this series is not to glorify war, but rather to discuss the origin of wars and show the parts various outstanding soldiers played in them. Included here are maps and battle plans. Unfortunately, it is hard to see how such a series could fail to arouse at least an interest in war on the part of young readers.

DISCOVERING ART   —McGraw-Hill
>   Batterberry, Michael
>   2640. Art of the Early Renaissance (1970)
>   2641. Art of the Middle Ages (1972)
>   2642. Chinese and Oriental Art (1969)
>   2643. Twentieth Century Art (1969)
>   Batterberry, Michael, and Ariane Ruskin
>   2644. Greek and Roman Art (1970)
>   Ruskin, Ariane
>   2645. Art of the High Renaissance (1970)
>   2646. Nineteenth Century Art (1969)
>   2647. Prehistoric and Ancient Art of the Near East (1971)
>   2648. Seventeenth and Eighteenth Century Art (1969)

The photos and illustrations for this excellent series are well chosen. For the older reader from grades 7 on up.

DISCOVERING SCIENCE   —World
>   Barrett, D. H.
>   2649. Heat (1972)
>   2650. Light (1972)
>   2651. Mechanics (1972)

These slim volumes are good introductions to the scientific principles involved in each subject. Commonplace examples clarify the principle under discussion. For grades 3 to 6.

DISCOVERING WHAT ANIMALS DO SERIES —McGraw-Hill
    Simon, Seymour
        2652. Discovering What Earthworms Do (1969)
        2653. Discovering What Frogs Do (1969)
        2654. Discovering What Gerbils Do (1971)
        2655. Discovering What Goldfish Do (1970)
Differs from other natural science series in that it deals with the collection and care
of animals as pets. Each book tells what the animal looks like, how it behaves, and
how to care for it. There are pronunciation guides given, as well as suggestions for
experiments, but there is no index. For grades 4 to 6.

DISCOVERY SERIES —Garrard
    Anderson, LaVere
        2656. Tad Lincoln: Abe's Son (1971)
    Ayars, James
        2657. John James Audubon: Bird Artist (1966)
    Beach, James
        2658. Theodore Roosevelt: Man of Action (1960)
    Berry, Erick
        2659. Leif the Lucky: Discoverer of America (1961)
        2660. Robert E. Peary: North Pole Conqueror (1963)
    Bishop, Claire
        2661. Lafayette: French-American Hero (1960)
    Blassingame, Wyatt
        2662. Ernest Thompson Seton: Scout and Naturalist (1971)
        2663. Franklin D. Roosevelt: Four Times President (1966)
        2664. Stephen Decatur: Fighting Sailor (1964)
    Campion, Nardi
        2665. Kit Carson: Pathfinder of the West (1963)
    Carmer, Carl
        2666. Henry Hudson: Captain of Ice-Bound Seas (1960)
    Carmer, Carl, and Elizabeth Carmer
        2667. Francis Marion: Swamp Fox of the Carolinas (1962)
    Colver, Anne
        2668. Abraham Lincoln: For the People (1960)
        2669. Florence Nightingale: War Nurse (1961)
        2670. Thomas Jefferson: Author of Independence (1963)
    Davidson, Mary
        2671. Buffalo Bill: Wild West Showman (1962)
        2672. Dolly Madison: Famous First Lady (1966)
    DeLeeuw, Adele
        2673. George Rogers Clark: Frontier Fighter (1967)
        2674. Richard E. Byrd: Adventurer to the Poles (1963)
    Epstein, Samuel, and Beryl Epstein
        2675. George Washington Carver: Negro Scientist (1960)
    Faber, Doris
        2676. Lucretia Mott: Foe of Slavery (1971)
        2677. Luther Burbank: Partner of Nature (1963)
    Graff, Stewart
        2678. George Washington: Father of Freedom (1964)
        2679. John Paul Jones: Sailor Hero (1961)
    Graff, Stewart, and Polly Graff
        2680. Helen Keller: Toward the Light (1965)
    Graves, Charles
        2681. Annie Oakley: The Shooting Star (1961)
        2682. Benjamin Franklin: Man of Ideas (1960)
        2683. Eleanor Roosevelt: First Lady of the World (1966)

DISCOVERY SERIES —Garrard
>2684. John F. Kennedy: New Frontiersman (1965)
2685. Paul Revere: Rider for Liberty (1964)
2686. Robert E. Lee: Hero of the South (1964)
Groh, Lynn
>2687. P. T. Barnum: King of the Circus (1966)
Kaufman, Mervyn
>2688. The Wright Brothers: Kings of the Air (1964)
2689. Thomas Alva Edison: Miracle Maker (1962)
Latham, Frank
>2690. Jed Smith: Trailblazer and Trapper (1968)
Latham, Jean
>2691. David Glasgow Farragut: Our First Admiral (1967)
2692. Eli Whitney: Great Inventor (1963)
2693. George W. Goethals: Panama Canal Engineer (1965)
2694. Sam Houston: Hero of Texas (1965)
2695. Samuel F. B. Morse: Artist-Inventor (1961)
Lomask, Milton
>2696. Robert H. Goddard: Space Pioneer (1972)
Luce, Willard, and Celia Luce
>2697. Jim Bridger: Man of the Mountains (1966)
Montgomery, Elizabeth
>2698. Alexander Graham Bell: Man of Sound (1963)
Moseley, Elizabeth
>2699. Davy Crockett: Hero of the Wild Frontier (1967)
Parlin, John
>2700. Amelia Earhart: Pioneer in the Sky (1962)
2701. Andrew Jackson: Pioneer and President (1962)
Patterson, Lillie
>2702. Booker T. Washington: Leader of His People (1962)
2703. Francis Scott Key: Poet and Patriot (1963)
2704. Frederick Douglass: Freedom Fighter (1965)
Peterson, Helen
>2705. Abigail Adams: "Dear Partner" (1967)
2706. Henry Clay: Leader in Congress (1964)
2707. Jane Addams: Pioneer of Hull House (1965)
Place, Marian
>2708. Marcus and Narcissa Whitman: Oregon Pioneers (1967)
Reeder, Red
>2709. Ulysses S. Grant: Horseman and Fighter (1964)
Rose, Mary C.
>2710. Clara Barton: Soldier of Mercy (1960)
Wilkie, Katharine
>2711. Daniel Boone: Taming the Wilds (1960)
2712. Maria Mitchell: Stargazer (1966)
2713. William Penn: Friend to All (1964)

These are short, easy-to-read biographies for beginning readers. The full-page color illustrations and large print should serve to make these enticing for grades 3 to 5.

DOLCH, EDWARD —Garrard
Folklore of the World
>2714. Stories from Alaska (1961)
2715. Stories from Canada (1964)
2716. Stories from France (1963)

DOLCH, EDWARD —Garrard   (cont'd)
    2717. Stories from Hawaii (1960)
    2718. Stories from India (1961)
    2719. Stories from Italy (1962)
    2720. Stories from Japan (1960)
    2721. Stories from Mexico (1960)
    2722. Stories from Old China (1964)
    2723. Stories from Old Egypt (1964)
    2724. Stories from Old Russia (1964)
    2725. Stories from Spain (1962)
Pleasure Reading
    2726. Aesop's Stories (1951)
    2727. Andersen Stories (1956)
    2728. Bible Stories (1950)
    2729. Fairy Stories (1950)
    2730. Famous Stories (1955)
    2731. Far East Stories (1953)
    2732. Gospel Stories (1951)
    2733. Greek Stories (1955)
    2734. Gulliver's Stories (1960)
    2735. Ivanhoe Stories (1961)
    2736. Old World Stories (1952)
    2737. Robin Hood Stories (1957)
    2738. Robinson Crusoe Stories (1958)
These simple adaptations of well-known stories, myths, and folktales use the Dolch Basic Vocabulary. They are easy to read, but the illustrations are completely unappealing. The chief benefit for the reluctant reader is the large print, the easy vocabulary, and the brevity of the stories. For grades 3 and 4.

DOUBLEDAY FIRST GUIDE TO . . .
    Kimball, Sabra, and Heathcote Kimball
      2739. Doubleday First Guide to Birds (1963)
    Selsam, Millicent
      2740. Doubleday First Guide to Wild Flowers (1964)
    Shuttlesworth, Dorothy
      2741. Doubleday First Guide to Rocks (1963)
    Swain, SuZan
      2742. Doubleday First Guide to Insects (1964)
    Watts, May
      2743. Doubleday First Guide to Trees (1964)
These books are good for identifying specific items, but there is no in-depth treatment of the material. Illustrations are colorful, and there is a pronunciation guide.

DOUBLEDAY SIGNAL BOOKS
    Bowen, Robert S.
      2744. Dirt Track Danger (1963)
    Brennan, Joe
      2745. Hot Rod Thunder (1962)
    Casewit, Curtis
      2746. Adventure in Deepmore Cave (1964)
    Cassiday, Bruce
      2747. Blast Off! (1964)
    Clarke, John
      2748. Black Soldier (1970)

DOUBLEDAY SIGNAL BOOKS (cont'd)
    2749. The Roar of Engines (1970)
Cohen, Tom
    2750. Three Who Dared (1969)
Finlayson, Ann
    2751. A Summer to Remember (1964)
    2752. Gracie (1965)
    2753. Runaway Teen (1970)
Fiore, Evelyn
    2754. Ginny Harris on Stage (1965)
    2755. Mystery at Lane's End (1969)
    2756. Mystery of the Third-Hand Shop (1967)
    2757. Nat Dunlap: Junior Medic (1964)
Fleischman, H. Samuel
    2758. Gang Girl (1967)
Forbes-Robertson, Diana
    2759. Footlights for Jean (1969)
Ford, Eliot
    2760. The Mystery of the Inside Room (1970)
Frankel, Haskell
    2761. Adventure in Alaska (1963)
    2762. Big Band (1965)
    2763. Pro Football Rookie (1964)
    2764. Rodeo Roundup (1965)
Gelman, Steve
    2765. Baseball Bonus Kid (1967)
    2766. Evans of the Army (1965)
    2767. Football Fury (1968)
Gilbert, Miriam
    2768. Shy Girl—The Story of Eleanor Roosevelt (1965)
Hanff, Helene
    2769. Queen of England—The Story of Elizabeth I (1969)
Heavlin, Jay
    2770. Fear Rides High (1970)
Kostka, Matthew
    2771. Climb to the Top (1962)
Laklan, Carli
    2772. Serving in the Peace Corps (1970)
    2773. Two Girls in New York (1964)
        See also fiction series about Nancy Kimball.
Lomas, Steve
    2774. Fishing Fleet Boy (1963)
McDonnell, Jack
    2775. The Ski Patrol (1965)
McDonnell, Virginia
    2776. Trouble at Mercy Hospital (1968)
Manus, Willard
    2777. Sea Treasure (1965)
    2778. The Mystery of the Flooded Mine (1964)
Oberreich, Robert
    2779. The Blood Red Belt (1963)
Parker, Robert
    2780. Carol Heiss: Olympic Biography (1962)

DOUBLEDAY SIGNAL BOOKS (cont'd)
    Pearson, M. J.
      2781. Pony of the Sioux (1966)
    Phillips, Maurice
      2782. Lightning on Ice (1963)
    Preston, Edward
      2783. Martin Luther King: Fighter for Freedom (1970)
    Priddy, Frances
      2784. The Ghosts of Lee House (1968)
    Robinson, Louis
      2785. Arthur Ashe: Tennis Champion (1967)
    Russell, Patrick
      2786. Going, Going, Gone (1967)
      2787. The Tommy Davis Story (1969)
    See, Ingram
      2788. The Jungle Secret (1963)
    Senseney, Dan
      2789. Austin of the Air Force (1962)
      2790. Scanlon of the Sub Service (1963)
    Simon, Tony
      2791. North Pole: The Story of Robert E. Peary (1964)
    Terzian, James
      2792. Pete Cass: Scrambler (1970)
      2793. The Kid from Cuba: Zoilo Versailles (1967)
    Terzian, James, and Kathryn Cramer
      2794. Mighty Hard Road: Cesar Chavez (1970)
    Thomas, Bob
      2795. Donna DeVarona: Gold Medal Swimmer (1968)
    Townsend, Doris
      2796. Dinny and Dreamdust (1963)
    Werstein, Irving
      2797. Civil War Sailor (1967)
      2798. Jack Wade—Fighter for Liberty (1963)
    Willcoxen, Harriett
      2799. First Lady of India: The Story of Indira Gandhi (1969)
    Williamson, Jack
      2800. Trapped in Space (1970)
    Woody, Regina
      2801. T.V. Dancer (1967)
    Wyckoff, James
      2802. Kendall of the Coast Guard (1961)
    Wyndham, Lee
      2803. Bonnie (1961)
    Zanger, Jack
      2804. Baseball Spark Plug (1966)
      2805. Hi Packett, Jumping Center (1968)
      2806. The Long Reach (1965)
Aimed at the reluctant reader. Although the books are primarily fiction, the series does include some biographies. The plots of the novels are based on high-interest topics, such as sports and mysteries. The biographies are about people who overcame various handicaps to reach success. For grades 7 on up.

DURANT SPORTS BOOKS —Hastings House
      Durant, John
            2807. Highlights of the Olympics (1965)
            2808. Highlights of the World Series (1970)
            2809. The Heavyweight Champions (1967)
            2810. The Sports of Our Presidents (1964)
Veteran sports writer John Durant has included much history in each book, as well as biographies of important sports figures. There are indices, photos, and records and charts where applicable. For grades 5 and up.

EARLY CULTURE —McGraw-Hill
      Collins, Robert
            2811. The Medes and the Persians (1972)
      Lansing, Elizabeth
            2812. The Sumerians: Inventors and Builders (1971)
      Van Duyn, Janet
            2813. The Egyptians: Pharoahs and Craftsmen (1971)
            2814. The Greeks (1972)
Another series on the subject of early civilizations. This one deals with the life-style and culture of different peoples, and also with the archaeological expeditions that led to our knowledge of them. For grades 5 through 9.

EBERLE, IRMENGARDE —Doubleday
            2815. A Chipmunk Lives Here (1966)
            2816. Bears Live Here (1966)
            2817. Elephants Live Here (1970)
            2818. Koalas Live Here (1967)
            2819. Moose Live Here (1971)
The full-page photographs alternating with a page of text create a more appealing format than one usually finds in animal biography series. This one is intended to capture the interest of the casual reader, as well as to provide information. For grades 3 to 6.

ECOLOGY —Childrens Press
      Hungerford, Harold
            2820. Ecology: The Circle of Life (1971)
The first book of this announced series deals well with the interrelationship of living things—the purpose of the series in general. Best of all, the photos and illustrations are quite good, and there are many illustrative examples of various kinds of food chains and other ecological chains. There is also a glossary and an index. For grades 4 through 9.

THE ENCHANTMENT OF AMERICA SERIES —Childrens Press
      Carpenter, John
            2821. Alabama (1968)
            2822. Alaska (1965)
            2823. Arizona (1966)
            2824. Arkansas (1967)
            2825. California (1964)
            2826. Colorado (1967)
            2827. Connecticut (1966)
            2828. Delaware (1967)
            2829. District of Columbia (1966)
            2830. Florida (1965)

2831. Georgia (1967)
2832. Hawaii (1966)
2833. Idaho (1968)
2834. Illinois (1963)
2835. Indiana (1966)
2836. Iowa (1964)
2837. Kansas (1965)
2838. Kentucky (1967)
2839. Louisiana (1967)
2840. Maine (1966)
2841. Maryland (1966)
2842. Massachusetts (1965)
2843. Michigan (1964)
2844. Minnesota (1966)
2845. Mississippi (1968)
2846. Missouri (1966)
2847. Montana (1968)
2848. Nebraska (1967)
2849. Nevada (1964)
2850. New Hampshire (1967)
2851. New Jersey (1965)
2852. New Mexico (1967)
2853. New York (1967)
2854. North Carolina (1965)
2855. North Dakota (1968)
2856. Ohio (1963)
2857. Oklahoma (1965)
2858. Oregon (1965)
2859. Pennsylvania (1966)
2860. Rhode Island (1968)
2861. South Carolina (1967)
2862. South Dakota (1966)
2863. Tennessee (1968)
2864. Texas (1965)
2865. Utah (1965)
2866. Vermont (1967)
2867. Virginia (1967)
2868. Washington (1966)
2869. West Virginia (1968)
2870. Wisconsin (1964)
2871. Wyoming (1966)

Carpenter, John
2872. Far Flung America (1966)

Cleveland, Libra
2873. High Country (1962)
2874. Pacific Shores (1962)

Wood, Dorothy
2875. Hills and Harbors (1962)
2876. Sea and Sunshine (1962)
2877. The Enchantment of Canada (1964)
2878. The Enchantment of New England Country (1962)

The books of this well-prepared series provide basic information on each state: climate, topography, history, famous people, education, and industry. Especially

THE ENCHANTMENT OF AMERICA SERIES —Childrens Press (cont'd)
valuable is the section on the larger cities; it is often difficult to find information
on them for this age level. The books are well indexed, with a quick reference section
in the back. The only drawback to the series is the fact that uninformative and often
unattractive illustrations have been used instead of photographs or more representational drawings. For grades 4 to 9.

THE ENCHANTMENT OF CENTRAL AND SOUTH AMERICA —Childrens Press
    Carpenter, John
        2879. Argentina (1969)
        2880. Brazil (1968)
        2881. Chile (1969)
        2882. Costa Rica (1971)
        2883. French Guiana (1970)
        2884. Guatemala (1971)
        2885. Panama (1971)
        2886. Paraguay (1970)
        2887. Peru (1970)
        2888. Uruguay (1969)
        2889. Venezuela (1970)
    Carpenter, John, and Eloise Baker
        2890. El Salvador (1971)
    Carpenter, John, and Tom Balow
        2891. British Honduras (1971)
        2892. Ecuador (1969)
        2893. Guyana (1970)
        2894. Honduras (1971)
        2895. Nicaragua (1971)
    Carpenter, John, and Jean Lyons
        2896. Bolivia (1970)
        2897. Colombia (1969)
        2898. Surinam (1970)
Similar to the Enchantment of America Series, with good, basic text and handy
reference guide (with statistics) in the back, plus photos, maps, and illustrations.
There is also space devoted to holidays and special events. The books are indexed.
For grades 4 to 9.

ENGLISH HERITAGE —Putnam
    Hart, Roger
        2899. English Life in the Eighteenth Century (1971)
        2900. English Life in the Nineteenth Century (1971)
        2901. English Life in the Seventeenth Century (1971)
The day-to-day life in England during the specified periods is presented through
the use of accounts from diaries, letters, and books written at the time; the result
is a first-hand view of what life was like. The narrative is lively and all levels of
society are examined, as well as the various historical events and social changes that
were taking place. There are both color and black-and-white illustrations, plus a
bibliography and index. For grades 6 through 8.

ENGLISH LIFE SERIES —Putnam
    Ashley, Maurice
        2902. Life in Stuart England (1964)
    Bagley, J. J.
        2903. Life in Medieval England (1960)

ENGLISH LIFE SERIES —Putnam (cont'd)
> Birley, Anthony
>> 2904. Life in Roman Britain (1965)
> Cecil, Robert
>> 2905. Life in Edwardian England (1970)
> Dodd, A. H.
>> 2906. Life in Elizabethan England (1962)
> Page, R. I.
>> 2907. Life in Anglo-Saxon England (1970)
> Reader, W. J.
>> 2908. Life in Victorian England (1965)
> Seaman, L. C. B.
>> 2909. Life in Britain between the Wars (1971)
> Tomkeieff, O. G.
>> 2910. Life in Norman England (1966)
> White, R. J.
>> 2911. Life in Regency England (1964)
> Williams, E. N.
>> 2912. Life in Georgian England (1962)
> Williams, Penry
>> 2913. Life in Tudor England (1965)

An excellent series on the life, social customs, and history of England. Each volume uses the drawings and paintings of the time as illustrations. Indexing is extensive. A must for any collection.

ETHNIC AND RACIAL HERITAGE —Messner
> Burt, Olive
>> 2914. Negroes in the Early West (1969)
> Dowdell, Joseph, and Dorothy Dowdell
>> 2915. The Chinese Helped Build America (1972)
>> 2916. The Japanese Helped Build America (1970)
> Feuerlicht, Roberta
>> 2917. In Search of Peace: The Story of Four Americans Who Won the Nobel Peace Prize (1970)
> Gay, Kathlyn
>> 2918. The Germans Helped Build America (1971)
> Henderson, Nancy
>> 2919. The Scots Helped Build America (1969)
> Kurtis, Arlene
>> 2920. Puerto Ricans: From Island to Mainland (1969)
>> 2921. The Jews Helped Build America (1970)
> McDonnell, Virginia
>> 2922. The Irish Helped Build America (1969)
> Sutton, Felix
>> 2923. Indian Chiefs of the West (1970)

Not as well done as the American Character series because this one indulges in the use of fictional characters to portray national characteristics and problems instead of relying on facts alone. Once these fictional characters have been dropped, the books become more valuable. There are good photographs and indices, and the straight text is generally well done.

EUROPEAN LIFE —Putnam
> Carr, John
>> 2924. Life in France under Louis XIV (1967)

EUROPEAN LIFE —Putnam (cont'd)
>   Chamberlin, E. R.
>   2925. Life in Medieval France (1967)
>   Cullen, L. M.
>   2926. Life in Ireland (1969)
>   Gage, John
>   2927. Life in Italy at the Time of the Medici (1968)
>   Kochan, Miriam
>   2928. Life in Russia under Catherine the Great (1969)
>   Lewis, Gwynne
>   2929. Life in Revolutionary France (1972)
>   Miller, Jack
>   2930. Life in Russia Today (1969)
>   Munz, Peter
>   2931. Life in the Age of Charlemagne (1969)

This series is a first cousin to the English Life series. There is the same informative text and extensive use of illustrations taken from paintings and drawings of the time. For grades 6 on up.

EVERYDAY LIFE —Putnam
>   Bray, Warwick
>   2932. Everyday Life of the Aztecs (1969)
>   Chamberlin, E. R.
>   2933. Everyday Life in Renaissance Times (1966)
>   Cowell, F. R.
>   2934. Everyday Life in Ancient Rome (1961)
>   Dunn, Charles
>   2935. Everyday Life in Traditional Japan (1969)
>   Edwardes, Michael
>   2936. Everyday Life in Early India (1969)
>   Lewis, Raphaela
>   2937. Everyday Life of the Ottoman Turks (1971)
>   Loewe, Michael
>   2938. Everyday Life in Early Imperial China (1968)
>   Quennell, Marjorie, and C. H. B. Quennell
>   2939. Everyday Life in Prehistoric Times (1960)
>   2940. Everyday Life in Roman and Anglo-Saxon Times (1960)
>   2941. Everyday Things in Ancient Greece (1954)
>   Rice, Tamara
>   2942. Everyday Life in Byzantium (1967)
>   Ross, Anne
>   2943. Everyday Life of the Pagan Celts (1970)
>   Rowling, Marjorie
>   2944. Everyday Life in Medieval Times (1968)
>   2945. Everyday Life of Medieval Travelers (1971)
>   Saggs, H. W. F.
>   2946. Everyday Life in Babylonia and Assyria (1965)
>   Simpson, Jacqueline
>   2947. Everyday Life in the Viking Age (1968)
>   Webster, T. B. L.
>   2948. Everyday Life in Classical Athens (1969)
>   White, Jon
>   2949. Everyday Life in Ancient Egypt (1964)

EVERYDAY LIFE —Putnam (cont'd)
>Willetts, R. F.
>>2950. Everyday Life in Ancient Crete (1969)
Another outstanding series from Putnam on the day-to-day life and customs of various civilizations. All strata of society are dealt with, as well as the architecture, history, poetry, and characteristics of the people and the area being investigated. The illustrations are excellent, with many maps, photos, and reproductions of the art, sculpture, and artifacts of the time. For grades 6 on up.

EVERYDAY LIFE IN AMERICA —Putnam
>Dodds, John
>>2951. Everyday Life in Twentieth Century America (1966)
>Walker, Robert
>>2952. Everyday Life in the Age of Enterprise, 1865-1900 (1967)
>Wright, Louis
>>2953. Everyday Life in Colonial America (1965)
>>2954. Everyday Life on the American Frontier (1968)
Closely related to the preceding series, both in format and in the type of information covered. For grades 6 and up.

EXPLORING OUR UNIVERSE —Crowell
>Branley, Franklyn
>>2955. Mars: Planet Number Four (1962)
>>2956. Earth: Planet Number Three (1966)
>>2957. The Milky Way: Galaxy Number One (1969)
>>2958. The Moon: Earth's Natural Satellite (1960)
>>2959. The Nine Planets (1971)
>>2960. The Sun: Star Number One (1964)
This author is a well-known authority on astronomy. His treatment of the various subjects here is quite detailed, with some photos and drawings and quite a few tables of planetary data. There is also a bibliography and an index in each book. For ages 11 on up.

EXPLORING SMALL WORLDS —Crowell
>Burgess, Robert
>>2961. Exploring a Coral Reef (1971)
>Evans, Eva
>>2962. Exploring a Fallen Log (1971)
>Kriger, M.
>>2963. Exploring a Sidewalk Crack (1971)
>>2964. Exploring a Tree Trunk (1971)
The authors examine plant life as well as insect and animal life, with the aim of showing readers just how much life is actually going on in a very small area. There are many photographs. These books will prove to be good supplementary sources for students interested in natural science.

EXPLORING SCIENCE —McGraw-Hill
>Bendick, Jeanne
>>2965. Electronics for Young People (1960)
>Berger, Melvin, and Frank Clark
>>2966. Science and Music (1961)
>Blackwood, Paul
>>2967. Push and Pull (1966)

EXPLORING SCIENCE —McGraw-Hill (cont'd)
>   Frankel, Edward
>   >   2968. DNA: Ladder of Life (1964)
>   Hyde, Margaret O.
>   >   2969. Animals in Science (1962)
>   >   2970. Atoms Today and Tomorrow (1966)
>   >   2971. Driving Today and Tomorrow (1965)
>   >   2972. Flight Today and Tomorrow (1970)
>   >   2973. Medicine in Action Today and Tomorrow (1964)
>   >   2974. Mind Drugs (1968)
>   >   2975. Molecules Today and Tomorrow (1963)
>   >   2976. Plants Today and Tomorrow (1960)
>   >   2977. This Crowded Planet (1961)
>   >   2978. Your Brain, Master Computer (1964)
>   Perry, John
>   >   2979. Our Wonderful Eyes (1955)
>   Poole, Lynn
>   >   2980. Carbon 14 (1961)
>   >   2981. Frontiers of Science (1958)
>   Raskin, Edith
>   >   2982. Watchers, Pursuers, and Masqueraders (1964)
>   Simon, Seymour
>   >   2983. Animals in Field and Laboratory (1968)
>   Tannenbaum, Beulah
>   >   2984. Understanding Food (1962)
>   >   2985. Understanding Light (1960)
>   >   2986. Understanding Maps (1957)
>   >   2987. Understanding Sound (1971)
>   >   2988. Understanding Time (1958)

Treatment of the various scientific topics covered is generally good, but the books are handicapped by few illustrations. Some experiments are included to illustrate the principles under discussion, and there is usually a glossary and an index. For grades 5 and 6.

EXPLORING MATHEMATICS —Doubleday
>   Razzell, Arthur, and K. G. O. Watts
>   >   2989. Circles and Curves (1968)
>   >   2990. Probability: The Science of Chance (1967)
>   >   2991. Question of Accuracy (1969)
>   >   2992. Symmetry (1968)
>   >   2993. This Is Four: The Idea of a Number (1967)
>   >   2994. 3 and the Shape of 3 (1969)

Each of these slender volumes examines one aspect of mathematics in simple terms, but in detail. New words are in boldface type, and the illustrations are not only good but occasionally funny. Good supplementary material for grades 4 through 7.

EXPLORING THE WORLD —Childrens Press
>   Cleater, P.
>   >   2995. Exploring the World of Archaeology (1966)
>   Lee, R.
>   >   2996. Exploring the World of Pottery (1967)
>   Matthews, W.
>   >   2997. Exploring the World of Fossils (1964)

EXPLORING THE WORLD —Childrens Press (cont'd)
>Richards, N.
>>2998. Giants in the Sky (1967)
>Telfer, Dorothy
>>2999. Exploring the World of Oceanography (1968)

For the most part, these books are general surveys of the topics, so there is no detailed treatment. There are many color illustrations and photographs. For grades 5 through 9.

FAMILY LIFE EDUCATION BOOKS —Follett
>May, Julian
>>3000. How We Are Born (1969)
>>3001. Living Things and Their Young (1969)
>>3002. Man and Woman (1969)
>Meeks, Esther, and Elizabeth Bagwell
>>3003. Families Live Together (1969)
>>3004. How New Life Begins (1969)
>>3005. The World of Living Things (1969)

A combination of sex education and family living. The books explore not just human families and relationships, but also those in the plant and animal kingdoms. For sex education, Lipke's Being Together series is far superior, but for a general overview of the world of living things this one is fine. For ages 8 through 12.

FAMOUS BIOGRAPHIES FOR YOUNG PEOPLE —Dodd
>Allen, Everett
>>3006. Famous American Humorous Poets (1968)
>Army Times, Editors
>>3007. Famous American Military Leaders of World War II (1962)
>>3008. Famous Fighters of World War I (1964)
>Bailey, Bernardine
>>3009. Famous Latin-American Liberators (1960)
>>3010. Famous Modern Explorers (1963)
>Benet, Laura
>>3011. Famous American Humorists (1959)
>>3012. Famous American Poets (1950)
>>3013. Famous New England Authors (1970)
>>3014. Famous Poets for Young People (1964)
>>3015. Famous Storytellers for Young People (1968)
>Bontemps, Arna
>>3016. Famous Negro Athletes (1964)
>Borie, Marcia
>>3017. Famous Presidents of the United States (1963)
>Burch, Gladys, and John Wolcott
>>3018. Famous Composers for Young People (1939)
>Cantwell, Robert
>>3019. Famous American Men of Letters (1956)
>Chandler, Caroline
>>3020. Famous Men of Medicine (1950)
>Coffman, Ramon, and Nathan Goodman
>>3021. Famous Authors for Young People (1943)
>>3022. Famous Explorers for Young People (1942)
>>3023. Famous Generals and Admirals for Young People (1948)
>>3024. Famous Kings and Queens for Young People (1945)

  3025. Famous Pioneers for Young People (1945)
Cournos, John, and Sybil Norton
  3026. Famous British Poets (1952)
  3027. Famous Modern American Novelists (1952)
Daniels, Patricia
  3028. Famous Labor Leaders (1970)
Donovan, Frank
  3029. Famous Twentieth Century Leaders (1964)
Eberle, Irmengarde
  3030. Famous Inventors for Young People (1965)
Ewen, David
  3031. Famous Conductors (1966)
  3032. Famous Instrumentalists (1965)
  3033. Famous Modern Conductors (1967)
Flynn, James
  3034. Famous Justices of the Supreme Court (1968)
Foley, Rae
  3035. Famous American Spies (1962)
  3036. Famous Makers of America (1963)
Heuman, William
  3037. Famous American Athletes (1963)
  3038. Famous Coaches (1968)
  3039. Famous Pro Basketball Stars (1970)
  3040. Famous Pro Football Stars (1967)
Hill, Frank E.
  3041. Famous Historians (1966)
Hughes, Langston
  3042. Famous American Negroes (1954)
  3043. Famous Negro Heroes of America (1958)
  3044. Famous Negro Music Makers (1955)
Jacobs, Helen Hull
  3045. Famous American Women Athletes (1964)
Lavine, Sigmund
  3046. Famous American Architects (1969)
  3047. Famous Industrialists (1961)
  3048. Famous Merchants (1965)
McGee, Dorothy
  3049. Famous Signers of the Declaration (1955)
McKinney, Roland
  3050. Famous American Painters (1955)
  3051. Famous French Painters (1960)
  3052. Famous Old Masters of Painting (1961)
Newlon, Clarke
  3053. Famous Mexican-Americans (1972)
  3054. Famous Pioneers in Space (1963)
Pickering, James
  3055. Famous Astronomers (1968)
Rollins, Charlemae
  3056. Famous American Negro Poets (1965)
  3057. Famous Negro Entertainers of Stage, Screen, and T.V. (1967)
Smaridge, Norah
  3058. Famous British Women Novelists (1967)
  3059. Famous Modern Storytellers for Young People (1969)

Stevens, William O.
3060. Famous American Statesmen (1953)
3061. Famous Scientists (1952)
3062. Famous Women of America (1950)
Wagner, Frederick
3063. Famous Underwater Adventurers (1962)

In general, these excellent biographies only touch on the early life of the individuals, and they deal primarily with whatever endeavors they were famous for. There is a section of photographs of the subjects in each volume, as well as a list of books or other works by the biographees, and an index.

FAMOUS DOG STORIES —Grosset

Balch, Glen
3064. White Ruff (1958)
Curwood, James O.
3065. Baree, Son of Kazan (1917)
3066. Kazan the Wolf Dog (1941)
Kjelgaard, Jim
3067. Irish Red (1951)
3068. Outlaw Red (1957)
3069. Snow Dog (1948)
Knight, Arthur
3070. Lassie Come Home (1940)
Lathrop, West
3071. Juneau the Sleigh Dog (1950)
Little, G. W.
3072. True Stories of Heroic Dogs (1958)
London, Jack
3073. Call of the Wild (1963)
3074. White Fang (1933)
Meek, S. P.
3075. Rusty, a Cocker Spaniel (1938)
O'Brien, Jack
3076. Return of Silver Chief (1943)
3077. Silver Chief, a Dog of the North (1950)
3078. Silver Chief to the Rescue (1937)
3079. Silver Chief's Big Game Trail (1961)
3080. Silver Chief's Revenge (1954)
3081. Valiant, Dog of the Timberline (1935)
Ollivant, Alfred
3082. Bob, Son of Battle (1898)
Saunders, Marshall
3083. Beautiful Joe (1920)

These books are cheap reissues of old stories, many of which should never have been resurrected. Fortunately, most of the good members of this series are available in sturdier, more appealing editions.

FAMOUS FIRSTS —Putnam

Cook, Joseph
3084. Famous Firsts in Baseball (1971)
Jakes, John
3085. Famous Firsts in Sports (1967)

FAMOUS FIRSTS —Putnam (cont'd)
>   Mason, Herbert
>>   3086. Famous Firsts in Exploration (1967)
>   Shenfield, Gary
>>   3087. Famous Firsts in Space (1971)

Although these works do cover "firsts" in the given subject areas, they do not present extensive information on any of the topics. There are many photos, but the main use of the books would be for pleasure reading.

FAMOUS HORSE STORIES —Grosset
>   Balch, Glen
>>   3088. Indian Paint (1942)
>>   3089. Lost Horse (1950)
>   Cooper, Page
>>   3090. Amigo—Circus Horse (1955)
>   Faralla, Dana
>>   3091. Magnificent Barb (1947)
>   Foote, John
>>   3092. Hoofbeats (1950)
>   Grew, David
>>   3093. Beyond Rope and Fence (1947)
>>   3094. Buckskin Colt (1962)
>>   3095. Sorrell Stallion (1951)
>   Hinkle, Thomas
>>   3096. Black Tiger (1952)
>   Holt, Stephen
>>   3097. Phantom Roan (1949)
>>   3098. Whistling Stallion (1950)
>>   3099. Wild Palomino (1946)
>   Lang, Don
>>   3100. Strawberry Roan (1964)
>   Larom, Henry
>>   3101. Mountain Pony (1946)
>>   3102. Mountain Pony and the Elkhorn Mystery (1950)
>>   3103. Mountain Pony and the Pinto Colt (1952)
>>   3104. Mountain Pony and the Rodeo Mystery (1949)
>   Lyons, Dorothy
>>   3105. Bluegrass Champion (1949)
>   McMeekin, Isabel
>>   3106. Kentucky Derby Winner (1949)
>   Meek, S. P.
>>   3107. Frog, the Horse That Knew No Master (1952)
>   Montgomery, Rutherford
>>   3108. Capture of the Golden Stallion (1951)
>>   3109. Midnight (1940)
>   Thompson, Harlan
>>   3110. Spook, the Mustang (1968)

The quality of the choices in this series is somewhat better than that in the Famous Dog Stories series; however, the format is still unappealing and the paper and binding are poor.

FAMOUS MUSEUM EXHIBITS SERIES —Hastings House
>   Colby, Jean
>>   3111. Mystic Seaport: The Age of Sail (1970)

FAMOUS MUSEUM EXHIBITS SERIES —Hastings House   (cont'd)
      3112. Plimoth Plantation: Then and Now (1970)
Franzen, Greta
      3113. The Great Ship "Vasa" (1971)
Hutchings, David
      3114. Edison at Work (1969)
Jackson, Caary Paul
      3115. Baseball's Shrine (1969)
Mason, George
      3116. The Moose Group (1968)
Shuttlesworth, Dorothy
      3117. Dodos and Dinosaurs (1968)
      3118. The Tower of London: Grim and Glamorous (1970)
There is no equivalent to this unusual series. It deals with a specific museum or an
exhibit within a museum: how it was obtained, the study that went into it, how
the exhibit was created, and the background history of whatever is on exhibit. There
are many photos and drawings of the various stages of preparation for each exhibit,
as well as an index.

FAVORITE FAIRY TALES . . . —Little
      Haviland, Virginia
      3119. Favorite Fairy Tales Told in Czechoslovakia (1966)
      3120. Favorite Fairy Tales Told in Denmark (1971)
      3121. Favorite Fairy Tales Told in England (1959)
      3122. Favorite Fairy Tales Told in France (1959)
      3123. Favorite Fairy Tales Told in Germany (1959)
      3124. Favorite Fairy Tales Told in Greece (1970)
      3125. Favorite Fairy Tales Told in Ireland (1961)
      3126. Favorite Fairy Tales Told in Italy (1965)
      3127. Favorite Fairy Tales Told in Norway (1961)
      3128. Favorite Fairy Tales Told in Poland (1963)
      3129. Favorite Fairy Tales Told in Russia (1961)
      3130. Favorite Fairy Tales Told in Scotland (1963)
      3131. Favorite Fairy Tales Told in Spain (1963)
      3132. Favorite Fairy Tales Told in Sweden (1966)
      Haviland, Virginia, and George Suyeoka
      3133. Favorite Fairy Tales Told in Japan (1967)
These are very attractive collections of fairy tales from various countries; some of
them are familiar, some not-so-familiar. The large print and color illustrations should
prove quite attractive, even to reluctant readers.

FIND A CAREER SERIES —Putnam
      Harrison, C. William
      3134. Find a Career in Auto Mechanics (1970)
      3135. Find a Career in Railroading (1968)
      Smith, Frances
      3136. Find a Career in Education (1960)
These books cover all the various places that one could find a job in each subject
area—for example, in colleges, public schools, private schools, prisons, etc. The
authors generally list famous people in these areas as well as giving information on
how to prepare for each career. Future potential in each career area is also discussed.

FIND OUT ABOUT . . . —Regnery
      Carlisle, Madelyn
          3137. Find Out about Glass (1972)
          3138. Find Out about Plastics (1972)
Similar to the New World of . . . series, but on a younger level. The author takes the reader behind the scenes to show how these materials are manufactured, where they are found, and the many different uses for them. For grades 2 to 4.

FINDING OUT ABOUT GEOGRAPHY —John Day
      Clayton, Robert
          3139. Central and East Africa (1971)
          3140. China (1971)
          3141. Mexico, Central America and the West Indies (1971)
          3142. The British Isles (1970)
          3143. The U.S.S.R. (1970)
          3144. Western Europe (1971)
It is absurd to attempt to cover such large geographic areas in books that average 48 pages. The illustrations are poor and the presentation is highly simplistic. Even the quality of the maps is inferior. Not recommended.

FINDING OUT ABOUT SCIENCE SERIES —John Day
      Brinton, Henry
          3145. Sound (1963)
          3146. The Telephone (1962)
      Edwards, D. J.
          3147. Growing Food (1969)
      Healy, Frederick
          3148. Light and Color (1962)
      Jackson, Francis
          3149. Our Living World (1964)
      Jervis, Derek, and Joan Veales
          3150. The Seasons (1963)
      Larsen, Egon
          3151. Atoms and Atomic Energy (1963)
      Lumsden, William
          3152. Liquids (1970)
      Lynch, Valerie
          3153. Exploring the Past (1970)
      Moore, Patrick
          3154. Telescopes and Observatories (1962)
      Roberson, Paul
          3155. Chemistry by Experiment (1965)
          3156. Engines (1965)
      Shepherd, Walter
          3157. Electricity (1964)
          3158. How Airplanes Fly (1972)
          3159. Jungles (1972)
          3160. Textiles (1972)
          3161. Wealth from the Ground (1962)
      Tyler, Margaret
          3162. Deserts (1970)
      Vale, C. P.
          3163. Plastics (1972)

FINDING OUT ABOUT SCIENCE SERIES —John Day (cont'd)
    Wellman, Alfred
        3164. Earthquakes and Volcanoes (1963)
Like the Find Out about Geography series, this one also has a simplistic text that,
in 48 pages, barely touches the basic material in these broad subject areas. There
is no index, but there is a brief glossary. At best, these could be used as introductory
books for grades 2 to 4, but there are other series that do the job better for that
age level (e.g., The Reason Why series).

FIREBIRD BOOKS —Four Winds
    Buckmaster, Henrietta
        3165. The Fighting Congressmen (1971)
    Emanuel, Myron
        3166. Faces of Freedom (1971)
    Fleming, Thomas
        3167. Give Me Liberty (1971)
    Graham, Lorenz
        3168. John Brown's Raid: A Picture History of the Attack on Harper's
               Ferry, Virginia (1972)
    Harbison, David
        3169. Reaching for Freedom (1972)
    McGovern, Ann
        3170. The Defenders (1970)
    Meltzer, Milton
        3171. To Change the World: A Picture History of Reconstruction (1971)
    Spencer, Philip
        3172. Three against Slavery (1972)
    Stiller, Richard
        3173. The Spy, the Lady, the Captain, and the Colonel (1970)
    Werstein, Irving
        3174. The Storming of Fort Wagner: Black Valor in the Civil War (1970)
    White, Anne Terry
        3175. The False Treaty: The Removal of the Cherokees from Georgia (1970)
Emphasis in these books is on the important but little-known roles played by
minority groups in important historical events. In each area, there are two companion
volumes—one of these is a historical overview, while the other is a biography. The
authors use maps, photos, etchings and documents from the period under discussion.
First-rate material for grades 4 through 8.

FIRST BOOK SERIES —Watts
    Abell, Elizabeth
        3176. The First Book of New Jersey (1968)
    Beck, Barbara
        3177. The First Book of Fruits (1967)
        3178. The First Book of Palaces (1964)
        3179. The First Book of the Ancient Maya (1965)
        3180. The First Book of the Aztecs (1966)
        3181. The First Book of the Incas (1966)
        3182. The First Book of Vegetables (1970)
        3183. The First Book of Venezuela (1969)
    Bendick, Jeanne
        3184. The First Book of Automobiles (1971)
        3185. The First Book of Fishes (1965)
        3186. The First Book of Ships (1959)

3187. The First Book of Time (1963)
Black, Algernon
3188. The First Book of Ethics (1965)
Blassingame, Wyatt
3189. The First Book of American Expansion (1957)
3190. The First Book of the Sea Shore (1964)
Bolian, Polly, and Shirley Hinds
3191. The First Book of Safety (1970)
Bothwell, Jean
3192. The First Book of India (1971)
3193. The First Book of Pakistan (1962)
Brandt, Sue
3194. The First Book of Facts about the Fifty States (1970)
3195. The First Book of How to Write a Report (1968)
Brewster, Benjamin
3196. The First Book of Baseball (1958)
3197. The First Book of Eskimos (1952)
3198. The First Book of Indians (1950)
Burnett, Bernice
3199. The First Book of Holidays (1955)
Burt, Olive
3200. The First Book of Copper (1968)
3201. The First Book of Salt (1965)
3202. The First Book of the Supreme Court (1958)
Carter, William
3203. The First Book of Bolivia (1963)
3204. The First Book of South America (1961)
Castor, Henry
3205. The First Book of the Spanish-American West (1963)
3206. The First Book of the War with Mexico (1964)
Cavanna, Betty
3207. The First Book of Fiji (1969)
3208. The First Book of Morocco (1970)
3209. The First Book of Wool (1966)
Chase, Sarah
3210. The First Book of Diamonds (1971)
3211. The First Book of Silver (1969)
Cobb, Vicki
3212. The First Book of Cells (1970)
3213. The First Book of Gases (1970)
Cohn, Angelo
3214. The First Book of the Netherlands (1971)
Colby, Carroll B.
3215. The First Book of Animal Signs (1966)
3216. The First Book of the Wild Bird World (1970)
Colorado, Antonio
3217. The First Book of Puerto Rico (1972)
Commager Henry Steele
3218. The First Book of American History (1957)
Cook, Fred
3219. The First Book of American Political Parties (1971)
Cormack, Maribelle
3220. The First Book of Stones (1950)

Coy, Harold
  3221. The First Book of Congress (1956)
  3222. The First Book of Presidents (1964)
  3223. The First Book of the Supreme Court (1958)
Csicsery-Ronay, Istvan
  3224. The First Book of Hungary (1967)
Deedy, John
  3225. The First Book of the Vatican (1970)
Dickinson, Alice
  3226. The First Book of Plants (1953)
  3227. The First Book of Prehistoric Animals (1954)
  3228. The First Book of Stone Age Man (1962)
Edison, Michael, and Susan Heimann
  3229. The First Book of Public Opinion Polls (1972)
Eichner, James
  3230. The First Book of Courts of Law (1969)
  3231. The First Book of Local Government (1964)
  3232. The First Book of the Cabinet (1968)
Elgin, Kathleen
  3233. The First Book of Mythology (1955)
Epstein, Edna
  3234. The First Book of the United Nations (1959)
Epstein, Samuel, and Beryl Epstein
  3235. The First Book of Electricity (1953)
  3236. The First Book of Italy (1958)
  3237. The First Book of Maps and Globes (1959)
  3238. The First Book of Measurement (1960)
  3239. The First Book of Mexico (1955)
  3240. The First Book of Switzerland (1964)
  3241. The First Book of the Ocean (1961)
  3242. The First Book of Washington, D.C. (1961)
Foster, F. Blanche
  3243. The First Book of Dahomey (1971)
  3244. The First Book of Kenya (1969)
Frame, Jean, and Paul Frame
  3245. The First Book of How to Give a Party (1972)
Gottlieb, Gerald
  3246. The First Book of France (1959)
Grant, Neil
  3247. The First Book of Cathedrals (1972)
  3248. The First Book of the Renaissance (1971)
Gurney, Gene, and Clare Gurney
  3249. The First Book of Colonial Maryland (1972)
Haines, Charles
  3250. The First Book of Florence: City of the Renaissance (1972)
Hamilton, Russel
  3251. The First Book of Trains (1956)
Harrison, C. William
  3252. The First Book of Hiking (1965)
  3253. The First Book of Modern California (1965)
Harrison, George
  3254. The First Book of Energy (1965)
  3255. The First Book of Lasers (1971)

3256. The First Book of Light (1962)

Hoke, Helen

3257. The First Book of Ants (1970)
3258. The First Book of Arctic Mammals (1969)
3259. The First Book of Etiquette (1970)
3260. The First Book of Solar Energy (1968)
3261. The First Book of Tropical Mammals (1958)
3263. The First Book of Turtles and Their Care (1970)

Hoke, John

3264. The First Book of Ecology (1971)
3265. The First Book of Photography (1965)
3266. The First Book of Snakes (1952)
3267. The First Book of the Guianas (1964)
3268. The First Book of the Jungle (1964)

Howard, Robert

3269. The First Book of Niagara Falls (1969)

Hughes, Langston

3270. The First Book of Africa (1960)

Icenhower, Joseph

3271. The First Book of Submarines (1957)
3272. The First Book of the Antarctic (1971)

Ingraham, Leonard

3273. The First Book of Slavery in the United States (1968)

Janes, Edward

3274. The First Book of Camping (1963)

Kay, Eleanor

3275. The First Book of Nurses (1968)
3276. The First Book of Skydiving (1971)
3277. The First Book of the Clinic (1971)
3278. The First Book of the Emergency Room (1970)
3279. The First Book of the Operating Room (1970)

Kinmond, William

3280. The First Book of Communist China (1972)

Klagsburn, Francine

3281. The First Book of Spices (1968)

Knight, David

3282. The First Book of Air (1961)
3283. The First Book of Berlin (1967)
3284. The First Book of Deserts (1964)
3285. The First Book of Mars (1966)
3286. The First Book of Meteors and Meteorites (1969)
3287. The First Book of Sound (1960)
3288. The First Book of the Sun (1968)

Kondo, Herbert

3289. The First Book of the Moon (1971)

Kubie, N. B.

3290. The First Book of Archaeology (1957)

Lacy, Dan

3291. The First Book of the Lost Colony (1972)

Lacy, Leslie

3292. The First Book of Black Africa on the Move (1969)

Lengyel, Emil

3293. The First Book of Iran (1972)

        3294. The First Book of Pakistan (1972)
        3295. The First Book of Turkey (1970)
Levenson, Dorothy
        3296. The First Book of Homesteaders and Indians (1971)
        3297. The First Book of the Civil War (1968)
        3298. The First Book of the Confederacy (1968)
        3299. The First Book of the Reconstruction (1970)
Lewis, Lucia
        3300. The First Book of Microbes (1955)
Limburg, Peter
        3301. The First Book of Engines (1969)
Lindop, Edmund
        3302. The First Book of Elections (1968)
Lineaweaver, Charles
        3303. The First Book of Canada (1955)
Liversidge, Douglas
        3304. The First Book of Arctic Exploration (1970)
        3305. The First Book of the Arctic (1967)
        3306. The First Book of the British Empire and Commonwealth of
            Nations (1971)
Lobsenz, Norman
        3307. The First Book of Denmark (1970)
        3308. The First Book of East Africa (1964)
        3309. The First Book of National Monuments (1968)
        3310. The First Book of National Parks (1968)
        3311. The First Book of the Peace Corps (1968)
        3312. The First Book of West Germany (1972)
Lowenstein, Dyno
        3313. The First Book of Graphs (1969)
Luhrmann, Winifred
        3314. The First Book of Gold (1968)
McKown, Robin
        3315. The First Book of the Colonial Conquest of Africa (1971)
Mahon, Julia
        3316. The First Book of Creative Writing (1968)
Marcus, Rebecca
        3317. The First Book of Cliff Dwellers (1968)
        3318. The First Book of Volcanoes and Earthquakes (1963)
Markun, Patricia
        3319. The First Book of Central America and Panama (1963)
        3320. The First Book of Politics (1970)
        3321. The First Book of the Panama Canal (1958)
Matthews, William
        3322. The First Book of Soils (1970)
        3323. The First Book of the Earth's Crust (1971)
Merrick, Helen
        3324. The First Book of Norway (1969)
        3325. The First Book of Sweden (1971)
Miller, Richard, and Lynn Katoh
        3326. The First Book of Japan (1969)
Moffett, Martha, and Robert Moffett
        3327. The First Book of Dolphins (1971)

Moore, Lamont
 3328. The First Book of Paintings (1960)
Morris, Richard
 3329. The First Book of the American Revolution (1956)
 3330. The First Book of the Constitution (1958)
 3331. The First Book of the Founding of the Republic (1968)
 3332. The First Book of the War of 1812 (1961)
Naden, Corinne
 3333. The First Book of Golf (1970)
 3334. The First Book of Grasslands around the World (1970)
 3335. The First Book of Rivers (1967)
Naylor, Penelope
 3336. The First Book of Sculpture (1971)
Nespojohn, Katherine
 3337. The First Book of Worms (1972)
Nolen, Barbara
 3338. The First Book of Ethiopia (1971)
Norman, Gertrude
 3339. The First Book of Music (1954)
Nourse, Alan
 3340. The First Book of Venus and Mercury (1972)
Peet, Bill
 3341. The First Book of Skyscrapers (1964)
Perry, John
 3342. The First Book of Zoos (1971)
Place, Marian
 3343. The First Book of the Santa Fe Trail (1966)
Poole, Frederick
 3344. The First Book of Indonesia (1971)
 3345. The First Book of Southeast Asia (1972)
 3346. The First Book of the Philippines (1971)
Powers, David
 3347. The First Book of How to Make a Speech (1963)
 3348. The First Book of How to Run a Meeting (1967)
Rich, Louise
 3349. The First Book of Early Settlers (1959)
 3350. The First Book of Lumbering (1967)
 3351. The First Book of New World Explorers (1960)
 3352. The First Book of the Fur Trade (1965)
 3353. The First Book of Vikings (1962)
Roberts, John
 3354. The First Book of the Industrialization of Japan (1971)
Robinson, Charles
 3355. The First Book of Ancient Crete and Mycenae (1964)
 3356. The First Book of Ancient Egypt (1961)
 3357. The First Book of Ancient Greece (1960)
 3358. The First Book of Ancient Rome (1959)
Rothkopf, Carol
 3359. The First Book of East Europe (1972)
 3360. The First Book of the Red Cross (1971)
 3361. The First Book of Yugoslavia (1971)
Schiffer, Don
 3362. The First Book of Basketball (1959)

    3363. The First Book of Football (1958)
    3364. The First Book of Swimming (1960)
Schuon, Keith
    3365. The First Book of Acting (1965)
Sevrey, O. Irene
    3366. The First Book of the Earth (1958)
Sheppard, Sally
    3367. The First Book of Brazil (1972)
Shilstone, Beatrice
    3368. The First Book of Oil (1969)
Sims, Carolyn
    3369. The First Book of Labor Unions in the U.S.A. (1971)
Slobodkin, Louis
    3370. The First Book of Drawing (1958)
Smith, Frances
    3371. The First Book of Conservation (1954)
    3372. The First Book of Mountains (1964)
    3373. The First Book of Swamps and Marshes (1969)
Snyder, Louis
    3374. The First Book of the Long Armistice (1964)
    3375. The First Book of the Soviet Union (1959)
    3376. The First Book of World War I (1958)
    3377. The First Book of World War II (1958)
Sobol, Donald J.
    3378. The First Book of Medieval Man (1959)
Steinberg, Fred
    3379. The First Book of Computers (1969)
Stevenson, Janet
    3380. The First Book of Women's Rights (1972)
Streatfeild, Noel
    3381. The First Book of Shoes (1967)
    3382. The First Book of the Opera (1966)
Stull, Edith
    3383. The First Book of Alaska (1965)
Thorne, Alma
    3384. The First Book of Hawaii (1961)
Tibbets, Albert
    3385. The First Book of Bees (1952)
Van der Horst, Brian
    3386. The First Book of Folk Music in America (1972)
Walker, Richard
    3387. The First Book of Ancient China (1969)
Walls, Fred
    3388. The First Book of Puzzles and Brain Twisters (1970)
Walsh, John
    3389. The First Book of Physical Fitness (1961)
    3390. The First Book of the Olympic Games (1971)
Warren, Ruth
    3391. The First Book of Modern Greece (1966)
Whitehead, Eric
    3392. The First Book of Ice Hockey (1969)
Whitehead, Robert
    3393. The First Book of Bears (1966)

FIRST BOOK SERIES —Watts (cont'd)
>   3394. The First Book of Eagles (1968)
>   Whitney, David
>   3395. The First Book of Facts and How to Find Them (1966)
>   Williamson, Margaret
>   3396. The First Book of Birds (1951)
>   3397. The First Book of Mammals (1967)
>   Wyler, Rose
>   3398. The First Book of Science Experiments (1971)
>   3399. The First Book of Weather (1956)
>   Young, Eleanor
>   3400. The First Book of Pearls (1970)
>   3401. The First Book of Rice (1971)
>   Young, Margaret
>   3402. The First Book of American Negroes (1967)

Since these books are not really intended for beginning readers, the title of the series may be somewhat of a misnomer. The information presented is introductory, but it is handled in a relatively complex manner. The print is comparatively small and, although there are some illustrations, there are not many photographs. The books are indexed. In many instances, these are the best books available in the subject areas. For grades 3 through 6.

FOCUS BOOKS —Watts
>   Barry, James
>   3403. Bloody Kansas, 1854-65, Guerilla Warfare Delays Peaceful American Settlement (1972)
>   3404. The Battle of Lake Erie, September 10, 1813 (1970)
>   3405. The Noble Experiment, 1920-33: The Eighteenth Amendment Prohibits Liquor in America (1972)
>   Castor, Henry
>   3406. 54-40 or Fight! A Showdown between America and England Settles the Oregon Question (1970)
>   3407. The Tripolitan War, 1801-05 (1971)
>   Cook, Fred
>   3408. The Army-McCarthy Hearings, April-December 1954 (1971)
>   Dickinson, Alice
>   3409. The Boston Massacre, March 5, 1770 (1968)
>   3410. The Stamp Act: "Taxation Without Representation Is Tyranny" (1970)
>   Fleischmann, Glen
>   3411. The Cherokee Removal, 1838 (1971)
>   Goodnough, David
>   3412. The Cherry Valley Massacre (1968)
>   Hiebert, Ray, and Roslyn Hiebert
>   3413. The Stock Market Crash, 1929 (1970)
>   Icenhower, Joseph
>   3414. The Panay Incident, December 12, 1937 (1971)
>   Knight, Ralph
>   3415. The Burr-Hamilton Duel (1968)
>   3416. The Naval War with France, 1798-1800 (1970)
>   3417. The Whiskey Rebellion (1968)
>   Kraske, Robert
>   3418. The Treason of Benedict Arnold, 1780 (1970)

FOCUS BOOKS —Watts (cont'd)
    Latham, Frank
        3419. F. D. R. and the Supreme Court Fight, 1937: The President Tries
              to Reorganize the Federal Judiciary (1972)
        3420. Lincoln and the Emancipation Proclamation, January 1, 1863
              (1969)
        3421. The Dred Scott Decision (1968)
        3422. The Panic of 1893 (1971)
        3423. The Rise and Fall of Jim Crow (1969)
        3424. The Trial of John Peter Zenger, August 1735: An Early Fight
              for America's Freedom of the Press (1970)
    Naden, Corinne
        3425. The Chicago Fire, October 8, 1871: The Blaze That Nearly
              Destroyed a City (1969)
        3426. The Haymarket Affair, Chicago, 1886 (1968)
        3427. The Triangle Shirtwaist Fire, March 25, 1911: The Blaze That
              Changed an Industry (1971)
    Rich, Louise
        3428. King Phillip's War, 1675-76: The New England Indians Fight the
              Colonists (1972)
    Roscoe, Theodore
        3429. The Lincoln Assassination, April 14, 1865 (1971)
    Stearns, Monroe
        3430. Shay's Rebellion (1968)
        3431. The Great Awakening, 1720-1760: Religious Revival Rouses
              America's Sense of Individual Liberties (1970)
    Stevenson, Janet
        3432. The Montgomery Bus Boycott, December 1955 (1971)
    Vaughan, Harold
        3433. The Citizen Genet Affair (1970)
        3434. The Hayes-Tilden Election of 1876: The Disputed Election in
              the Gilded Age (1972)
    Walsh, John
        3435. The Mayflower Contract, November 11, 1620 (1971)
        3436. The Sinking of the "U.S.S. Maine," February 15, 1898 (1969)
    Webb, Robert
        3437. The Bonus March on Washington, May 1932: U.S. Veterans
              Protest for Rights and Pay (1970)
        3438. The Raid on Harper's Ferry, October 17, 1859 (1971)
Each of these books centers on an important incident in American history, providing
a background to the events that led up to the incident as well as to the people involved, and explaining how the incident progressed. The authors also discuss the
implications each happening had for future generations. There are bibliographies
and indices, photos and drawings. Excellent supplementary material for ages 12
and up.

FORGE OF FREEDOM —Crowell
    Alderman, Clifford
        3439. The Rhode Island Colony (1969)
    Brown, Ira
        3440. The Georgia Colony (1970)
    Cook, Fred
        3441. The New Jersey Colony (1969)

FORGE OF FREEDOM   —Crowell (cont'd)
 Giffen, Daniel
  3442. The New Hampshire Colony (1970)
 Johnston, Johanna
  3443. The Connecticut Colony (1969)
 Mason, F. VanWyck
  3444. The Maryland Colony (1969)
 Nurenberg, Thelma
  3445. The New York Colony (1969)
 Powell, William
  3446. The North Carolina Colony (1969)
 Reed, H. Clay
  3447. The Delaware Colony (1970)
 Smith, Robert
  3448. The Massachusetts Colony (1969)
 Steedman, Marguerite
  3449. The South Carolina Colony (1970)
 Stevens, S. K.
  3450. The Pennsylvania Colony (1970)
 Thane, Elswyth
  3451. The Virginia Colony (1969)
Each of the 13 colonies is examined from the founding of the colony through the
beginnings of the Revolution. Some attention is paid to what life was like then, in
addition to the discussions of political, governmental, and historical factors. There
is a list of important dates and places to visit, as well as a bibliography and an index.
Most of the illustrations are taken from paintings of the time. Excellent material.

FRANKLIN INSTITUTE BOOKS   —Westminster
 Bova, Ben
  3452. The Amazing Laser (1971)
 Struble, Mitch
  3453. Stretching a Point (1971)
This new series is being written by scientists in cooperation with the Franklin
Institute. Each subject is treated in depth, with many experiments for readers to
try out.

FRANKLIN WATTS REFERENCE LIBRARY
 Burton, Maurice
  3454. The Animal World: Birds, Fish, Insects (1969)
 Edwards, Lovett
  3455. Russia and Her Neighbors (1969)
 MacKinnon, Cleodie
  3456. Stories of Courage (1968)
 Moore, Patrick
  3457. Exploring the World (1968)
 Petrie, Jean
  3458. The Earth (1968)
 Ronan, Colin
  3459. The Universe (1966)
 Zinkin, Taya
  3460. India and Her Neighbours (1968)
Various and somewhat unrelated areas are investigated in the volumes of this
series. The text material is short, but there are many illustrations (most of them
in color) and an index. For ages 8 through 10.

FREEDOM TO WORSHIP —McKay
    Elgin, Kathleen
        3461. The Episcopalians (1970)
        3462. The Mormons (1969)
        3463. The Quakers (1968)
        3464. The Unitarians (1971)
An outstanding series on a subject which has received virtually no treatment. Ms. Elgin discusses both the history and the beliefs of each religious group and shows the position of the church today. The type is large and easy to read. There is a section of questions and answers covering the questions most often asked about each denomination. Each book contains a chart of the organization of the church, as well as brief biographies of famous members. A must for any library.

FRESH LOOK AT AMERICAN HISTORY —Sterling
    Woodin, G. Bruce
        3465. Modern America (1877-1968) (1971)
        3466. Pioneers (1707-1850) (1971)
        3467. Revolution and Constitution (1763-1799) (1969)
        3468. Slavery (1850-1877) (1971)
        3469. The Founding of America (1492-1763) (1969)
An in-depth treatment of American history, presented in several volumes. The writing is interesting, and it is a refreshing change to have the history of America cogently divided rather than crammed into one volume. For ages 10 to 14.

FROM FARM TO MARKET —Coward
    Hammond, Winifred
        3470. Corn: From Farm to Market (1972)
        3471. Cotton: From Farm to Market (1968)
        3472. Sugar: From Farm to Market (1967)
        3473. Wheat: From Farm to Market (1970)
Each agricultural product in this series is followed through all the steps of its existence: from planting through harvesting and processing to marketing. There are many maps, photos, and illustrations, as well as a list of projects to do at the end of each chapter, related to the subjects covered therein. The author also provides pronunciation guides, as well as the history, uses, and worldwide locations of the products. Excellent material for grades 4 through 6.

FRONTIERS OF AMERICA —Childrens Press
    James, Harry C.
        3474. Grizzly Adams (1963)
    Jones, Helen
        3475. Over the Mormon Trail (1963)
    McCall, Edith
        3476. Cowboys and Cattle Drives (1964)
        3477. Explorers in a New World (1960)
        3478. Forts in the Wilderness (1968)
        3479. Gold Rush Adventures (1962)
        3480. Heroes of the Western Outposts (1960)
        3481. Hunters Blaze the Trail (1959)
        3482. Log Fort Adventures (1958)
        3483. Mail Riders (1961)
        3484. Men on Iron Horses (1960)
        3485. Pioneer Show Folk (1963)
        3486. Pioneer Traders (1964)

FRONTIERS OF AMERICA —Childrens Press (cont'd)
>   3487. Pioneering on the Plains (1962)
>   3488. Pioneers on Early Waterways (1961)
>   3489. Pirates and Privateers (1963)
>   3490. Settlers on a Strange Shore (1960)
>   3491. Stalwart Men of Early Texas (1970)
>   3492. Steamboats to the West (1959)
>   3493. The Cumberland Gap and Trails West (1961)
>   3494. Wagons Over the Mountains (1961)

It is questionable whether these books should be used for biographical material, since they present the stories of real people in a fictionalized form. Because they are easy to read, however, and because they deal with exciting episodes in our country's history, perhaps they can be used to fan the interest of readers in grades 3 and 4.

FUN TO READ CLASSICS SERIES —Childrens Press
>   Andersen, Hans Christian
>   3495. Andersen's Fairy Tales (1970)
>   Baum, L. Frank
>   3496. The Wizard of Oz (1969)
>   Carroll, Lewis
>   3497. Alice in Wonderland and Through the Looking Glass (1969)
>   Collodi, Carlo
>   3498. Pinocchio (1968)
>   Dodge, Mary Mapes
>   3499. Hans Brinker or the Silver Skates (1969)
>   Doyle, Arthur Conan
>   3500. The Casebook of Sherlock Holmes (1968)
>   Grimm, Jacob, and Wilhelm Grimm
>   3501. Sleeping Beauty and Other Tales (1969)
>   Kingsley, Charles
>   3502. Heroes (1968)
>   Kipling, Rudyard
>   3503. Captains Courageous (1969)
>   3504. The Jungle Book (1968)
>   Lang, Andrew
>   3505. The Arabian Nights (1968)
>   Lipman, Michel
>   3506. Paul Bunyan (1968)
>   London, Jack
>   3507. Call of the Wild (1968)
>   3508. White Fang (1970)
>   Poe, Edgar Allan
>   3509. The Gold Bug and Other Tales of Mystery (1969)
>   Pyle, Howard
>   3510. The Book of King Arthur (1969)
>   3511. The Merry Adventures of Robin Hood (1968)
>   Sewell, Anna
>   3512. Black Beauty (1969)
>   Stevenson, Robert Louis
>   3513. Kidnapped (1969)
>   3514. The Black Arrow (1970)
>   3515. Treasure Island (1968)

FUN TO READ CLASSICS SERIES   —Childrens Press (cont'd)
    Swift, Jonathan
        3516. Gulliver's Travels (1970)
    Twain, Mark
        3517. The Adventures of Tom Sawyer (1970)
        3518. The Prince and the Pauper (1969)
    Verne, Jules
        3519. Around the World in Eighty Days (1969)
        3520. Twenty Thousand Leagues under the Sea (1968)
    Wells, H. G.
        3521. The Time Machine and the Invisible Man (1969)
    Wister, Owen
        3522. The Virginian (1968)
    Wyss, Johann
        3523. Swiss Family Robinson (1968)
Yet another addition to the many series of classics, this one differs in that it provides
marginal notes for easier comprehension, plus vocabulary definitions, many illustrations, and background information on both the author and the story. There is a
definite attempt to reach the reluctant reader with this series.

GALLANT, ROY   —Doubleday
        3524. Exploring Chemistry (1958)
        3525. Exploring Mars (1968)
        3526. Exploring the Moon (1966)
        3527. Exploring the Planets (1967)
        3528. Exploring the Sun (1958)
        3529. Exploring the Universe (1968)
        3530. Exploring the Weather (1969)
        3531. Exploring under the Earth (1960)
These oversized books provide good basic introductory material on the areas covered.
Best of all are the many color and black-and-white illustrations. The books on
astronomy are especially well prepared, with information on the evolution of the
planets in addition to physical descriptions of them. Each book is indexed.

GARRARD SPORTS LIBRARY
    Epstein, Samuel, and Beryl Epstein
        3532. The Baseball Hall of Fame: Stories of Champions (1965)
        3533. The Game of Baseball (1965)
    Finlayson, Ann
        3534. Champions at Bat (1970)
        3535. Decathlon Men: Greatest Athletes in the World (1966)
        3536. Stars of the Modern Olympics (1967)
    Newcombe, Jack
        3537. The Game of Football (1967)
    Reeder, Red
        3538. On the Mound: Three Great Pitchers (1966)
    Sullivan, George
        3539. Hockey Heroes: The Game's Great Players (1969)
        3540. Pass to Win: Pro Football Greats (1968)
        3541. Pro Football's Greatest Upsets (1972)
    VanRiper, Guernsey
        3542. Four Famous Contests (1970)
        3543. The Game of Basketball (1967)
        3544. The Mighty Macs: Three Famous Baseball Managers (1972)

GARRARD SPORTS LIBRARY (cont'd)
      3545. World Series Highlights (1964)
      3546. Yea, Coach! (1966)
History of the sport and biographies of some outstanding players are featured in these books. Many of the biographical entries have been chosen with an eye toward promoting interracial understanding. Although there is duplication here with the contents of other series, this one is on a lower reading level, with large type and brief sentences. For grades 3 to 6.

GATEWAY BOOKS —Random House
    Adelson, Leonie, and Lilian Moore
      3547. Mr. Twitmeyer and the Poodle (1963)
      3548. Old Rosie and the Horse Nobody Understood (1960)
      3549. The Terrible Mr. Twitmeyer (1952)
    Andrews, Roy Chapman
      3550. In the Days of Dinosaurs (1959)
    Asimov, Isaac
      3551. Satellites in Outer Space (1964)
    Austin, Elizabeth
      3552. Birds That Stopped Flying (1969)
      3553. Penguins: The Birds with Flippers (1968)
    Crosby, Alexander
      3554. The World of Rockets (1965)
    Davidson, Mickie
      3555. The Pirate Book (1965)
    Epstein, Samuel, and Beryl Epstein
      3556. Hurricane Guest (1964)
    Feld, Freidrich
      3557. The Mystery of the Musical Umbrella (1962)
    Freeman, Mae
      3558. Finding Out about the Past (1967)
      3559. Stars and Stripes: The Story of the American Flag (1964)
      3560. The Story of Chemistry (1962)
      3561. The Story of Electricity (1961)
      3562. The Story of the Atom (1960)
      3563. The Sun, the Moon, and the Stars (1959)
      3564. Your Wonderful World of Science (1957)
    Gannett, Ruth
      3565. Katie and the Sad Noise (1961)
    Hayes, Florence
      3566. The Boy in the Forty-Ninth Seat (1963)
      3567. The Boy in the Rooftop School (1967)
    Hitte, Kathryn
      3568. Hurricanes, Tornadoes, and Blizzards (1960)
    Holland, Marion
      3569. No Room for a Dog (1959)
    Johnson, Pat
      3570. The Story of Horses (1968)
    Kohn, Bernice
      3571. All Kinds of Seals (1968)
    Lauber, Patricia
      3572. Adventure at Black Rock Cave (1959)
      3573. Bats: Wings in the Night (1968)
      3574. Champ: Giant Collie (1960)

GATEWAY BOOKS —Random House (cont'd)
    3575. Found: One Orange-Brown Horse (1957)
    3576. Runaway Flea Circus (1958)
    3577. The Friendly Dolphins (1963)
    3578. The Story of Dogs (1966)
    3579. The Story of Numbers (1961)
    3580. The Surprising Kangaroos and Other Pouched Mammals (1965)
    3581. Your Body and How It Works (1962)
McClung, Robert
    3582. Mammals and How They Live (1963)
    3583. The Mighty Bears (1967)
    3584. The Swift Deer (1966)
McGovern, Ann
    3585. The Story of Christopher Columbus (1963)
    3586. Why It's a Holiday (1960)
Moore, Lilian
    3587. Everything Happens to Stevey (1960)
    3588. The Snake That Went to School (1957)
Polgreen, John, and Cathleen Polgreen
    3589. The Earth in Space (1963)
Poole, Lynn, and Gray Poole
    3590. Danger! Iceberg Ahead! (1961)
Sharp, Elizabeth
    3591. Simple Machines and How They Work (1959)
Shuttlesworth, Dorothy
    3592. All Kinds of Bees (1967)
Simon, Seymour
    3593. Exploring with a Microscope (1969)
White, Anne Terry
    3594. Rocks All around Us (1959)
Some of these easy-to-read books are fiction, while others deal with some aspect
of science. The print is large and the sentences are short. There are quite a few
photos, maps, and illustrations to make the books appealing. Good basic books for
beginning readers, grades 2 to 5.

GETTING TO KNOW SERIES —Coward
    Ayer, Margaret
    3595. Getting to Know Thailand (1959)
    Bahar, Hushang
    3596. Getting to Know Iran and Iraq (1963)
    Breetveld, Jim
    3597. Getting to Know Alaska (1958)
    3598. Getting to Know Brazil (1960)
    3599. Getting to Know Chile (1960)
    3600. Getting to Know Lebanon (1958)
    Burchell, S. C.
    3601. Getting to Know the Suez Canal (1971)
    Craz, Albert
    3602. Getting to Know Italy (1961)
    3603. Getting to Know the Mississippi River (1965)
    Davis, Burke
    3604. Getting to Know Jamestown (1971)
    3605. Getting to Know Thomas Jefferson's Virginia (1971)

GETTING TO KNOW SERIES —Coward (cont'd)
    Davis, Fanny
        3606. Getting to Know Turkey (1971)
    Day, Dee
        3607. Getting to Know Panama (1958)
        3608. Getting to Know Spain (1957)
    Deming, Angus
        3609. Getting to Know Algeria (1971)
    Ferguson, Charles
        3610. Getting to Know the U.S.A. (1963)
    Fink, William B.
        3611. Getting to Know New York State (1971)
        3612. Getting to Know the Hudson River (1970)
    Gemming, Elizabeth
        3613. Getting to Know New England (1970)
    Gomez, Barbara
        3614. Getting to Know Mexico (1959)
    Griffin, Ella
        3615. Getting to Know UNESCO (1962)
    Halsell, Grace
        3616. Getting to Know Colombia (1964)
        3617. Getting to Know Guatemala and the Two Honduras (1964)
        3618. Getting to Know Peru (1964)
    Harris, Miles
        3619. Getting to Know the World Meteorological Organization (1966)
    Holbrook, Sabra
        3620. Getting to Know the Two Germanys (1966)
        3621. Getting to Know the Virgin Islands (1959)
    Ingalls, Leonard
        3622. Getting to Know Kenya (1963)
        3623. Getting to Know South Africa (1965)
    Jakeman, Alan
        3624. Getting to Know Japan (1966)
    Johnston, Richard
        3625. Getting to Know the Two Koreas (1965)
    Joy, Charles
        3626. Getting to Know Costa Rica, El Salvador, and Nicaragua (1964)
        3627. Getting to Know England, Scotland, and Ireland (1966)
        3628. Getting to Know Israel (1960)
        3629. Getting to Know Tanzania (1966)
        3630. Getting to Know the River Amazon (1963)
        3631. Getting to Know the Sahara (1963)
        3632. Getting to Know the South Pacific (1961)
        3633. Getting to Know the Tigris and Euphrates Rivers (1965)
        3634. Getting to Know the Two Chinas (1960)
    King, Seth
        3635. Getting to Know Malaysia and Singapore (1964)
    Laschever, Barnett
        3636. Getting to Know Cuba (1962)
        3637. Getting to Know Hawaii (1965)
        3638. Getting to Know India (1960)
        3639. Getting to Know Pakistan (1961)
        3640. Getting to Know Venezuela (1962)

Lauber, Patricia
   3641. Getting to Know Switzerland (1960)
Ogle, Ed
   3642. Getting to Know the Arctic (1961)
Olden, Sam
   3643. Getting to Know Africa's French Community (1961)
   3644. Getting to Know Argentina (1961)
   3645. Getting to Know Nigeria (1960)
Parke, Margaret
   3646. Getting to Know Australia (1962)
Phillips, Ted
   3647. Getting to Know Saudi Arabia (1963)
Redford, Lora
   3648. Getting to Know the Central Himalayas (1964)
   3649. Getting to Know the Northern Himalayas (1964)
Robins, Eric
   3650. Getting to Know the Congo River (1965)
Rollins, Frances
   3651. Getting to Know Canada (1966)
   3652. Getting to Know Puerto Rico (1967)
Smith, Ralph Lee
   3653. Getting to Know the World Health Organization (1963)
Soni, Welthy
   3654. Getting to Know the River Ganges (1964)
Taylor, Carl
   3655. Getting to Know Burma (1962)
   3656. Getting to Know Indonesia (1961)
Teltsch, Kathleen
   3657. Getting to Know the U.N. Peace Forces (1966)
Thompson, Hildegard
   3658. Getting to Know the American Indians Today (1965)
Tor, Regina
   3659. Getting to Know Greece (1959)
   3660. Getting to Know the Philippines (1958)
Underwood, Paul
   3661. Getting to Know Eastern Europe (1966)
Veglahn, Nancy
   3662. Getting to Know the Missouri River (1972)
Wallace, John
   3663. Getting to Know Egypt (1961)
   3664. Getting to Know France (1962)
   3665. Getting to Know Poland (1960)
   3666. Getting to Know the Soviet Union (1964)
West, Fred
   3667. Getting to Know the Two Vietnams (1963)
Witker, Jim
   3668. Getting to Know Scandinavia (1963)
The usefulness of these volumes is somewhat limited. Some of them are written in a story format, which curtails their use for school subjects. In many of them (e.g., the book on Vietnam), the material is outdated and the attitudes are goody-goody. Most of the books on the countries are well handled, but the approach is still rather simplistic. For grades 3 through 6.

GIDAL, TIM, and SONIA GIDAL   —Pantheon
        3669. My Village in Austria (1956)
        3670. My Village in Brazil (1968)
        3671. My Village in Denmark (1963)
        3672. My Village in England (1963)
        3673. My Village in Finland (1966)
        3674. My Village in France (1965)
        3675. My Village in Germany (1964)
        3676. My Village in Ghana (1970)
        3677. My Village in Greece (1960)
        3678. My Village in India (1956)
        3679. My Village in Ireland (1957)
        3680. My Village in Israel (1959)
        3681. My Village in Italy (1962)
        3682. My Village in Japan (1966)
        3683. My Village in Korea (1968)
        3684. My Village in Morocco (1964)
        3685. My Village in Norway (1958)
        3686. My Village in Portugal (1972)
        3687. My Village in Spain (1962)
        3688. My Village in Switzerland (1961)
        3689. My Village in Thailand (1970)
        3690. My Village in Yugoslavia (1957)
The point of view of these books is that of a child in a foreign country. The text
is in story form, although the authors do provide maps and glossaries. Only a brief
page of background on the country itself is provided in each volume. Supplementary
material at best.

GLUBOK, SHIRLEY
        3691. The Art of Africa (Harper, 1965)
        3692. The Art of Ancient Egypt (Atheneum, 1962)
        3693. The Art of Ancient Greece (Atheneum, 1963)
        3694. The Art of Ancient Mexico (Harper, 1968)
        3695. The Art of Ancient Peru (Harper, 1966)
        3696. The Art of Ancient Rome (Harper, 1965)
        3697. The Art of Colonial America (Macmillan, 1970)
        3698. The Art of India (Macmillan, 1969)
        3699. The Art of Japan (Macmillan, 1970)
        3700. The Art of Lands of the Bible (Atheneum, 1963)
        3701. The Art of the Eskimo (Harper, 1964)
        3702. The Art of the Etruscans (Harper, 1967)
        3703. The Art of the New American Nation (Macmillan, 1972)
        3704. The Art of the North American Indian (Harper, 1964)
        3705. The Art of the Old West (Macmillan, 1971)
        3706. The Art of the Southwest Indians (Macmillan, 1971)
These slender but enthralling volumes take the reader on a quick survey of art
during a specific period or by specific groups of people. The many reproductions,
some in color, far overwhelm the text. Still, the illustrations alone are worth the
price of the book; also, in many cases this is the only material available on the arts
and artifacts of certain eras.

GOLDEN NATURE GUIDES
     Abbott, R. Tucker
        3707. Sea Shells of the World (1962)

GOLDEN NATURE GUIDES   (cont'd)
    Fichter, George
        3708. Insect Pests (1966)
    Hoffmeister, Donald
        3709. Zoo Animals (1971)
    Lehr, Paul, and R. Will Burnett
        3710. Weather (1963)
    Reid, George K.
        3711. Pond Life (1967)
    Zim, Herbert
        3712. Zoology (1958)
    Zim, Herbert, and Robert Baker
        3713. Stars (1956)
    Zim, Herbert, and Clarence Cottam
        3714. Insects (1956)
    Zim, Herbert, and Ira Gabrielson
        3715. Birds (1960)
    Zim, Herbert, and Donald Hoffmeister
        3716. Mammals (1955)
    Zim, Herbert, and Lester Ingle
        3717. Seashores (1955)
    Zim, Herbert, and Alexander Martin
        3718. Flowers (1950)
        3719. Trees (1956)
    Zim, Herbert, and Robert Mitchell
        3720. Butterflies and Moths (1964)
    Zim, Herbert, and Paul Shaffer
        3721. Rocks and Minerals (1957)
    Zim, Herbert, Paul Shaffer, and Frank Rhodes
        3722. Fossils (1962)
    Zim, Herbert, and Hurst Shoemaker
        3723. Fishes (1956)
    Zim, Herbert, and Floyd Shuttleworth
        3724. Non-Flowering Plants (1967)
    Zim, Herbert, and Hobart Smith
        3725. Reptiles and Amphibians (1953)
    Zim, Herbert, and Alexander Sprunt
        3726. Gamebirds (1961)
These books are standard reference materials for the identification of various species. All the illustrations are in color, and the authors provide one paragraph of brief information on each specimen of wildlife under discussion. There is a general introduction in each book, as well as an index.

GOVERNMENT SERVICE THE WORLD OVER —Hastings House
    Torbert, Floyd
        3727. Firefighters the World Over (1967)
        3728. Park Rangers the World Over (1968)
        3729. Policemen the World Over (1971)
        3730. Postmen the World Over (1966)
The duties and operations of various civil servants in different countries are summarized in these books. The author discusses not only what the job entails, but also the equipment and uniforms worn in each country. The lively writing should interest readers in grades 3 to 6.

GREAT BATTLES SERIES   —Macmillan
    Barnett, Correlli
        3731. The Battle of El Alamein (1964)
    Conroy, Robert
        3732. The Battle of Bataan: America's Greatest Defeat (1969)
        3733. The Battle of Manila Bay: The Spanish War in the Philippines (1968)
    Cowley, Robert
        3734. 1918, Gamble for Victory (1964)
    Cuneo, John
        3735. The Battles of Saratoga (1967)
    Dupuy, Trevor
        3736. The Battle of Austerlitz (1968)
    Fehrenback, T. R.
        3737. Crossroads in Korea (1966)
    Goldston, Robert
        3738. The Battles of the "Constitution": Old Ironsides and the
                Freedom of the Seas (1969)
    Hough, Richard
        3739. The Battle of Britain: Triumph of R.A.F. Fighter Pilots (1971)
        3740. The Battle of Midway: Victory in the Pacific (1970)
    Irving, Clifford
        3741. The Battle of Jerusalem : The Six-Day War of June, 1967 (1970)
    Komroff, Manuel
        3742. The Battle of Waterloo (1964)
    Palmer, Bruce
        3743. Chancellorsville (1967)
        3744. First Bull Run (1965)
    Sammis, Edward
        3745. Last Stand at Stalingrad: The Battle That Saved the World (1966)
    Suskind, Richard
        3746. The Battle of Belleau Wood (1969)
    Tinkle, Lon
        3747. The Valiant Few (1964)
    Villiers, Alan
        3748. The Battle of Trafalgar (1965)
In this excellent series on important individual battles throughout history, the
authors provide background information on the events leading up to the battle, and
a complete breakdown of what happened during the battle. There are many maps and
photos of the battle sites and of the troop positions at various stages. At the end of
each book the authors provide a chart of the chain of command of each of the
armies involved. There are also bibliographies and indices.

GREAT CIVILIZATIONS SERIES   —Dufour
    Burland, Cottie
        3749. Ancient China (1961)
        3750. Ancient Egypt (1962)
        3751. Ancient Greece (1961)
        3752. Ancient Rome (1961)
        3753. Inca Peru (1962)
        3754. The Vikings (1961)
Small as they are, these books cover a multitude of subject areas. The author discusses
everything from architecture to education, clothing, industry, theater, and social life
of the various classes of each society. The illustrations are clear, not decorative, and
there is an index. This series is a must.

GREAT COMPOSERS SERIES —Crowell
    Chissell, Joan
        3755. Chopin (1965)
    Fenby, Eric
        3756. Delius (1972)
    Harding, James
        3757. Rossini (1972)
    Helm, Everett
        3758. Bartok (1972)
    Holst, Imogen
        3759. Bach (1965)
        3760. Britten (1965)
    Hurd, Michael
        3761. Elgar (1965)
        3762. Mendelssohn (1971)
        3763. Vaughan Williams (1970)
    Padmore, Elaine
        3764. Wagner (1972)
    Sadie, Stanley
        3765. Beethoven (1967)
        3766. Handel (1968)

This good biographical series treats many outstanding composers as well as others who are less well known. The authors deal primarily with the development of the composer's personality through artistic ferment. Not too much attention is paid to childhood unless the musical ability showed itself then. Background information is also provided about the time during which the composers wrote, and samples of their music are included. For ages 10 on up.

GREAT MEN OF SCIENCE —John Day
    Silverstein, Alvin, and Virginia Silverstein
        3767. Carl Linnaeus (1969)
        3768. Frederick Sanger (1969)
        3769. Harold Urey (1971)

The emphasis here is on the important scientific discoveries that each man proposed. The authors place special emphasis on the scientific achievements and even list formulas and examples of experiments , in order to stress the meaning of what each scientist achieved. There are photos and illustrations, as well as a list of important events in the life of each man. For grades 4 to 9.

GREAT MYSTERIES OF SCIENCE —Basic Books
    Clymer, Eleanor
        3770. The Case of the Missing Link (1958)
    Grey, Vivian
        3771. The Secret of the Mysterious Rays (1966)
    Simon, Tony
        3772. The Heart Explorers (1966)
        3773. The Search for Planet X (1962)

The quasi-fictional writing style of these books detracts greatly from their usefulness as objective, scientific books. Ms. Clymer's work is particularly at fault here; the other authors are somewhat more self-contained. Each book does have a glossary, bibliography, and index. For grades 4 to 7.

GREEK MYTHS SERIES —Viking
> Gates, Doris
>> 3774. Lord of the Sky: Zeus (1972)
>> 3775. The Warrior Goddess: Athena (1972)

Many of the legends surrounding a particular deity are collected into a single volume. The books of this series, attractive in format, should appeal to the casual reader as well as to the serious student of mythology.

HELFMAN, HARRY —Morrow
>> 3776. Fun with Your Fingers (1968)
>> 3777. Making Pictures Move (1969)
>> 3778. Strings on Your Fingers (1965)
>> 3779. Tricks with Your Fingers (1967)

This unusual series combines crafts with tricks and games—all of them intended to keep idle hands occupied. The illustrations, showing how to make and do things, are quite clear. Although there is no index, the table of contents should be sufficient for locating projects. For grades 3 on up.

HELLO SERIES —Grosset
> Bowen, J. David
>> 3780. Hello Brazil (1967)
>> 3781. Hello South America (1968)
> Karen, Ruth
>> 3782. Hello Guatemala (1970)
> Weeks, Morris
>> 3783. Hello Mexico (1970)
>> 3784. Hello Venezuela (1968)
>> 3785. Hello West Indies (1971)

This series is best when it deals with the histories of the countries involved. Although there is information on such topics as industry and education today, not as much information is to be found here as in other series, such as the Lands and Peoples series.

HERE IS YOUR HOBBY SERIES —Putnam
> Braverman, Bill, and Bill Neumann
>> 3786. Here Is Your Hobby: Slot Car Racing (1969)
> Cetin, Frank
>> 3787. Here Is Your Hobby: Stamp Collecting (1962)
> Felsen, Henry
>> 3788. Here Is Your Hobby: Car Customizing (1965)
> Foss, William O.
>> 3789. Here Is Your Hobby: Skiing (1964)
> Henderson, Dion
>> 3790. Here Is Your Hobby: Hunting (1963)
> Holcomb, Hank
>> 3791. Here Is Your Hobby: Outboard Boating (1965)
> Joseph, James
>> 3792. Here Is Your Hobby: Snowmobiling (1972)
> Lessin, Andrew
>> 3793. Here Is Your Hobby: Art (1963)
> Moore, William
>> 3794. Here Is Your Hobby: Fishing (1962)
>> 3795. Here Is Your Hobby: Science Equipment (1962)

HERE IS YOUR HOBBY SERIES —Putnam (cont'd)
>   Neumann, Bill
>> 3796. Here Is Your Hobby: Model Car Building (1971)
>   Powers, William
>> 3797. Here Is Your Hobby: Indian Dancing and Costumes (1966)
>   Roth, Bernhard
>> 3798. Here Is Your Hobby: Archery (1962)
>   Wels, Byron G.
>> 3799. Here Is Your Hobby: Amateur Radio (1968)
>> 3800. Here Is Your Hobby: Magic (1967)
>   Young, Helen
>> 3801. Here Is Your Hobby: Doll Collecting (1964)

All facets of a hobby are presented in this series: the history, the rules for collecting or making the items involved, the type and cost of equipment necessary, and information on displaying items. Each book also provides a glossary and an index, and some of them offer lists of the publications, clubs, and manufacturers of supplies pertinent to the hobby.

HISTORICAL CHARACTERS SERIES —McGraw-Hill
>   Bellis, H.
>> 3802. Admiral Nelson (1970)
>> 3803. Captain Cook (1970)
>   Purton, R. W.
>> 3804. Captain Scott (1970)
>> 3805. Doctor Livingstone (1970)

These are short, easy-to-read biographies of people who are not the usual subjects of such series. Although the authors sometimes invoke fiction, using a story format, these are nonetheless presentable introductory biographies. Glossaries and bibliographies are provided. For ages 10 on up.

HISTORICAL EVENTS SERIES —McGraw-Hill
>   Gray, Peter
>> 3806. D-Day (1970)
>> 3807. The Battle of Hastings (1968)
>> 3808. The Invincible Armada (1970)

Another easy-to-read historical series from McGraw-Hill. This one introduces readers to important individual events in history. The incidents are related with a verve that should capture the imagination of the casual reader as well as the student of a particular event. For ages 9 through 13.

HISTORY IN PICTURES SERIES —John Day
>   Whittle, Tyler
>> 3809. Classical Greece (1971)
>> 3810. The Birth of Greece (1971)

As the series title suggests, these slim books are primarily photos and drawings. There is no table of contents and no index, so the books are extremely difficult to use— especially considering the little information they provide. The chief use for the books would be purely supplemental for those students who would need pictures and illustrations of what life was like during these eras.

HOGEBOOM, AMY —Vanguard
>> 3811. Birds and How to Draw Them (1952)
>> 3812. Boats and How to Draw Them (1950)
>> 3813. Cats and How to Draw Them (1939)

HOGEBOOM, AMY —Vanguard (cont'd)
        3814. Dogs and How to Draw Them (1934)
        3815. Familiar Animals and How to Draw Them (1951)
        3816. Forest Animals and How to Draw Them (1950)
        3817. Horses and How to Draw Them (1938)
        3818. Planes and How to Draw Them (1956)
        3819. Sea Animals and How to Draw Them (1951)
        3820. Trains and How to Draw Them (1953)
        3821. Wild Animals and How to Draw Them (1937)
This series differs a little from other how-to-draw series in that it provides a photograph of an object for the artist to draw from. Ms. Hogeboom also provides the
reader with some information about the object—how it works, what it does—to
make the drawing somewhat easier. The next few pages are then devoted to showing
the various stages leading up to a completed drawing. For ages 9 to 12.

HOLIDAY BOOK SERIES —Garrard
      Epstein, Samuel, and Beryl Epstein
        3822. European Folk Festivals (1968)
      Graves, Charles
        3823. The Fourth of July (1963)
      Groh, Lynn
        3824. New Year's Day (1964)
      Guilfoile, Elizabeth
        3825. Valentine's Day (1965)
      Morrow, Betty, and Louis Hartman
        3826. Jewish Holidays (1967)
      Parlin, John
        3827. Patriot's Day (1964)
      Patterson, Lillie
        3828. Christmas Feasts and Festivals (1968)
        3829. Christmas in America (1969)
        3830. Christmas in Britain and Scandinavia (1970)
        3831. Easter (1966)
        3832. Halloween (1963)
        3833. Holiday Books: Birthdays (1965)
      Wyndham, Lee
        3834. Thanksgiving (1963)
The history, customs, and traditions of the respective holidays are the subject of
these books. Written in an easy-to-read format, with plenty of illustrations, the books
can be used for class work or just for pleasure reading, since the authors usually
include story, poem, and legend information along with facts about the holiday.

HORIZON CARAVEL SERIES —American Heritage
      Andrist, Ralph
        3835. Heroes of Polar Exploration (1962)
      Bixby, William
        3836. The Universe of Galileo and Newton (1964)
      Blacker, Irwin
        3837. Cortez and the Aztec Conquest (1965)
      Burchell, S. C.
        3838. Building the Suez Canal (1966)
      Donovan, Frank
        3839. The Vikings (1964)

Dowd, D. L.
    3840. The French Revolution (1965)
Hawkes, Jacquette
    3841. Pharoahs of Egypt (1965)
Herold, Christopher
    3842. The Battle of Waterloo (1967)
Hibbert, Christopher
    3843. The Search for King Arthur (1969)
Horizon, Editors
    3844. Shakespeare's England (1964)
Howard, Cecil
    3845. Pizarro and the Conquest of Peru (1968)
Isenberg, Irwin
    3846. Caesar (1964)
Jacobs, David
    3847. Beethoven (1970)
    3848. Constantinople, City on the Golden Horn (1969)
    3849. Master Builders of the Middle Ages (1969)
Karp, Walter
    3850. Charles Darwin and the Origin of the Species (1968)
Kotker, Norman
    3851. The Holy Land in the Time of Jesus (1967)
McKendrick, Melveena
    3852. Ferdinand and Isabella (1968)
Mee, Charles
    3853. Lorenzo de' Medici and the Renaissance (1969)
Mercer, Charles
    3854. Alexander the Great (1962)
Moscow, Henry
    3855. Russia under the Czars (1962)
Pfeiffer, John
    3856. The Search for Early Man (1963)
Rugoff, Milton
    3857. Marco Polo's Adventures in China (1964)
Sears, Stephen
    3858. The Desert War in North Africa (1967)
Shipton, Eric
    3859. Mountain Conquest (1966)
Sterling, Thomas
    3860. The Exploration of Africa (1963)
Warner, Oliver
    3861. Captain Cook and the South Pacific (1963)
    3862. Nelson and the Age of Fighting Sail (1963)
Williams, Jay
    3863. Joan of Arc (1964)
    3864. Knights of the Crusades (1962)
    3865. Leonardo da Vinci (1965)
    3866. The Spanish Armada (1966)
Winston, Richard
    3867. Charlemagne (1968)

This outstanding series is a companion to the American Heritage Series. The illustrations here are equally lavish color and black-and-white reproductions of paintings,

HORIZON CARAVEL SERIES —American Heritage (cont'd)
drawings, and etchings of the time. The writing styles of the various authors are
without exception fluent and fascinating. The scholarship is impeccable. All
volumes have indices and bibliographies. A must for any collection.

HOW AND WHY WONDER BOOKS SERIES —Grosset
    Barr, Donald
       3868. The How and Why Wonder Book of Atomic Energy (1961)
       3869. The How and Why Wonder Book of Building (1964)
       3870. The How and Why Wonder Book of Primitive Man (1961)
    Bethell, Jean
       3871. The How and Why Wonder Book of Famous Scientists (1961)
    Coe, Geoffrey
       3872. The How and Why Wonder Book of Trees (1964)
    Coe, Geoffrey, and Felix Sutton
       3873. The How and Why Wonder Book of Fish (1964)
    Ferguson, Grace
       3874. The How and Why Wonder Book of Wild Flowers (1962)
    Geis, Darlene
       3875. The How and Why Wonder Book of Dinosaurs (1960)
    Gelinas, Paul
       3876. The How and Why Wonder Book of Coins and Currency (1965)
    Grossman, Shelly, and Mary Grossman
       3877. The How and Why Wonder Book of Ecology (1960)
    Highland, Harold
       3878. The How and Why Wonder Book of Flight (1961)
       3879. The How and Why Wonder Book of Light and Color (1963)
       3880. The How and Why Wonder Book of Mathematics (1961)
       3881. The How and Why Wonder Book of Planets and Interplanetary
           Travel (1962)
    Hoss, Norman
       3882. The How and Why Wonder Book of Stars (1960)
    Hyler, Nelson
       3883. The How and Why Wonder Book of Rocks and Minerals (1960)
    Keen, Martin
       3884. The How and Why Wonder Book of Chemistry (1961)
       3885. The How and Why Wonder Book of Electronics (1969)
       3886. The How and Why Wonder Book of Magnets and Magnetism (1963)
       3887. The How and Why Wonder Book of Prehistoric Mammals (1965)
       3888. The How and Why Wonder Book of Science Experiments (1962)
       3889. The How and Why Wonder Book of Sound (1962)
       3890. The How and Why Wonder Book of the Human Body (1961)
       3891. The How and Why Wonder Book of the Microscope (1961)
       3892. The How and Why Wonder Book of Wild Animals (1962)
    Keen, Martin, and Claire Cundiff
       3893. The How and Why Wonder Book of Air and Water (1969)
    Knight, Clayton
       3894. The How and Why Wonder Book of Rockets and Missiles (1962)
    Liberty, Gene
       3895. The How and Why Wonder Book of Time (1963)
    Low, Donald
       3896. The How and Why Wonder Book of Sea Shells (1961)
    Matthewson, Robert
       3897. The How and Why Wonder Book of Birds (1960)

HOW AND WHY WONDER BOOKS SERIES —Grosset (cont'd)
>   3898. The How and Why Wonder Book of Reptiles and Amphibians (1960)
Miers, Earl Schenck
>   3899. The How and Why Wonder Book of the Civil War (1961)
Notkin, Jerome
>   3900. The How and Why Wonder Book of Beginning Science (1960)
>   3901. The How and Why Wonder Book of Electricity (1960)
>   3902. The How and Why Wonder Book of Machines (1960)
Robbin, Irving
>   3903. The How and Why Wonder Book of Basic Inventions (1965)
>   3904. The How and Why Wonder Book of Caves to Skyscrapers (1963)
>   3905. The How and Why Wonder Book of Dogs (1962)
>   3906. The How and Why Wonder Book of Explorations and Dis-
>   coveries (1961)
>   3907. The How and Why Wonder Book of Guns (1963)
>   3908. The How and Why Wonder Book of Polar Regions (1965)
Rood, Ronald
>   3909. The How and Why Wonder Book of Ants and Bees (1962)
>   3910. The How and Why Wonder Book of Insects (1960)
Scharff, Robert
>   3911. The How and Why Wonder Book of Oceanography (1964)
Self, Margaret
>   3912. The How and Why Wonder Book of Horses (1961)
Sutton, Felix
>   3913. The How and Why Wonder Book of Deserts (1965)
>   3914. The How and Why Wonder Book of Our Earth (1969)
>   3915. The How and Why Wonder Book of the Moon (1963)
>   3916. The How and Why Wonder Book of World War II (1962)
Webb, Robert
>   3917. The How and Why Wonder Book of Florence Nightingale (1962)
The question and answer approach of this series covers not only the appearance
and characteristics of the subject under discussion, but various myths and stories
connected with it and (where applicable) collection and preservation of specimens.
The format is two-column, with rather small typeface. The illustrations are in color,
but there is no index; the reader must depend on the table of contents to locate
the needed material.

HOW DO THEY . . . SERIES —Westminster
Hilton, Suzanne
>   3918. How Do They Cope with It? (1972)
>   3919. How Do They Get Rid of It? (1970)
Sullivan, George
>   3920. How Do They Build It? (1972)
>   3921. How Do They Grow It? (1968)
>   3922. How Do They Make It? (1965)
>   3923. How Do They Run It? (1971)
>   3924. More How Do They Make It? (1969)
This is an excellent series that covers all kinds of oddities—how macaroni is made,
how sandpaper is made, etc. The books are also good for school assignments,
especially *How Do They Get Rid of It?*, which deals with recycling. There are many
photos and drawings, and the volumes are indexed.

100

HOW IT WORKS SERIES   —Putnam
>   Cook, Joseph
>   >   3925. The Electronic Brain, How It Works (1969)
>   Harvey, Tad
>   >   3926. Television, How It Works (1968)
>   Jones, Raymond
>   >   3927. Radar, How It Works (1972)
>   Lukashok, Alvin
>   >   3928. Communications Satellites, How They Work (1967)
>   McFarland, Kenton
>   >   3929. Airplanes, How They Work (1966)
>   Stambler, Irwin
>   >   3930. Weather Instruments, How They Work (1967)
>   Yerkow, Charles
>   >   3931. Automobiles, How They Work (1965)
>   >   3932. Motorcycles, How They Work (1971)

All of the mechanics and principles that go into these various devices are examined. The authors also discuss the various designs throughout history, as well as safety factors involved in their manufacture and use. There are glossaries and indices.

HOW THEY LIVE AND WORK SERIES   —Praeger
>   Austin, Paul Britten
>   >   3933. The Swedes: How They Live and Work (1970)
>   Bryant, Andrew
>   >   3934. The Italians: How They Live and Work (1971)
>   Carroll, Joseph
>   >   3935. The French: How They Live and Work (1971)
>   Dicks, T. R. B.
>   >   3936. The Greeks: How They Live and Work (1972)
>   Foster, Dereck
>   >   3937. The Argentines: How They Live and Work (1972)
>   Hoffman, Ann
>   >   3938. The Dutch: How They Live and Work (1971)
>   Peck, Reginald
>   >   3939. The West Germans: How They Live and Work (1970)
>   Perceval, Michael
>   >   3940. The Spaniards: How They Live and Work (1970)
>   Wallace, Martin
>   >   3941. The Irish: How They Live and Work (1972)

While presenting the contemporary life of peoples in various foreign lands, the authors discuss the living conditions of various segments of society as well as the national character and social organization of those societies. Information is also given on the government, politics, industry, arts, education, and entertainment of each country. The authors also often compare such aspects with their American counterparts. An outstanding series on life as it is lived abroad.

HOW THEY LIVED SERIES   —Garrard
>   Andrews, Mary
>   >   3942. When Jamestown Was a Colonial Capital (1970)
>   Berry, Erick
>   >   3943. When Wagon Trains Rolled to Santa Fe (1966)
>   Blassingame, Wyatt
>   >   3944. Bent's Fork: Crossroad of the Great West (1967)

Cavanah, Frances
    3945. When Americans Came to New Orleans (1970)
Douty, Esther
    3946. Mr. Jefferson's Washington (1970)
Emerson, Caroline
    3947. New Amsterdam: Old Holland in the New World (1967)
Epstein, Samuel, and Beryl Epstein
    3948. Young Paul Revere's Boston (1966)
Glendinning, Richard
    3949. Circus Days under the Big Top (1969)
    3950. When Mountain Men Trapped Beaver (1967)
Groh, Lynn
    3951. The Pilgrims, Brave Settlers of Plymouth (1968)
Janes, Edward
    3952. When Cape Cod Men Saved Lives (1968)
    3953. When Men Panned Gold in the Klondike (1968)
Luce, Williard, and Celia Luce
    3954. Sutter's Fort (1969)
McCague, James
    3955. Flatboat Days on the Frontier Rivers (1968)
    3956. Mississippi Steamboat Days (1967)
    3957. When Chicago Was Young (1971)
    3958. When Clipper Ships Ruled the Seas (1968)
    3959. When Cowboys Rode the Chisholm Trail (1969)
    3960. When Men First Flew (1969)
    3961. When the Rails Ran West (1967)
Meadowcroft, Enid
    3962. When Nantucket Men Went Whaling (1966)
Montgomery, Elizabeth
    3963. Old Ben Franklin's Philadelphia (1967)
    3964. When a Ton of Gold Reached Seattle (1968)
    3965. When Pioneers Pushed West to Oregon (1970)
Patterson, Lillie
    3966. Lumberjacks of the North Woods (1967)
Voight, Virginia
    3967. Stagecoach Days and Stagecoach Kings (1970)

The volumes of this colorful series are based on first-hand journals, diaries, and letters written by people during these exciting times in American history. There are many illustrations, most of which are in color. The format is enticing, and the books can be used either for enjoyment reading or as a basis for school assignments.

HOW THINGS ARE MADE SERIES —Dodd

Cooke, David C.
    3968. How Atomic Submarines Are Made (1967)
    3969. How Automobiles Are Made (1972)
    3970. How Books Are Made (1963)
    3971. How Helicopters Are Made (1961)
    3972. How Money Is Made (1962)
    3973. How Paper Is Made (1959)
    3974. How Superhighways Are Made (1968)

These books give step-by-step information on how each item is made, alternating one page of photos with one page of text. Most interesting for casual readers and

HOW THINGS ARE MADE SERIES —Dodd (cont'd)
school-related subjects; unfortunately, there are no indices, and there is not always
a table of contents. For ages 9 to 11.

HOW THINGS WORK SERIES —World
    Meyer, Jerome
        3975. Engines (1972)
        3976. Machines (1972)
        3977. Prisms and Lenses (1972)
        3978. Sound and Its Reproduction (1972)
In its examination of the principles of certain types of machinery and natural
phenomena, this new series is similar to several other series. These books also
examine various types of devices—e.g., types of engines, types of prisms, etc.
For grades 4 through 6.

HOW THE INDIANS LIVED SERIES —Morrow
    Hofsinde, Robert
        3979. Indian Arts (1971)
        3980. Indian Beadwork (1958)
        3981. Indian Costumes (1968)
        3982. Indian Fishing and Camping (1963)
        3983. Indian Games and Crafts (1957)
        3984. Indian Hunting (1962)
        3985. Indian Medicine Man (1966)
        3986. Indian Music Makers (1967)
        3987. Indian Picture Writing (1959)
        3988. Indian Sign Language (1956)
        3989. Indian Warriors and Their Weapons (1965)
        3990. Indians at Home (1964)
        3991. Indians on the Move (1970)
The author, who has been adopted into an Indian tribe, has prepared a first-rate
account of various aspects of Indian life. The black-and-white illustrations are
excellent, the books are factual and interestingly written (although not always
indexed). The main difficulty is that these books cover general topics, and do not
examine closely the practices of individual tribes. Thus, if a student needs information
on Seminole crafts, he may have difficulty in finding more than just a few sentences.
Sonja Bleeker's series is more valuable for this type of use.

HOW TO DRAW SERIES —Abelard
    Zaidenburg, Arthur
        3992. How to Draw a Circus (1969)
        3993. How to Draw and Compose Pictures (1971)
        3994. How to Draw Athletes in Action (1965)
        3995. How to Draw Ballet and Other Dancers (1968)
        3996. How to Draw Birds, Fish, and Reptiles (1962)
        3997. How to Draw Butterflies, Bees, and Reptiles (1963)
        3998. How to Draw Costumes and Clothes (1964)
        3999. How to Draw Dogs, Cats, and Horses (1959)
        4000. How to Draw Farm Animals (1959)
        4001. How to Draw Flowers, Fruit, and Vegetables (1964)
        4002. How to Draw Heads and Faces (1966)
        4003. How to Draw Historic and Modern Bridges (1962)
        4004. How to Draw Houses (1968)
        4005. How to Draw Landscapes, Seascapes, and Cityscapes (1963)

HOW TO DRAW SERIES —Abelard (cont'd)
       4006. How to Draw Military and Civilian Uniforms (1965)
       4007. How to Draw Motors, Machines, and Tools (1970)
       4008. How to Draw Musicians and Musical Instruments (1969)
       4009. How to Draw People at Work (1970)
       4010. How to Draw Period Costumes (1970)
       4011. How to Draw Prehistoric and Mythical Animals (1967)
       4012. How to Draw Shakespeare's People (1967)
       4013. How to Draw Ships, Trains, Cars and Airplanes (1961)
       4014. How to Draw the Wild West (1971)
       4015. How to Draw Wild Animals (1958)

These books assume that the user has some prior knowledge of sketching. The author shows both rough and finished drawings, but he does not discuss the basic principles of sketching. Nonetheless, the series provides many samples and ideas for the budding artist to choose from.

HOW TO STAR . . . SERIES —Four Winds
     Batterman, Charles
       4016. How to Star in Swimming and Diving (1970)
     Masin, Herman
       4017. How to Star in Baseball (1966)
       4018. How to Star in Basketball (1966)
       4019. How to Star in Football (1966)
     O'Connor, W. Harold
       4020. How to Star in Track and Field (1969)
     Vogelsinger, Herbert
       4021. How to Star in Soccer (1967)

Comparable to the Better Sports Series in that it shows how to play various sports. These books also discuss conditioning, which is not done in the other series, and, where applicable, basic plays and maneuvers.

HUMAN BODY SERIES —Watts
     Elgin, Kathleen
       4022. The Brain (1967)
       4023. The Ear (1967)
       4024. The Eye (1967)
       4025. The Female Reproductive System (1969)
       4026. The Glands (1971)
       4027. The Hand (1968)
       4028. The Heart (1968)
       4029. The Male Reproductive System (1969)
       4030. The Respiratory System (1970)
       4031. The Skeleton (1971)
       4032. The Skin (1970)

Although this easy-to-read series on human anatomy is very simple in content, it will still serve as a basic introduction for readers in grades 2 to 4. The print is large and the illustrations are clear; the volumes are indexed.

IMMORTALS' BIOGRAPHIES SERIES —Watts
     Bendick, Jeanne
       4033. Archimedes and the Door of Science (1962)
     Cormack, Maribelle
       4034. Imhotep: Builder in Stone (1965)

IMMORTALS' BIOGRAPHIES SERIES —Watts (cont'd)
    May, Charles
        4035. James Clerk Maxwell and Electromagnetism (1962)
        4036. Michael Faraday and the Electric Dynamo (1961)
    Pittenger, W. Norman
        4037. Plato: His Life and Teaching (1971)
        4038. The Life of Saint Peter (1971)
    Sims, Bennett
        4039. Lao-Tzu and the Tao Te Ching (1971)
    Stearns, Monroe
        4040. Charlemagne (1971)
        4041. Dante: Poet of Love (1965)
        4042. Elizabeth I of England (1970)
        4043. Julius Caesar: Master of Men (1971)
        4044. Louis XIV of France (1971)
        4045. Mark Twain (1965)
        4046. Wolfgang Amadeus Mozart: Master of Pure Music (1968)
In this excellent series for grades 7 to 12, the authors not only present biographical material, but also place the subject against the background of his time, against
the beliefs and customs prevalent then. Volumes include a chronology of the
biographee's life, a bibliography, an index, and, where applicable, listening suggestions.

IN THE STEPS OF THE GREAT AMERICAN NATURALISTS SERIES —M. Evans
    Clark, James
        4047. In the Steps of the Great American Naturalists: Museum Collector
            Carl Ethan Akeley (1968)
    Forbes, John
        4048. In the Steps of the Great American Naturalists: Zoologist
            William Temple Hornaday (1967)
    Pallister, John
        4049. In the Steps of the Great American Naturalists: Entomologist
            Frank Eugene Lutz (1967)
    Wright, A. Gilbert
        4050. In the Steps of the Great American Naturalists: Herpetologist
            Karl Patterson Schmidt (1967)
In addition to covering the careers of various naturalists, these biographies also
suggest nature projects along the same lines as those followed by the subjects.
For supplementary use.

INDIAN BOOKS SERIES —Garrard
    Anderson, LaVere
        4051. Sitting Bull: Great Sioux Chief (1970)
    Blassingame, Wyatt
        4052. Osceola: Seminole War Chief (1967)
        4053. Sacagawea: Indian Guide (1965)
    Graff, Stewart, and Polly Graff
        4054. Squanto: Indian Adventurer (1965)
    McCague, James
        4055. Tecumseh: Shawnee Warrior-Statesman (1970)
    Meadowcroft, Enid
        4056. Crazy Horse: Sioux Warrior (1965)
    Montgomery, Elizabeth
        4057. Chief Joseph: Guardian of His People (1969)
        4058. Chief Seattle: Great Statesman (1966)

INDIAN BOOKS SERIES —Garrard (cont'd)
>   Voight, Virginia
>   4059. Massasoit: Friend of the Pilgrims (1971)
>   Wilkie, Katharine
>   4060. Pocahontas: Indian Princess (1969)

While the publisher states that the purpose of these dramatized biographies is to promote knowledge of the Indians, the chief intent actually seems to be popularization. There are better, more factual biographies of these same individuals to be found elsewhere.

INDIAN NATIONS SERIES —Putnam
>   Gridley, Marion
>   4061. The Story of the Haida (1972)
>   4062. The Story of the Iroquois (1969)
>   4063. The Story of the Navajo (1971)
>   4064. The Story of the Seminole (announced)
>   4065. The Story of the Sioux (1972)

The colorful illustrations and large print make this a more attractive series than Bleeker, although the books are shorter and less detailed. Ms. Gridley describes the history of each tribe, how they lived and raised their children, their beliefs, festivals, crafts, and so forth. She also presents biographies of famous members of the tribe and a brief last chapter that discusses what the tribe is like today.

INTERNATIONAL LIBRARY —McGraw-Hill
>   Bauer, Ernst
>   4066. The Mysterious World of Caves (1971)
>   Duche, Jean
>   4067. The Great Trade Routes (1969)
>   Duffey, Eric
>   4068. The Conservation of Nature (1970)
>   Girardi, Roland
>   4069. Olympic Games (1972)
>   Goldstein, Kenneth
>   4070. The World of Tomorrow (1969)
>   Herbert, Wally
>   4071. Polar Deserts (1971)
>   Hinkelbein, Albert
>   4072. Energy and Power (1971)
>   Lloyd, Christopher
>   4073. Sea Fights under Sail (1970)
>   Melegari, Vezio
>   4074. Great Sieges (1970)
>   Nitsche, Roland
>   4075. Money (1971)
>   Quilici, Folco
>   4076. The Great Desert (1969)
>   Rondiere, Pierre
>   4077. Purity or Pollution: The Struggle for Water (1971)
>   Stephen, David, and James Lockie
>   4078. Nature's Way (1969)

The authors of these volumes hail from various countries abroad. In fact, that is the theme tying the books together, since the authors write about any subject that may be of international concern. Attractively presented, with both color and black-and-white illustrations, nonetheless much of the information is available in other series.

INTRODUCING MODERN SCIENCE SERIES —Lippincott
    Allen, Richard J.
        4079. Cryogenics (1964)
    Dilson, Jesse
        4080. Curves and Automation: The Scientist's Plot (1971)
    Drummond, A. H.
        4081. Molecules in the Service of Man (1972)
    Hellman, Hal
        4082. High Energy Physics (1968)
    Klein, H. Arthur
        4083. Biolumenescence (1964)
        4084. Fuel Cells (1966)
        4085. Holography (1970)
        4086. Masers and Lasers (1963)
        4087. Oceans and Continents in Motion (1972)
        4088. The New Gravitation: Key to Incredible Energies (1971)
    Latham, Donald
        4089. Transistors and Integrated Circuits (1966)
    Marteka, Vincent
        4090. Bionics (1965)
    Milne, Lorus, and Margery Milne
        4091. The Nature of Animals (1969)
    Nickelsburg, Janet
        4092. Ecology: Habitats, Niches, and Food Chains (1969)
    Thomas, Paul D.
        4093. Abiogenesis (1969)
        4094. Gases and Plasmas (1966)
    Wohlrabe, Raymond
        4095. Crystals (1962)
        4096. Fundamental Physical Forces (1969)
        4097. Metals (1964)
    Woodburn, John
        4098. Excursions into Chemistry (1965)
        4099. Radioisotopes (1962)
This outstanding series presents detailed treatment of very unusual scientific topics. The texts are interestingly written—although they are not simple—and the authors provide some photographs in addition to bibliographies and indices. A must for grades 6 through 12.

INVESTIGATING SCIENCE SERIES —Addisonian
    White, Laurence
        4100. Investigating Science with Coins (1969)
        4101. Investigating Science with Nails (1970)
        4102. Investigating Science with Paper (1970)
        4103. Investigating Science with Rubber Bands (1969)
The physical properties of each object are explored: why it is constructed as it is, and the uses each object has. Through such examination, the author illustrates the various scientific principles involved, such as magnetism, heat conduction, etc. Interesting experiments are included. For grades 3 to 6.

JACKSON, ROBERT B. —Walck
        4104. Championship Trail (1970)
        4105. Grand Prix at the Glen (1965)
        4106. Road Race Round the World (1965)

JACKSON, ROBERT B. —Walck (cont'd)
      4107. Stock Car Racing (1968)
Mr. Jackson discusses the history of racing and outstanding individual events. Using many photos, he delves into the sport itself, the history and various kinds of cars, and the men involved in automobile racing.

JUNIOR REFERENCE BOOK SERIES —Dufour
      Brinton, Henry
          4108. Man in Space (1969)
      Cunnington, Phyllis
          4109. Costume (1968)
      Darlow, Denys
          4110. Musical Instruments (1962)
      Davey, John
          4111. Coal Mining (1962)
      Dumpleton, John
          4112. Law and Order, the Story of the Police (1963)
      Forbes, Duncan
          4113. Life before Man (1968)
      Hoare, Robert
          4114. The Story of Aircraft and Travel by Air (1966)
          4115. Travel by Sea (1965)
      Huggett, Frank
          4116. Farming (1963)
      Male, David
          4117. The Story of the Theatre (1960)
      Manning, Rosemary
          4118. Heraldry (1966)
      Moore, Patrick
          4119. Stars and Space (1966)
      Page, Robert
          4120. The Story of the Post (1967)
      Ransome-Wallis, P.
          4121. British Railways Today (1964)
      Turland, Frank
          4122. Furniture in England (1962)
      Unstead, R. J.
          4123. A History of Houses (1965)
          4124. Monasteries (1961)
          4125. Travel by Road through the Ages (1967)
      Wilkinson, Frederick
          4126. Arms and Armour (1963)
      Wright, John
          4127. Deep Sea Fishing (1961)
These short works, on many and varied subjects, have attractive layouts with good color illustrations and large type. The authors also present a bibliography and index. Some of the information may be inapplicable, since the series was originally published in England.

JUNIOR SCIENCE BOOKS SERIES —Garrard
      Anderson, Dorothy
          4128. Junior Science Book of Sound (1962)
      Collins, Henry
          4129. Junior Science Book of Turtles (1962)

JUNIOR SCIENCE BOOKS SERIES —Garrard (cont'd)
    Crosby, Alexander
        4130. Junior Science Book of Beavers (1960)
        4131. Junior Science Book of Canada Geese (1966)
        4132. Junior Science Book of Pond Life (1964)
    Crosby, Phoebe
        4133. Junior Science Book of Rock Collecting (1962)
        4134. Junior Science Book of Stars (1960)
    Epstein, Samuel, and Beryl Epstein
        4135. Junior Science Book of Seashells (1963)
    Feravolo, Rocco
        4136. Junior Science Book of Electricity (1960)
        4137. Junior Science Book of Flying (1960)
        4138. Junior Science Book of Heat (1964)
        4139. Junior Science Book of Light (1961)
        4140. Junior Science Book of Magnets (1960)
        4141. Junior Science Book of Water Experiments (1965)
        4142. Junior Science Book of Weather Experiments (1963)
    Larrick, Nancy
        4143. Junior Science Book of Rain, Hail, Sleet, and Snow (1961)
    Lauber, Patricia
        4144. Junior Science Book of Icebergs and Glaciers (1961)
        4145. Junior Science Book of Penguins (1963)
        4146. Junior Science Book of Volcanoes (1965)
    Lemmon, Robert
        4147. Junior Science Book of Big Cats (1962)
        4148. Junior Science Book of Trees (1960)
    Lietz, Gerald
        4149. Junior Science Book of Bacteria (1964)
    Peterson, Ottis
        4150. Junior Science Book of Water (1966)
    Pierce, Georgia
        4151. Junior Science Book of Bird Life (1967)
    Sheldon, William
        4152. Junior Science Book of Elephants (1961)
In this science series for younger readers, the sentences are short, the print is
large, and the examination of each subject is handled simply. Each volume is
indexed, but there are not as many photos as would be desirable for grades 2 to 4.

KETTELKAMP, LARRY —Morrow
        4153. Drums, Rattles, and Bells (1960)
        4154. Flutes, Whistles, and Reeds (1962)
        4155. Horns (1964)
        4156. Singing Strings (1958)
This is the only series which presents a history of musical instruments. The author
also shows how readers may make similar instruments out of materials found in the
home. Each member of the orchestral family is covered; volumes contain glossaries,
but they are not indexed.

KEY CONCEPTS IN POLITICAL SCIENCE SERIES —Praeger
    Albrow, Martin
        4157. Bureaucracy (1970)
    Birch, A. H.
        4158. Representation (1972)

    Calvert, Peter
        4159. Revolution (1970)
    Chapman, Brian
        4160. The Police State (1970)
    Davies, Ioan
        4161. Social Mobility and Political Change (1970)
    Frankel, Joseph
        4162. The National Interest (1970)
    Partridge, P. H.
        4163. Consent and Consensus (1971)
    Plamenatz, John
        4164. Ideology (1970)
    Rees, John
        4165. Equality (1972)
    Schapiro, Leonard
        4166. Totalitarianism (1972)
    Tudor, Henry
        4167. Political Myth (1972)
    Wilkinson, Paul
        4168. Social Movements (1971)

An outstanding series concerning various facets of political science. The authors discuss the origin of the concept under examination, its changes through the years, and various important people who molded the concepts. Also discussed are the influences these concepts have on political life today, as well as the various interpretations of these ideas by different groups. For grades 7 and up.

KEYS TO THE CITIES SERIES —Lippincott
    Douglas, Marjory
        4169. The Key to Paris (1960)
    Jackson, Charlotte
        4170. The Key to San Francisco (1961)
    King, Martha
        4171. The Key to Chicago (1961)
    Loder, Dorothy
        4172. The Key to Philadelphia (1960)
    Robinson, W. W.
        4173. The Key to Los Angeles (1963)
    Salisbury, Harrison
        4174. The Key to Moscow (1963)
    Seifert, Shirley
        4175. The Key to St. Louis (1963)
    Sheldon, Walter
        4176. The Key to Tokyo (1962)
    Terrell, John
        4177. The Key to Washington (1962)
    Tinkle, Lon
        4178. The Key to Dallas (1965)
    Wohlrabe, Raymond
        4179. The Key to Vienna (1961)

Although this series is well written and well organized, covering the history and character of each city, all of the books are outdated by now and have been superseded by other series with more recent titles.

LANDMARK SERIES —Random House
    Adams, Samuel
        4180. General Brock and Niagara Falls (1957)
        4181. The Erie Canal (1953)
        4182. The Pony Express (1950)
        4183. The Santa Fe Trail (1951)
    Alderman, Clifford
        4184. The Story of the Thirteen Colonies (1956)
    Blassingame, Wyatt
        4185. Combat Nurses of World War II (1967)
        4186. Medical Corps Heroes of World War II (1969)
        4187. The French Foreign Legion (1965)
        4188. U.S. Frogmen of World War II (1964)
    Bliven, Bruce
        4189. From Casablanca to Berlin (1965)
        4190. From Pearl Harbor to Okinawa (1960)
        4191. The American Revolution (1958)
        4192. The Story of D-Day: June 6, 1944 (1956)
    Boylston, Helen
        4193. Clara Barton: Founder of the American Red Cross (1955)
    Brown, John M.
        4194. Daniel Boone: The Opening of the Wilderness (1952)
    Brown, Slater
        4195. Ethan Allen and the Green Mountain Boys (1956)
    Bryan, Joe
        4196. The World's Greatest Showman: P. T. Barnum (1956)
    Buck, Pearl
        4197. The Man Who Changed China: Sun Yat Sen (1953)
    Buckmaster, Henrietta
        4198. Walter Raleigh: Man of Two Worlds (1964)
    Carter, Hodding
        4199. Commandoes of World War II (1966)
        4200. Marquis de Lafayette: Bright Sword for Freedom (1959)
        4201. Robert E. Lee and the Road to Honor (1955)
    Castillo, Edmund
        4202. Flat-tops: The Story of Aircraft Carriers (1969)
        4203. Midway: Battle for the Pacific (1968)
        4204. The Seabees of World War II (1963)
    Castor, Henry
        4205. America's First World War (1957)
        4206. Teddy Roosevelt and the Rough Riders (1954)
    Comay, Joan
        4207. Ben-Gurion and the Birth of Israel (1967)
    Considine, Bob
        4208. The Panama Canal (1951)
    Costain, Thomas
        4209. William the Conqueror (1963)
    Cousins, Margaret
        4210. Ben Franklin of Old Philadelphia (1952)
        4211. The Story of Thomas Alva Edison (1965)
    Crouse, Anna, and Russell Crouse
        4212. Alexander Hamilton and Aaron Burr (1958)
        4213. Peter Stuyvesant of Old New York (1954)

LANDMARK SERIES —Random House (cont'd)
Daniel, Anita
 4214. The Story of Albert Schweitzer (1957)
Daniels, Jonathan
 4215. Stonewall Jackson (1959)
Daugherty, James
 4216. Magna Charta (1956)
 4217. The Landing of the Pilgrims (1950)
 4218. Trappers and Traders of the Far West (1952)
Davenport, Marcia
 4219. Garibaldi: Father of Modern Italy (1957)
Day, A. Grove
 4220. The Story of Australia (1960)
Dobie, J. Frank
 4221. Up the Trail from Texas (1955)
Dolson, Hildegarde
 4222. Disaster at Johnstown: The Great Flood (1965)
 4223. William Penn (1961)
Douglas, William O.
 4224. Exploring the Himalaya (1958)
Fehrenback, T. R.
 4225. The United Nations in War and Peace (1968)
Fermi, Laura
 4226. The Story of Atomic Energy (1961)
Fisher, Dorothy
 4227. Our Independence and the Constitution (1956)
 4228. Paul Revere and the Minutemen (1950)
Forester, C. S.
 4229. The Barbary Pirates (1953)
Fosdick, Harry
 4230. Jesus of Nazareth (1959)
 4231. Martin Luther (1956)
 4232. The Life of Saint Paul (1962)
Gottlieb, Gerald
 4233. The Adventures of Ulysses (1959)
Gunther, John
 4234. Alexander the Great (1953)
 4235. Julius Caesar (1959)
Gurney, Gene
 4236. Americans into Orbit: Project Mercury (1962)
 4237. Flying Aces of World War I (1965)
 4238. Walk in Space: The Story of Project Gemini (1967)
Hahn, Emily
 4239. Leonardo da Vinci (1956)
 4240. Mary Queen of Scots (1953)
Hansen, Harry
 4241. Old Ironsides, the Fighting "Constitution" (1955)
Havighurst, Walter
 4242. Buffalo Bill's Great Wild West Show (1957)
Henry, Will
 4243. The Texas Rangers (1957)
Hill, Ralph
 4244. Doctors Who Conquered Yellow Fever (1957)
 4245. Robert Fulton and the Steamboat (1954)

LANDMARK SERIES —Random House (cont'd)

Hillyer, Clement
4246. The U.S. Border Patrol (1963)
Holbrook, Stewart
4247. Davy Crockett (1955)
4248. Swamp Fox of the Revolution (1959)
4249. The Golden Age of Railroads (1960)
4250. Wild Bill Hickok Tames the West (1952)
4251. Wyatt Earp: U.S. Marshall (1956)
Hornblow, Arthur, and Leonora Hornblow
4252. Cleopatra of Egypt (1961)
Hume, Ruth
4253. Florence Nightingale (1960)
4254. Great Men of Medicine (1961)
Hunt, George
4255. The Story of the U.S. Marines (1951)
Jackson, Shirley
4256. The Witchcraft of Salem Village (1956)
Janeway, Elizabeth
4257. The Early Day of Automobiles (1956)
4258. The Vikings (1951)
Jennings, John
4259. Clipper Ship Days (1952)
Johnson, William
4260. Captain Cortes Conquers Mexico (1960)
4261. Sam Houston, the Tallest Texan (1953)
Kane, Harnett
4262. Young Mark Twain and the Mississippi (1966)
Kantor, MacKinlay
4263. Gettysburg (1952)
4264. Lee and Grant at Appomattox (1950)
Kelly, Regina
4265. Lincoln and Douglas: The Years of Decision (1954)
Kielty, Bernardine
4266. Marie Antoinette (1955)
4267. The Fall of Constantinople (1957)
Kieran, John, and Margaret Kieran
4268. John James Audubon (1954)
Kjelgaard, Jim
4269. The Coming of the Mormons (1953)
4270. The Explorations of Pere Marquette (1951)
Kuhn, Ferdinand
4271. Commodore Perry and the Opening of Japan (1955)
4272. The Story of the Secret Service (1957)
Lamb, Harold
4273. Chief of the Cossacks (1959)
4274. Genghis Kahn and the Mongol Horde (1954)
Lawson, Marie
4275. Pocahontas and Captain John Smith (1950)
Lawson, Ted, and Bob Considine
4276. Thirty Seconds over Tokyo (1953)
Leckie, Robert
4277. The Battle for Iwo Jima (1967)
4278. The War in Korea (1963)

LANDMARK SERIES —Random House (cont'd)
Lewis, Oscar
    4279. Hawaii, Gem of the Pacific (1954)
Loomis, Robert
    4280. Great American Fighter Pilots of World War II (1961)
    4281. The Story of the U.S. Air Force (1959)
MacLean, Alistair
    4282. Lawrence of Arabia (1962)
McNeer, May
    4283. The Alaska Gold Rush (1960)
    4284. The California Gold Rush (1950)
    4285. War Chief of the Seminoles (1954)
Marriott, Alice
    4286. Sequoyah: Leader of the Cherokees (1956)
Mason, F. VanWyck
    4287. The Winter at Valley Forge (1953)
Mayer, Jane
    4288. Betsy Ross and the Flag (1952)
    4289. Dolly Madison (1954)
Moos, Malcolm
    4290. Dwight D. Eisenhower (1964)
Morenus, Richard
    4291. The Hudson's Bay Company (1956)
Nathan, Adele
    4292. The Building of the First Transcontinental Railroad (1950)
    4293. The First Transatlantic Cable (1959)
Nathan, Dorothy
    4294. Women of Courage (1964)
Neuburger, Richard
    4295. The Lewis and Clark Expedition (1951)
    4296. The Royal Canadian Mounted Police (1953)
Norman, Charles
    4297. The Flight and Adventures of Charles II (1958)
North, Sterling
    4298. Abe Lincoln: Log Cabin to White House (1956)
    4299. George Washington: Frontier Colonel (1957)
Owen, Russell
    4300. The Conquest of the North and South Poles (1952)
Payne, Elizabeth
    4301. The Pharoahs of Ancient Egypt (1964)
Pinkerton, Robert
    4302. The First Overland Mail (1953)
Place, Marian
    4303. Copper Kings of Montana (1961)
Pond, Seymour
    4304. Ferdinand Magellan: Master Mariner (1957)
Pratt, Fletcher
    4305. The "Monitor" and the "Merrimac" (1951)
Rachlis, Eugene
    4306. The Story of the U.S. Coast Guard (1961)
    4307. The Voyages of Henry Hudson (1962)
Reeder, Red
    4308. Medal of Honor Heroes (1965)

LANDMARK SERIES —Random House (cont'd)
    Reeder, Red, and Nardi Campion
        4309. The West Point Story (1956)
    Reynolds, Quentin
        4310. Custer's Last Stand (1951)
        4311. The Battle of Britain (1953)
        4312. The Life of Saint Patrick (1955)
        4313. The Story of the F.B.I. (1954)
        4314. The Wright Brothers (1950)
        4315. Winston Churchill (1963)
    Riesenberg, Felix
        4316. Balboa: Swordsman and Conquistador (1965)
        4317. The Story of the Naval Academy (1958)
    Robinson, Mabel
        4318. King Arthur and IIis Knights (1963)
    Ross, Nancy
        4319. Heroines of the Early West (1950)
        4320. Joan of Arc (1953)
    Scherman, Katherine
        4321. Catherine the Great (1957)
        4322. The Slave Who Freed Haiti: Toussaint Louverture (1954)
    Sheean, Vincent
        4323. Thomas Jefferson: Father of Democracy (1953)
    Shippen, Katherine
        4324. Andrew Carnegie and the Age of Steel (1958)
        4325. Mr. Bell Invents the Telephone (1952)
    Shirer, William L.
        4326. The Rise and Fall of Adolf Hitler (1961)
        4327. The Sinking of the "Bismarck" (1962)
    Smith, Bradford
        4328. Rogers's Rangers and the French and Indian War (1956)
    Sperry, Armstrong
        4329. Captain Cook Explores the South Seas (1955)
        4330. John Paul Jones: Fighting Sailor (1963)
        4331. The Voyages of Christopher Columbus (1950)
    Stewart, George
        4332. To California by Covered Wagon (1954)
    Streatfield, Noel
        4333. Queen Victoria (1958)
    Tallant, Robert
        4334. Evangeline and the Arcadians (1957)
        4335. The Louisiana Purchase (1952)
        4336. The Pirate Lafitte and the Battle of New Orleans (1951)
    Thompson, Laurence
        4337. The Story of Scotland Yard (1955)
    Tinkle, Lon
        4338. The Story of Oklahoma (1962)
    Toland, John
        4339. The Battle of the Bulge (1966)
        4340. The Flying Tigers (1963)
    Tregaskis, Richard
        4341. Guadalcanal Diary (1955)
        4342. John F. Kennedy and P.T. 109 (1962)

LANDMARK SERIES —Random House (cont'd)
    Walsh, Richard W.
        4343. The Adventures and Discoveries of Marco Polo (1953)
    Warren, Robert Penn
        4344. Remember the Alamo (1958)
    Weller, George
        4345. The Story of the Paratroops (1958)
        4346. The Story of Submarines (1962)
    West, Anthony
        4347. The Crusades (1954)
    Whipple, A. B. C.
        4348. Famous Pirates of the New World (1958)
        4349. Hero of Trafalgar: The Story of Lord Nelson (1963)
        4350. The Mysterious Voyage of Captain Kidd (1970)
    White, Anne Terry
        4351. George Washington Carver (1953)
        4352. Prehistoric America (1951)
        4353. The First Men in the World (1953)
        4354. Will Shakespeare and the Globe Theater (1955)
    Whitridge, Arnold
        4355. Simon Bolivar: The Great Liberator (1954)
    Williams, Jay
        4356. The Battle for the Atlantic (1959)
    Winwar, Frances
        4357. Napoleon and the Battle of Waterloo (1953)
        4358. Queen Elizabeth and the Spanish Armada (1954)
    Young, Stanley
        4359. Tippecanoe and Tyler Too (1957)
This huge series presents various outstanding people and events in both world and
American history. The authors write with flair and present these incidents in a somewhat novelistic style to entertain as well as to teach. Unfortunately, the binding is
not the sturdiest, nor the paper the best. Still, these are generally good additions to
any collection.

LANDMARK GIANTS SERIES —Random House
    Bliven, Bruce, and Naomi Bliven
        4360. New York: The Story of the World's Most Exciting City (1969)
    Boorstin, Daniel
        4361. The Landmark History of the American People from Appomattox
            to the Moon (1970)
        4362. The Landmark History of the American People from Plymouth
            to Appomattox (1968)
    Brandon, William, and Anne Terry White
        4363. The American Indian (1963)
    Cross, Helen
        4364. Life in Lincoln's America (1964)
    Faber, Harold, and Doris Faber
        4365. American Heroes of the Twentieth Century (1967)
    Gail, Marzieh
        4366. Life in the Renaissance (1968)
    Gurney, Gene
        4367. Americans to the Moon, the Story of Project Apollo (1970)
    Hollander, Zander
        4368. Great American Athletes of the Twentieth Century (1966)

LANDMARK GIANTS SERIES —Random House (cont'd)
>   Katz, Fred
>   4369. Great American Athletes of the Sixties (1970)
>   Leckie, Robert
>   4370. Great American Battles (1968)
>   4371. The Story of Football (1965)
>   4372. The Story of World War I (1965)
>   4373. The Story of World War II (1964)
>   Rosenburg, John
>   4374. The Story of Baseball (1964)
>   Smith, Howard K.
>   4375. Washington, D.C. (1967)
>   Speare, Elizabeth George
>   4376. Life in Colonial America (1963)
>   Stearns, Monroe
>   4377. The Story of New England (1967)
>   Whitehead, Don
>   4378. The F.B.I. Story (1963)
>   Williams, Jay
>   4379. Life in the Middle Ages (1966)

While this series bears the same title as Landmark Books, the quality of binding and paper is far better here. The large print and plentiful use of photos make this series more attractive as well as more durable.

LANDS AND PEOPLES SERIES —Macmillan
>   Bryan, D.
>   4380. The Land and People of China (1965)
>   Cairns, G. O.
>   4381. The Land and People of Australia (1954)
>   Charnock, Joan
>   4382. The Land and People of Poland (1968)
>   Colvin, Gerard
>   4383. The Land and People of Central America (1962)
>   Evans, M. Filmer
>   4384. The Land and People of Korea (1963)
>   Exell, F. K.
>   4385. The Land and People of Thailand (1961)
>   Feldman, Hubert
>   4386. The Land and People of Pakistan (1958)
>   Gordon, R. L.
>   4387. The Land and People of Canada (1954)
>   Grundy, Kenneth
>   4388. The Land and People of Kenya, Tanzania, and Uganda (1968)
>   MacDonald, Norman
>   4389. The Land and People of Brazil (1959)
>   Martin, Rupert
>   4390. The Land and People of Morocco (1968)
>   Maxwell-Lefroy, C.
>   4391. The Land and People of Burma (1965)
>   4392. The Land and People of Ceylon (1966)
>   Pendle, George
>   4393. The Land and People of Argentina (1957)
>   4394. The Land and People of Chile (1960)
>   4395. The Land and People of Paraguay and Uruguay (1958)

LANDS AND PEOPLES SERIES —Macmillan (cont'd)
>4396. The Land and People of Peru (1968)
Shearman, John
>4397. The Land and People of Iran (1963)
Tillyard, Angela
>4398. The Land and People of Yugoslavia (1963)

Much like the Portraits of the Nations Series, this one devotes more space to the
geographical sections of each country, and not as much to such aspects as industry
and education. Unfortunately, there are not many photographs, and too many
books of the series still in print contain information that was long ago outdated.

LEEMING, JOSEPH —Lippincott
>4399. Fun for Young Collectors (1953)
>4400. Fun with Artificial Flowers (1959)
>4401. Fun with Boxes (1937)
>4402. Fun with Clay (1944)
>4403. Fun with Fabrics (1950)
>4404. Fun with Greeting Cards (1960)
>4405. Fun with Leather (1941)
>4406. Fun with Magic (1943)
>4407. Fun with Paper (1939)
>4408. Fun with Pencil and Paper (1955)
>4409. Fun with Puzzles (1946)
>4410. Fun with Shells (1958)
>4411. Fun with Wire (1956)
>4412. Fun with Wood (1942)

Each book describes the equipment necessary to make gifts from the medium
under consideration. Suggestions range from novelties to gifts and jewelry. Where
applicable, Mr. Leeming indicates how to identify various types of clay, fabric, shells,
or wood. He also lists places where readers can buy materials, but most of these lists
are now out of date.

LEGACY BOOKS SERIES —Random House
Barker, Shirley
>4413. The Trojan Horse (1959)
Benchley, Nathaniel
>4414. Sinbad the Sailor (1960)
Clark, Eleanor
>4415. The Song of Roland (1960)
Dolbier, Maurice
>4416. Paul Bunyan (1959)
Fadiman, Clifton
>4417. The Adventures of Hercules (1960)
>4418. The Story of Young King Arthur (1961)
>4419. The Voyages of Ulysses (1959)
Scherman, Katherine
>4420. William Tell (1960)
Schmitt, Gladys
>4421. The Heroic Deeds of Beowulf (1962)
Warren, Robert Penn
>4422. The Gods of Mount Olympus (1959)
Williams, Jay
>4423. Medusa's Head (1960)

LEGACY BOOKS SERIES —Random House (cont'd)
This series consists of myths, legends, and tall tales retold by well-known authors.
The illustrations are not extraordinary, but exciting versions of these adventures are
a welcome addition to any collection.

LENSKI, LOIS —Lippincott
    Regional Stories
        4424. Bayou Suzette (1943)
        4425. Blue Ridge Billy (1946)
        4426. Boom Town Boy (1948)
        4427. Coal Camp Girl (1959)
        4428. Corn-Farm Boy (1954)
        4429. Cotton in My Sack (1949)
        4430. Deer Valley Girl (1968)
        4431. Flood Friday (1956)
        4432. Houseboat Girl (1957)
        4433. Judy's Journey (1947)
        4444. Mama Hattie's Girl (1953)
        4445. Prairie School (1951)
        4446. San Francisco Boy (1955)
        4447. Shoo-Fly Girl (1963)
        4448. Strawberry Girl (1945)
        4449. Texas Tomboy (1950)
        4450. To Be a Logger (1967)
    Roundabout America Stories
        4451. Berries in the Scoop (1956)
        4452. High-Rise Secret (1966)
        4453. Little Sioux Girl (1958)
        4454. Peanuts for Billy Ben (1952)
        4455. Project Boy (1959)
        4456. We Live by the River (1956)
        4457. We Live in the City (1954)
        4458. We Live in the Country (1963)
        4459. We Live in the North (1965)
        4460. We Live in the South (1952)
Ms. Lenski is an outstanding author who wrote about children from various under-
privileged areas and walks of life long before anyone else thought about it. These
books explore the ways of life in various areas of our country, and much of what
she has to say still applies today. *Strawberry Girl* won the Newbery Award.

LET'S GO SERIES —Putnam
    Borreson, Mary Jo
        4461. Let's Go to Colonial Williamsburg (1961)
        4462. Let's Go to Mount Vernon (1962)
        4463. Let's Go to Plymouth with the Pilgrims (1963)
        4464. Let's Go to South America (1969)
    Buchheimer, Naomi
        4465. Let's Go to a Dentist (1959)
        4466. Let's Go to a Firehouse (1956)
        4467. Let's Go to a Television Station (1958)
        4468. Let's Go to School (1958)
        4469. Let's Go to the Library (1957)
        4470. Let's Go to the Post Office (1964)
        4471. Let's Take a Trip to the Post Office (1964)

4472. Let's Take a Trip to the Telephone Company (1958)

Butler, Roger

4473. Let's Go to an Automobile Factory (1961)

4474. Let's Go to the U.S. Coast Guard Academy (1964)

Chester, Michael

4475. Let's Go on a Space Trip (1963)

4476. Let's Go to Stop Air Pollution (1968)

4477. Let's Go to Stop Water Pollution (1969)

4478. Let's Go to the Moon (1965)

Chester, Michael, and William Nephew

4479. Let's Go to a Rocket Base (1961)

Cochrane, Joanna

4480. Let's Go to the United Nations Headquarters (1958)

Cooke, David C.

4481. Let's Go to India (1969)

Goodspeed, J. M.

4482. Let's Go to a Dairy (1956)

4483. Let's Go to a Garage (1957)

4484. Let's Go to a Supermarket (1958)

4485. Let's Go to Watch a Building Go Up (1957)

Green, Erma

4486. Let's Go to a Steel Mill (1957)

Hamill, Lloyd, and Rose Hamill

4487. Let's Go to a National Park (1962)

Hamilton, Lee

4488. Let's Go Aboard an Atomic Submarine (1965)

4489. Let's Go to a Dam (1963)

4490. Let's Go to West Point (1962)

Hammond, Diana

4491. Let's Go to a Harbor (1959)

Harris, Joanna

4492. Let's Go to a Sanitation Department (1972)

Lazarus, Henry

4493. Let's Go to a Clothing Factory (1961)

McCarthy, Agnes

4494. Let's Go to Court (1961)

4495. Let's Go to Vote (1962)

Mercer, Charles

4496. Let's Go to Africa (1968)

4497. Let's Go to Europe (1968)

Mitchell, Barbara

4498. Let's Go to the Peace Corps (1968)

Perkins, Lynn

4499. Let's Go to a Paper Mill (1969)

Place, Marian

4500. Let's Go to a Fish Hatchery (1966)

Polking, Kirk

4501. Let's Go to an Atomic Energy Town (1968)

4502. Let's Go to See Congress at Work (1966)

4503. Let's Go with Lewis and Clark (1963)

Reisdorf, Patricia, and Margo McWilliams

4504. Let's Go to Build a Highway (1971)

LET'S GO SERIES —Putnam (cont'd)
    Rosenfield, Bernard
        4505. Let's Go to the Capitol (1959)
        4506. Let's Go to the F.B.I. (1960)
        4507. Let's Go to the Supreme Court (1960)
        4508. Let's Go to the U.S. Mint (1960)
        4509. Let's Go to the White House (1959)
    Rowland, Florence
        4510. Let's Go to a Hospital (1958)
    Sootin, Laura
        4511. Let's Go to a Bank (1957)
        4512. Let's Go to a Circus (1960)
        4513. Let's Go to a Farm (1958)
        4514. Let's Go to a Newspaper (1956)
        4515. Let's Go to a Police Station (1957)
        4516. Let's Go to an Airport (1957)
        4517. Let's Go to the Zoo (1959)
    Spiegelman, Judith
        4518. Let's Go to the Battle of Gettysburg (1965)
    Talmadge, Marion, and Iris Gilmore
        4519. Let's Go to a Truck Terminal (1964)
    Williams, Barbara
        4520. Let's Go to an Indian Cliff Dwelling (1965)
    Wolfe, Louis
        4521. Let's Go to a Planetarium (1958)
        4522. Let's Go to a Weather Station (1959)
        4523. Let's Go to City Hall (1959)
        4524. Let's Go to the Louisiana Purchase (1963)
The simple text of these books is designed to introduce youngsters to various
experiences. Each book is written as though the reader himself is participating in
the event. For this reason, the authors discuss not only what a visitor would find
at each place, but also the correct behavior and things to look for. For grades 3 to 5.

LET'S LOOK SERIES —Whitman
    Bowman, Gerald
        4525. Let's Look at Ships (1965)
    Carter, Ernest
        4526. Let's Look at Trains (1964)
    Cooper, Edmund
        4527. Let's Look at Costumes (1965)
    Morey, Joan
        4528. Let's Look at Houses and Homes (1969)
    Philpott, A. R.
        4529. Let's Look at Puppets (1966)
    Rhodes, C. O.
        4530. Let's Look at Musical Instruments and the Orchestra (1969)
    Warwick, Alan
        4531. Let's Look at Castles (1965)
        4532. Let's Look at Prehistoric Animals (1966)
Concise and well written, these books are non-academic examinations of the
various subjects. Illustrations are clear, and each book has an index. For grades 4 to 8.

LET'S TRAVEL IN ... SERIES —Childrens Press
    Currie, Gordon
        4533. Let's Travel in Australia (1968)
    Downing, Joan
        4534. Let's Travel in Canada (1968)
    Dyra, Frances
        4535. Let's Travel in West Germany (1968)
    Geis, Darlene
        4536. Let's Travel in China (1962)
        4537. Let's Travel in England (1961)
        4538. Let's Travel in France (1960)
        4539. Let's Travel in Greece (1964)
        4540. Let's Travel in Hawaii (1960)
        4541. Let's Travel in Hong Kong (1965)
        4542. Let's Travel in India (1960)
        4543. Let's Travel in Italy (1964)
        4544. Let's Travel in Japan (1960)
        4545. Let's Travel in Mexico (1961)
        4546. Let's Travel in Spain (1964)
        4547. Let's Travel in Switzerland (1964)
        4548. Let's Travel in Thailand (1965)
        4549. Let's Travel in the Holy Land (1961)
        4550. Let's Travel in the Philippines (1965)
        4551. Let's Travel in the South Seas (1961)
        4552. Let's Travel in the Soviet Union (1964)
    Irwin, Theodore
        4553. Let's Travel in Holland (1964)
    Kittler, Glenn
        4554. Let's Travel in Nigeria and Ghana (1962)
        4555. Let's Travel in the Congo (1961)
The format of this series consists of a full-page color photo alternating with one page
of information on a specific place within each country or an occurrence, such as a
festival or bull fight, representative of the country. Because of this format, the
treatment of individual areas of information is sparse. There are better series available to supplement geography and social studies courses.

LET'S VISIT SERIES —John Day
    Caldwell, John
        4556. Let's Visit Argentina (1961)
        4557. Let's Visit Australia (1963)
        4558. Let's Visit Brazil (1961)
        4559. Let's Visit Canada (1964)
        4560. Let's Visit Central America (1964)
        4561. Let's Visit Chile (1963)
        4562. Let's Visit China (1972)
        4563. Let's Visit Formosa (1965)
        4564. Let's Visit India (1960)
        4565. Let's Visit Ireland (1969)
        4566. Let's Visit Japan (1959)
        4567. Let's Visit Korea (1959)
        4568. Let's Visit Malaysia (1968)
        4569. Let's Visit Mexico (1965)
        4570. Let's Visit Micronesia, Guam (1969)
        4571. Let's Visit Middle Africa (1963)

LET'S VISIT SERIES —John Day (cont'd)
    4572. Let's Visit New Zealand (1963)
    4573. Let's Visit Pakistan (1960)
    4574. Let's Visit Peru (1962)
    4575. Let's Visit Russia (1968)
    4576. Let's Visit Scotland (1967)
    4577. Let's Visit Southeast Asia (1967)
    4578. Let's Visit Thailand (1967)
    4579. Let's Visit the Middle East (1972)
    4580. Let's Visit the Philippines (1961)
    4581. Let's Visit the South Pacific (1969)
    4582. Let's Visit the West Indies (1963)
    4583. Let's Visit Turkey (1969)
    4584. Let's Visit Venezuela (1962)
    4585. Let's Visit Vietnam (1966)
    4586. Let's Visit West Africa (1969)
Caldwell, John, and Noel Barber
    4587. Let's Visit the U.S.A. (1968)
Caldwell, John, and Vernon Bartlett
    4588. Let's Visit Italy (1968)
Caldwell, John, and Nicholas Freville
    4589. Let's Visit Nigeria (1970)
Caldwell, John, and Garry Lyle
    4590. Let's Visit Greece (1971)
Moore, James
    4591. Let's Visit Germany (1970)
Newman, Bernard
    4592. Let's Visit France (1967)
    4593. Let's Visit South Africa (1968)
Popescu, Julian
    4594. Let's Visit Yugoslavia (1969)
Like most series on foreign countries, this one provides information on industry,
education, geography, and history. The authors also attempt to type the people
in various countries, which seems a somewhat questionable approach. Pronunciation
guides are furnished.

LIBRARY OF AMERICAN HEROES SERIES —Follett
    Brett, Grace
        4595. Tom Paine (1965)
    Garst, Shannon
        4596. Red Cloud (1965)
    Herschler, Mildred
        4597. Frederick Douglass (1968)
    Howard, Robert
        4598. Eli Whitney (1966)
    Judson, Clara
        4599. Admiral Christopher Columbus (1965)
    Kelly, Regina
        4600. John Adams (1965)
        4601. John F. Kennedy (1968)
        4602. Marquette and Joliet (1965)
    Milgrim, Shirley
        4603. Haym Solomon (1966)

LIBRARY OF AMERICAN HEROES SERIES —Follett (cont'd)
    Mooney, Booth
        4604. General Billy Mitchell (1968)
        4605. Henry Clay (1966)
        4606. Jane Addams (1968)
        4607. Sam Houston (1966)
        4608. Woodrow Wilson (1968)
    Seymour, Alta
        4609. Charles Steinmetz (1965)
    Wallower, Lucille
        4610. William Penn (1968)
In this good series of biographies of various outstanding Americans, the authors
generally avoid fictionalizing the lives of the individuals. Photographs are only
in the front of the books, instead of being distributed throughout, and unfortunately
there are not always indices or bibliographies.

LIFE CYCLE LIBRARY SERIES —Holiday
    Adrian, Mary
        4611. Fiddler Crab (1953)
        4612. Garden Spider (1951)
        4613. Gray Squirrel (1955)
        4614. Honeybee (1952)
    Conklin, Gladys
        4615. Chimpanzee (1970)
        4616. Giraffe (1971)
    DeSeyn, Donna
        4617. Termite (1967)
    Jenkins, Marie
        4618. Moon Jelly (1969)
    Marcher, Marion
        4619. Monarch Butterfly (1954)
    Peterson, Barbara, and Russell Peterson
        4620. Whitefoot Mouse (1959)
    Schwartz, Elizabeth, and Charles Schwartz
        4621. Cottontail Rabbit (1957)
    Sears, Paul
        4622. Barn Swallow (1955)
        4623. Downy Woodpecker (1953)
        4624. Firefly (1956)
    Stephens, William, and Peggy Stephens
        4625. Hermit Crab (1969)
        4626. Octopus (1968)
        4627. Sea Horse (1969)
        4628. Sea Turtle (1971)
This series tells of the life of an individual animal in biographical form. There are no
photos, but the color illustrations are quite good. Because of its fictionalized format,
however, the series will be of only marginal use.

LIFE IN ANCIENT LANDS SERIES —Putnam
    Burland, C. A.
        4629. Life in Peru under the Incas (1968)
    Mellersh, H. E. L.
        4630. Life in Minoan Crete (1968)

LIFE IN ANCIENT LANDS SERIES —Putnam (cont'd)
      Sewell, Barbara
          4631. Egypt under the Pharoahs (1968)
      Strong, Donald
          4632. The Early Etruscans (1968)
An outstanding series on ancient civilizations. In an interesting fashion the authors present the geography, the origins, customs, and history of these cultures. There are lavish color illustrations as well as maps, glossaries, bibliographies, and indices. Each author is extremely well qualified to write on his particular subject. For grades 7 to 12.

LIFE LONG AGO SERIES —Coward
      Miller, Shane
          4633. The Romans: In the Days of the Empire (1963)
      Ochsenschlager, E., and Shane Miller
          4634. The Egyptians: In the Middle Kingdom (1963)
      Powers, Richard
          4635. The Cave Dwellers: In the Old Stone Age (1963)
      Weisgard, Leonard
          4636. The Athenians: In the Classical Period (1963)
          4637. The Beginning of Cities: In Mesopotamia (1968)
          4638. The First Farmers: In the New Stone Age (1966)
These oversized books present huge, colorful illustrations, as well as information on various archaeologists and their findings. There are also glossaries, indices, and bibliographies. The illustrations, however, completely overshadow the text and are the strong point of the series.

LIFE NATURE LIBRARY —Time-Life
      Beiser, Arthur
          4639. The Earth (1968)
      Bergamini, David
          4640. The Universe (1968)
      Carr, Archie
          4641. The Reptiles (1968)
      Carrington, Richard
          4642. The Mammals (1967)
      Eimerl, Saul, and Irven DeVore
          4643. The Primates (1968)
      Engel, Leonard
          4644. The Sea (1967)
      Howell, F. Clark
          4645. Early Man (1968)
      Leopold, A. Starker
          4646. The Desert (1967)
      Moore, Ruth
          4647. Evolution (1968)
      Ommanney, F. D.
          4648. The Fishes (1968)
      Peterson, Roger
          4649. The Birds (1967)
      Tinbergen, Niko
          4650. Animal Behavior (1968)
Adapted from the Time-Life series for adults. The illustrations are excellent, and the text is both detailed and fascinating. A must for all libraries.

THE LIFE OF ANIMALS SERIES   —World
    Smith, Bradley
        4651. The Life of the Elephant (1972)
        4652. The Life of the Giraffe (1972)
        4653. The Life of the Hippopotamus (1972)
This series studies the animals involved in their own surroundings: how they live and eat, how they raise their young, how they react to danger. Color photographs illuminate the text. For grades 3 to 6.

LITTLE CRAFT BOOKS SERIES   —Sterling
    Alkema, Chester
        4654. Masks (1971)
        4655. Puppet Making (1969)
        4656. Crafting with Nature's Materials (1972)
    Banister, Manly
        4657. Lithographic Prints from Stone and Plate (1972)
    Bauzen, Peter, and Susanne Bauzen
        4658. Flower Pressing (1970)
    Bernstein, Marion
        4659. Off-Loom Weaving (1971)
    Boulay, R.
        4660. Make Your Own Elegant Jewelry (1972)
    Christensen, Jo
        4661. Trapunto: Decorative Quilting (1972)
    Christensen, Jo, and Soni Ashner
        4662. Needlepoint Simplified (1972)
        4663. Bargello Stitchery (1972)
        4664. Tole Painting (1972)
    Conroy, Norma
        4665. Making Shell Flowers (1971)
    DeBrouwer, Ab
        4666. Creating with Flexible Foam (1971)
    Eppens-VanVeen, J. H.
        4667. Colorful Glasscrafting (1972)
    Ficarotta, Phyllis
        4668. Sewing without a Pattern (1970)
    Fish, Harriet
        4669. Creative Lace-Making with Thread and Yarn (1972)
    Fressard, M. J.
        4670. Creating with Burlap (1970)
    Groe, Lini
        4671. Scissorscraft (1970)
    Gruber, Elmar
        4672. Metal and Wire Sculpture (1969)
        4673. Nail Sculpture (1969)
    Hoppe, H.
        4674. Whittling and Wood Carving (1971)
    Janvier, Jacqueline
        4675. Felt Crafting (1970)
    Kelly, Sandra
        4676. How to Add Designer Touches to Your Wardrobe (1972)
    Konijnenberg-DeGroot, Jo
        4677. Cellophane Creations (1972)

LITTLE CRAFT BOOKS SERIES —Sterling (cont'd)
    LaCroix, Grethe
        4678. Beads Plus Macrame (1971)
        4679. Creating with Beads (1969)
    Lozier, Herb
        4680. Model Boat Building (1970)
    Meriel-Bussy, Yves
        4681. Repoussage (1970)
    Nussbaumer, Hanny
        4682. Lacquer and Crackle (1969)
    Pesch, Imelda
        4683. Macrame (1970)
    Priolo, Joan
        4684. Ideas for Collage (1972)
    Ritchie, Carson
        4685. Scrimshaw (1972)
    Schilt, Stephen, and Donna Weir
        4686. Enamel without Heat (1970)
    Seitz, Marianne
        4687. Creating Silver Jewelry with Beads (1972)
    Strom, Nils, and Anders Enestrom
        4688. Big Knot Macrame (1972)
    Strose, Susanne
        4689. Candle-Making (1968)
        4690. Coloring Papers (1968)
        4691. Making Paper Flowers (1969)
        4692. Potato Printing (1968)
    Van Voorst, Dick
        4693. Corrugated Carton Crafting (1969)
    Von Bornstedt, Marianne, and Ulla Prytz
        4694. Folding Table Napkins (1972)
The books in this unusual craft series show how to make various types of gifts and personal objects in the very latest crafts. Each book covers the basics, the materials used, and the projects. These books could be used either with adults or with juveniles from grade 5 on up.

LITTLE LEAGUE LIBRARY SERIES —Random House
    Bisher, Furman
        4695. Strange But True Baseball Stories (1966)
    Brosnan, Jim
        4696. Great Baseball Pitchers (1965)
        4697. Great Rookies of the Major Leagues (1966)
        4698. Little League to Big League (1968)
    Graham, Frank
        4699. Great No-Hit Games of the Major Leagues (1968)
        4700. Great Pennant Races of the Major Leagues (1967)
        4701. Great Pitchers of the Major Leagues (1969)
    Peters, Alexander
        4702. Heroes of the Major Leagues (1967)
    Robinson, Ray
        4703. Greatest World Series Thrillers (1965)
    Smith, Robert
        4704. Secrets of Big League Play (1965)

LITTLE LEAGUE LIBRARY SERIES —Random House (cont'd)
    Vecsey, George
        4705. Baseball's Most Valuable Players (1966)
    Wolf, Dave
        4706. Amazing Baseball Teams (1970)
    Zanger, Jack
        4707. Great Catchers of the Major Leagues (1970)
This is a run-of-the-mill sports series which features collected biographies of various important sports figures and incidents. Plenty of photos and attractive format may entice the reluctant reader as well as the fan.

LIVES-TO-REMEMBER SERIES —Putnam
    Alter, Robert
        4708. Henry M. Stanley (1967)
    Becker, Beril
        4709. Jules Verne (1966)
    Beckhard, Arthur
        4710. Albert Einstein (1959)
    Bobbe, Dorothie
        4711. Abigail Adams (1966)
        4712. DeWitt Clinton (1968)
        4713. John Quincy Adams (1971)
    Cetin, Frank
        4714. Nobody Stops Cushing: Civil War Hero William Baker Cushing
            (1966)
    David, Heather
        4715. Admiral Rickover and the Nuclear Navy (1970)
        4716. Wernher von Braun (1967)
    Davis, Burke
        4717. Amelia Earhart (1972)
    Faber, Doris
        4718. John Jay (1966)
    Keating, Vern
        4719. Chaka: King of the Zulus (1968)
        4720. Zebulon Pike: Young America's Frontier Scout (1965)
    Lipman, David
        4721. Mr. Baseball: The Story of Branch Rickey (1966)
    McKee, James
        4722. Martin Luther King (1969)
    McKown, Robin
        4723. Benjamin Franklin (1963)
    Marble, Harriet
        4724. James Monroe (1970)
    Mellor, William
        4725. General Patton: The Last Cavalier (1971)
    Moore, Patrick
        4726. Isaac Newton (1958)
    Noel-Baker, Francis
        4727. Fridtjof Nansen: Arctic Explorer (1958)
    Orrmont, Arthur
        4728. Chinese Gordon: Hero of Khartoum (1966)
    Pallenberg, Corrado
        4729. Pope Paul VI (1968)

LIVES-TO-REMEMBER SERIES   —Putnam (cont'd)
    Russell, Jack
        4730. Clive of India (1965)
    Silverberg, Robert
        4731. John Muir: Prophet among the Glaciers (1972)
        4732. Socrates (1965)
    Sims, Lydel
        4733. Thaddeus Lowe: Uncle Sam's First Airman (1964)
    Steinberg, Alfred
        4734. Daniel Webster (1959)
        4735. Douglas MacArthur (1961)
        4736. Dwight David Eisenhower (1967)
        4737. Harry S. Truman (1963)
        4738. Herbert Hoover (1967)
        4739. James Madison (1965)
        4740. John Adams (1969)
        4741. John Marshall (1968)
        4742. The Kennedy Brothers (1969)
        4743. Woodrow Wilson (1961)
    Sutton, Felix
        4744. Master of Ballyhoo: The Story of P. T. Barnum (1968)
    Tate, Allen
        4745. Jefferson Davis (1969)
    Thomas, Henry
        4746. Franklin Delano Roosevelt (1961)
    Thompson, John
        4747. Nelson: Hero of Trafalgar (1969)
    Tibble, S. W., and Anne Tibble
        4748. Helen Keller (1958)
    Wells, Bob
        4749. Mad Anthony Wayne (1970)
    Whipple, Chandler
        4750. William F. Halsey: Fighting Admiral (1968)
    Whitehouse, Arch
        4751. John J. Pershing (1964)
    Wise, Winifred
        4752. Aaron Burr (1968)
        4753. Alexander Hamilton (1963)
        4754. Fanny Kemble: Actress, Author, Abolitionist (1966)
        4755. Harriet Beecher Stowe: Woman with a Cause (1965)
The texts of these biographies are usually interesting, and the authors provide
bibliographies and indices. It is generally a good series, including among its
biographees some unusual people (General Gordon, Clive, and William Cushing,
to name a few). For grades 6 through 9.

LIVING CITIES AROUND THE WORLD SERIES   —Nelson
    Boardman, Gwenn
        4756. Living in Singapore (1971)
        4757. Living in Tokyo (1970)
    Perl, Lila
        4758. Living in Lisbon (1971)
        4759. Living in Naples (1970)
The main values of these books are their currency and the fact that they cover

LIVING CITIES AROUND THE WORLD SERIES —Nelson (cont'd)
cities omitted from other foreign cities series. The material presented in each
book deals with culture, social customs, education, industry, and religion—all
applicable to the country in general, so that these books would be good for
use in conjunction with social studies courses.

LIVING IN TODAY'S WORLD SERIES —Garrard
    Grant, Clara, and Jane Watson
        4760. Mexico: Land of the Plumed Serpent (1968)
    Paloheimo, Leonora, and Jane Watson
        4761. Finland: Champion of Independence (1969)
    Watson, Jane
        4762. Canada: Giant Nation of the North (1968)
        4763. Egypt: Child of the Nile (1967)
        4764. Ethiopia: Mountain Kingdom (1966)
        4765. Greece: Land of Golden Light (1967)
        4766. India: Old Land, New Nation (1966)
        4767. Iran: Crossroads of Caravans (1966)
        4768. Japan: Islands of the Rising Sun (1968)
        4769. Nigeria: Republic of a Hundred Kings (1967)
        4770. Peru: Land Astride the Andes (1967)
        4771. Thailand: Rice Bowl of Asia (1966)
A unique feature of this series is that the authors present not only facts about
the geography, history, and social life of the various countries, but also stories,
tales, and legends associated with the countries. Illustrations include art by
native artists as well as color photographs.

LIVING THINGS OF THE WORLD SERIES —Doubleday
    Baker, Jeffrey
        4772. The Vital Process: Photosynthesis (1969)
    Bowman, John
        4773. On Guard (1969)
    DeWaard, E. John
        4774. Plants and Animals in the Air (1969)
        4775. The Color of Life (1971)
        4776. The Shape of Living Things (1969)
    Klein, Stanley
        4777. A World of Difference (1971)
These books discuss in detail various scientific discoveries like photosynthesis,
recounting step-by-step the experiments leading up to these discoveries, with a
discussion of what these discoveries mean to life today.

LIVING WORLD SERIES —Lippincott
    Austing, G. Ronald
        4778. The World of the Red-Tailed Hawk (1964)
        4779. The World of the White-Tailed Deer (1962)
    Austing, G. Ronald, and John Holt
        4780. The World of the Great Horned Owl (1965)
    Caldwell, David, and Melba Caldwell
        4781. The World of the Bottlenosed Dolphin (1971)
    Costello, David
        4782. The World of the Ant (1968)
        4783. The World of the Gull (1971)
        4784. The World of the Porcupine (1966)

LIVING WORLD SERIES —Lippincott (cont'd)
    4785. The World of the Prairie Dog (1970)
Harrison, Hal
    4786. The World of the Snake (1971)
Keefe, James
    4787. The World of the Opossum (1967)
Park, Ed
    4788. The World of the Bison (1969)
    4789. The World of the Otter (1971)
Porter, George
    4790. The World of the Frog and the Toad (1967)
Rue, Leonard
    4791. The World of the Beaver (1964)
    4792. The World of the Raccoon (1964)
    4793. The World of the Red Fox (1969)
Rutter, Russell, and Douglas Pimlott
    4794. The World of the Wolf (1967)
Schoonmaker, W. J.
    4795. The World of the Grizzly Bear (1968)
    4796. The World of the Woodchuck (1966)
VanWormer, Jo
    4797. The World of the American Elk (1969)
    4798. The World of the Black Bear (1966)
    4799. The World of the Bobcat (1964)
    4800. The World of the Canada Goose (1968)
    4801. The World of the Coyote (1964)
    4802. The World of the Pronghorn (1969)
Individual animals are treated in great detail in this excellent series. In spite of the
extensive use of photographs, the series is better suited to the older reader (grades
6 through 12). Full of information interestingly presented, these books will make
a fine addition to any library's collection.

LOOK! READ! LEARN! SERIES —Melmont
    Clark, Ann Nolan
        4803. Little Indian Basket Maker (1957)
        4804. Little Indian Pottery Maker (1955)
    Dobrin, Norma
        4805. The Delawares (1963)
    Estep, Irene
        4806. The Iroquois (1961)
        4807. The Seminoles (1963)
    Falk, Elsa
        4808. Tohi, a Chumash Boy (1959)
    Harvey, Lois
        4809. Toyanuki's Rabbit (1964)
    Hood, Flora
        4810. Something for the Medicine Man (1962)
    Israel, Marion
        4811. The Apaches (1959)
        4812. The Cherokees (1961)
        4813. The Dakotas (1959)
        4814. The Ojibway (1962)
    James, Harry
        4815. A Day in Oraibi (1959)

LOOK! READ! LEARN! SERIES —Melmont (cont'd)
>   4816. A Day with Honau (1957)
>   Leavitt, J.
>   4817. America and Its Indians (1963)
>   Morris, Loverne
>   4818. The American Indian as a Farmer (1963)
>   Russell, Solveig
>   4819. Navaho Land (1961)
>   Shannon, Terry
>   4820. A Dog Team for Ongluk (1962)
>   4821. A Playmate for Puna (1963)
>   Worthylake, Mary
>   4822. Children of the Seed Gatherers (1964)
>   4823. Nika Illahee (My Homeland) (1962)

An easy-to-read series about various Indian tribes and their ways of life. Although the informational content is not high, the books will nevertheless serve as early introductions to the American Indian. For grades 2 to 4.

LOOK-IT-UP-BOOKS SERIES —Random House
>   Blassingame, Wyatt
>   4824. The Look-It-Up Book of Presidents (1968)
>   Freeman, Ira
>   4825. The Look-It-Up Book of Space (1969)
>   Kohn, Bernice
>   4826. The Look-It-Up Book of Transportation (1968)
>   Lauber, Patricia
>   4827. The Look-It-Up Book of Mammals (1967)
>   4828. The Look-It-Up Book of Stars and Planets (1967)
>   4829. The Look-It-Up Book of the Fifty States (1967)
>   Simon, Seymour
>   4830. The Look-It-Up Book of the Earth (1968)

Arrangement is alphabetical by subject, and at the end of each article is a "see also" reference to related subjects. The photos and illustrations are excellent, and the books are indexed. While the treatment is not in detail, these books are still a good source of supplementary material.

LOOKING AT OUR COUNTRIES SERIES —Lippincott
>   Arbman, Maj
>   4831. Looking at Sweden (1971)
>   Ashby, Gwynneth
>   4832. Looking at Japan (1969)
>   4833. Looking at Norway (1967)
>   Church, Harrison
>   4834. Looking at France (1970)
>   Kirby, George
>   4835. Looking at Germany (1972)
>   Loman, Anna
>   4836. Looking at Holland (1966)
>   Martin, Rupert
>   4837. Looking at Italy (1967)
>   4838. Looking at Spain (1969)
>   Noel-Baker, Francis
>   4839. Looking at Greece (1968)

LOOKING AT OUR COUNTRIES SERIES   —Lippincott   (cont'd)
    Rutland, Jonathan
        4840. Looking at Denmark (1968)
        4841. Looking at Israel (1970)
This geographic series provides much information on cities and provinces in each
country. Subjects like schools and sports are covered only briefly, and some topics,
such as religion, are not touched on at all. The format is attractive, but this series
must be considered marginal for the basic collection.

LOOKING GLASS LIBRARY SERIES   —Random House
    Baum, L. Frank
        4842. The Wizard of Oz and the Land of Oz (1960)
    Doyle, Arthur Conan
        4843. The Hound of the Baskervilles (1961)
        4844. The Lost World (1959)
    Gorey, Edward
        4845. The Haunted Looking Glass (1959)
    Hale, Lucretia
        4846. The Peterkin Papers (1959)
    Hope, Anthony
        4847. The Prisoner of Zenda (1961)
    Hughes, Richard
        4848. The Spider's Palace (1960)
    Lang, Andrew
        4849. The Blue Fairy Book (1959)
        4850. The Green Fairy Book (1960)
        4851. The Red Fairy Book (1960)
    Lear, Edward
        4852. The Book of Nonsense (1959)
    Leavitt, Holt
        4853. The Comic Looking Glass (1961)
        4854. The Looking Glass Book of Stories (1960)
    MacDonald, George
        4855. The Princess and the Curdie (1960)
        4856. The Princess and the Goblin (1959)
    Molesworth, Mrs.
        4857. The Tapestry Room (1961)
    Nesbit, Mrs.
        4858. Five Children and It (1959)
        4859. The Book of Dragons (1961)
        4860. The Phoenix and the Carpet (1960)
        4861. The Story of the Amulet (1960)
    Pyle, Howard
        4862. Otto of the Silver Hand (1960)
    Seton, Ernest
        4863. Wild Animals I Have Known (1959)
    Smith, Janet
        4864. The Looking Glass Book of Verse (1959)
    Stockton, Frank
        4865. Buccaneers and Pirates of Our Coasts (1960)
    Wells, H. G.
        4866. The War of the Worlds (1960)
    Williamson, Henry
        4867. Tarka the Otter (1960)

LOOKING GLASS LIBRARY SERIES —Random House (cont'd)
      Yonge, Charlotte
          4868. Countess Kate (1960)
Although this short, squat series offers many unusual titles, the general format is
unappealing. The print is tiny, the space between lines negligible, and the illustrations few. For ages 8 on up.

McCLUNG, ROBERT —Morrow
          4869. Black Jack, Last of the Big Alligators (1967)
          4870. Blaze, the Story of a Striped Skunk (1969)
          4871. Bufo, the Story of a Toad (1954)
          4872. Buzztail, the Story of a Rattlesnake (1958)
          4873. Green Darner (1956)
          4874. Honker (1965)
          4875. Horseshoe Crab (1967)
          4876. Ladybug (1966)
          4877. Leaper, the Story of an Atlantic Salmon (1957)
          4878. Luna, the Story of a Moth (1957)
          4879. Major, the Story of a Black Bear (1956)
          4880. Opossum (1963)
          4881. Otus, the Story of a Screech Owl (1959)
          4882. Redbird, the Story of a Cardinal (1968)
          4883. Ruby Throat (1950)
          4884. Screamer, Last of the Eastern Panthers (1964)
          4885. Shag, Last of the Plains Buffalo (1960)
          4886. Sphinx, the Story of a Caterpillar (1949)
          4887. Spike, the Story of a Whitetail Deer (1952)
          4888. Spotted Salamander (1964)
          4889. Stripe, the Story of a Chipmunk (1951)
          4890. Thor, Last of the Sperm Whales (1971)
          4891. Tiger (1953)
          4892. Vulcan, the Story of a Bald Eagle (1955)
          4893. Whitefoot, the Story of a Wood Mouse (1961)
          4894. Whooping Crane (1959)
Like Mary Adrian, Mr. McClung offers readers the stories of individual animals to
represent the entire species. While this often proves interesting reading, the applica-
bility of these books to school use is marginal.
      How They Live
          4895. Aquatic Insects and How They Live (1970)
          4896. Caterpillars and How They Live (1965)
          4897. Mammals and How They Live (1963)
          4898. Moths and Butterflies and How They Live (1966)
This series is far more useful for science students than the preceding one. The
author presents all the facets of each species, without fictionalizing them. For
grades 4 through 6.

MACMILLAN CLASSICS
      Alcott, Louisa May
          4899. Little Men (1963)
          4900. Little Women (1962)
      Andersen, Hans Christian
          4901. Andersen's Fairy Tales (1963)

MACMILLAN CLASSICS (cont'd)
    Asbjornsen, P. C.
        4902. East of the Sun and West of the Moon (1963)
    Austen, Jane
        4903. Pride and Prejudice (1962)
    Baum, L. Frank
        4904. The Wizard of Oz (1962)
    Bronte, Charlotte
        4905. Jane Eyre (1962)
    Carroll, Lewis
        4906. Alice in Wonderland and Through the Looking Glass (1963)
    Church, Alfred
        4907. The Aeneid for Boys and Girls (1962)
        4908. The Iliad and Odyssey of Homer (1964)
    Collodi, Carlo
        4909. The Adventures of Pinocchio (1963)
    Crane, Stephen
        4910. The Red Badge of Courage (1962)
    Dickens, Charles
        4911. A Christmas Carol (1963)
        4912. A Tale of Two Cities (1962)
        4913. David Copperfield (1962)
    Doyle, Arthur Conan
        4914. Tales of Sherlock Holmes (1963)
    Dumas, Alexandre
        4915. The Three Musketeers (1962)
    Grimm, Jacob, and Wilhelm Grimm
        4916. Grimm's Fairy Tales (1963)
    Irving, Washington
        4917. Rip Van Winkle and The Legend of Sleepy Hollow (1963)
    Jacobs, Joseph
        4918. The Fables of Aesop (1964)
    Kipling, Rudyard
        4919. The Jungle Books (1964)
    Lamb, Charles, and Mary Lamb
        4920. Tales from Shakespeare (1963)
    Lanier, Sidney
        4921. King Arthur and His Knights (1963)
    London, Jack
        4922. Call of the Wild (1963)
    MacDonald, George
        4923. At the Back of the North Wind (1964)
    Melville, Herman
        4924. Moby Dick (1962)
    Orczy, Baroness
        4925. The Scarlet Pimpernel (1964)
    Poe, Edgar Allan
        4926. The Tales and Poems of Edgar Allan Poe (1963)
    Sewell, Anna
        4927. Black Beauty (1962)
    Sidney, Margaret
        4928. Five Little Peppers and How They Grew (1962)
    Spyri, Johanna
        4929. Heidi (1962)

MACMILLAN CLASSICS (cont'd)
    Steel, Flora
        4930. English Fairy Tales (1962)
    Stevenson, Robert Louis
        4931. Treasure Island (1963)
    Swift, Jonathan
        4932. Gulliver's Travels (1962)
    Twain, Mark
        4933. The Adventures of Huckleberry Finn (1962)
        4934. The Adventures of Tom Sawyer (1962)
    Verne, Jules
        4935. Twenty Thousand Leagues under the Sea (1962)
    Wiggin, Kate Douglas
        4936. Rebecca of Sunnybrook Farm (1962)
One of the best of the children's classics series. The binding is very sturdy, the illustrations are plentiful, and the large print is appealing.

MADE IN . . . SERIES —Knopf
    Ayer, Margaret
        4937. Made in Thailand (1964)
    Bonner, Mary
        4938. Made in Canada (1943)
    Golden, Grace
        4939. Made in Iceland (1958)
    Jarecka, Louise
        4940. Made in Poland (1949)
    Ross, Patricia
        4941. Made in Mexico (1952)
    Spencer, Cornelia
        4942. Made in China (1958)
        4943. Made in India (1946)
        4944. Made in Japan (1963)
    Toor, Frances
        4945. Made in Italy (1957)
The arts and crafts of each country (including, in some cases, miscellaneous items such as tea ceremonies, gardens, and festivals) are the subjects of these books. Some history of the country is presented, along with a lengthy description of the origins and practices of the crafts. An excellent series, except that there are few illustrations or reproductions of the items mentioned.

MAJOR CULTURES OF THE WORLD SERIES —World
    Chubb, Thomas C.
        4946. Slavic Peoples (1962)
        4947. The Byzantines (1959)
        4948. The Northmen (1964)
    Cottrell, Leonard
        4949. The Land of the Pharoahs (1960)
        4950. The Land of the Two Rivers (1962)
    Duggan, Alfred
        4951. The Romans (1964)
    Ellis, Harry
        4952. The Arabs (1958)
    Fairservis, Walter
        4953. Horsemen of the Steppes (1962)

          4954. India (1961)
     Turnbull, Colin
          4955. The Peoples of Africa (1962)
     Von Hagen, Victor
          4956. The Incas, People of the Sun (1961)
          4957. The Maya: Land of the Turkey and Deer (1960)
          4958. The Sun Kingdom of the Aztecs (1958)
     Yutang, Lin
          4959. The Chinese Way of Life (1972)
This is an excellent series on various ancient world cultures. It deals with many
peoples not covered before, treating all aspects of the civilizations—history, religion, education, etc. There are bibliographies, indices, and chronological charts.

MAJOR LEAGUE LIBRARY SERIES —Random House
     Klein, Dave
          4960. Great Infielders of the Major Leagues (1972)
     Libby, Bill
          4961. Star Pitchers of the Major Leagues (1971)
     Liss, Howard
          4962. Baseball's Zaniest Stars (1971)
          4963. More Strange But True Baseball Stories (1972)
A typical series on sports, providing information about various exciting incidents
and players in baseball. Especially good for use with reluctant readers.

MAJOR RIVERS OF THE UNITED STATES SERIES —Walck
     Lord, Beman
          4964. On the Banks of the Delaware (1971)
          4965. On the Banks of the Hudson (1971)
Two other series exist on rivers, but they concentrate on rivers throughout the
world, while this series is concerned with American rivers. All the series are useful,
but this one is somewhat more up to date, including treatment of pollution problems.

MANNING-SANDERS, RUTH —Dutton
          4966. A Book of Charms and Changelings (1972)
          4967. A Book of Dragons (1965)
          4968. A Book of Dwarfs (1965)
          4969. A Book of Ghosts and Goblins (1969)
          4970. A Book of Giants (1963)
          4971. A Book of Mermaids (1968)
          4972. A Book of Princes and Princesses (1970)
          4973. A Book of Witches (1966)
          4974. A Book of Wizards (1966)
These are retellings of both well-known and not-so-well-known fairy tales. Each
collection contains stories from various countries. In addition to being excellent
storytelling sources, these books are also handsomely illustrated by Robin Jacques.

MARLIN PERKINS' WILD KINGDOM SERIES —Doubleday
     Cromer, Richard, and Don Meier
          4975. The Miracle of Flight (1968)
     Eckert, Allan
          4976. Bayou Backwaters (1968)
          4977. In Search of a Whale (1970)

        Martin, Robert
            4978. Yesterday's People (1970)
        Walker, Lewis
            4979. Survival Under the Sun (1971)
The subjects of these books are examined from both a historical and a physical
standpoint. The color illustrations are beautiful, subjects are examined in depth,
and the books are indexed. For grades 4 through 7.

MASON, GEORGE   —Morrow
            4980. Animal Appetites (1966)
            4981. Animal Baggage (1961)
            4982. Animal Clothing (1955)
            4983. Animal Feet (1970)
            4984. Animal Habits (1959)
            4985. Animal Homes (1947)
            4986. Animal Sounds (1948)
            4987. Animal Tails (1958)
            4988. Animal Teeth (1965)
            4989. Animal Tools (1951)
            4990. Animal Tracks (1943)
            4991. Animal Vision (1968)
            4992. Animal Weapons (1949)
The format for this series features a full-page drawing of an animal, with its
scientific name, facing a page of text. Since one page only is devoted to each
animal under discussion, no detailed information is provided for any one animal.
The books do provide, however, an excellent examination of the varying characteristics among different animals. Unfortunately, not all the volumes are indexed.

MASTERS OF MUSIC SERIES   —David White
        Young, Percy
            4993. Beethoven (1967)
            4994. Britten (1968)
            4995. Debussy (1968)
            4996. Dvorak (1971)
            4997. Handel (1967)
            4998. Haydn (1970)
            4999. Mozart (1966)
            5000. Schubert (1971)
            5001. Stravinsky (1970)
            5002. Tchaikowsky (1969)
In addition to information on the early lives of these composers, the author also
provides extensive material on their creative lives. There are also excerpts from
their works and listening suggestions. For grades 4 on up.

MEN AT WORK SERIES   —Putnam
        Lent, Henry
            5003. Men at Work in New England (1967)
            5004. Men at Work in the Great Lakes States (1971)
            5005. Men at Work in the Middle Atlantic States (1970)
            5006. Men at Work in the South (1969)
            5007. Men at Work on the West Coast (1968)

  Rubicam, Harry
    5008. Men at Work in Hawaii (1967)
    5009. Men at Work in the Great Plains States (1968)
    5010. Men at Work in the Mountain States (1960)
  Smith, Frances
    5011. Men at Work in Alaska (1967)
These works provide information on various industries in different parts of the country, but the indexing is bad. No references are given to the individual states, with the result that information on "cotton growing" is indexed, but information on "cotton growing in Virginia" is not. This limitation handicaps the reader and precludes his making full use of the books of the series.

MESSNER BIOGRAPHIES
  Abodaher, David
    5012. Freedom Fighter: Casimir Pulaski (1969)
    5013. Rebel on Two Continents: Thomas Meagher (1970)
    5014. Warrior on Two Continents: Thaddeus Kosciuszko (1968)
  Apsler, Alfred
    5015. Fighter for Independence: Jawaharlal Nehru (1963)
    5016. Iron Chancellor: Otto von Bismarck (1968)
    5017. Ivan the Terrible (1971)
    5018. Prophet of Revolution: Karl Marx (1967)
    5019. Sun King: Louis XIV of France (1965)
  Archer, Jules
    5020. African Firebrand: Kenyatta of Kenya (1969)
    5021. Angry Abolitionist: William Lloyd Garrison (1969)
    5022. Battlefield President: Dwight D. Eisenhower (1967)
    5023. Colossus of Europe: Metternich (1970)
    5024. Fighting Journalist: Horace Greeley (1966)
    5025. Front Line General: Douglas MacArthur (1963)
    5026. Man of Steel: Joseph Stalin (1965)
    5027. Red Rebel: Tito of Yugoslavia (1968)
    5028. Science Explorer: Roy Chapman Andrews (1968)
    5029. Strikes, Bonds, and Bullets: Big Bill Haywood and the I.W.W. (1972)
    5030. Twentieth Century Caesar: Benito Mussolini (1964)
    5031. World Citizen: Woodrow Wilson (1967)
  Archibald, Joe
    5032. Commander of the Flying Tigers: Claire Lee Chenault (1966)
  Bailey, Bernardine
    5033. Abe Lincoln's Other Mother: The Story of Sarah Bush Lincoln
         (1941)
  Baker, Rachel
    5034. America's First Trained Nurse: Linda Richards (1959)
    5035. Angel of Mercy: The Story of Dorothea Lynde Dix (1955)
    5036. Chaim Weizmann: Builder of a Nation (1950)
    5037. Doctor Morton: Pioneer in the Use of Ether (1946)
    5038. Sigmund Freud (1952)
    5039. The First Woman Doctor: The Story of Elizabeth Blackwell, M.D.
         (1944)
  Baker, Rachel, and Johanna Merlen
    5040. America's First Woman Astronomer: Maria Mitchell (1960)
  Beard, Charles
    5041. The Presidents in American History (1969)

MESSNER BIOGRAPHIES (cont'd)
> Beaty, John
>> 5042. Luther Burbank: Plant Magician (1943)
> Beckhard, Arthur
>> 5043. Black Hawk (1957)
>> 5044. Electrical Genius: Nikola Tesla (1959)
> Beckhard, Arthur, and William Crane
>> 5045. Cancer, Cocaine, and Courage: The Story of Doctor William
>>> Halsted (1960)
> Bishop, Curtis
>> 5046. Lone Star Leader: Sam Houston (1961)
> Bolton, Ivy
>> 5047. Father Junipero Serra (1952)
> Bryan, Florence
>> 5048. Susan B. Anthony: Champion of Women's Rights (1947)
> Buchman, Dian
>> 5049. The Sherlock Holmes of Medicine: Doctor Joseph Goldberger (1969)
> Burt, Olive
>> 5050. Brigham Young (1956)
>> 5051. First Woman Editor: Sarah J. Hale (1960)
>> 5052. Jedediah Smith: Fur Trapper of the Old West (1951)
>> 5053. Jim Beckwourth (1957)
>> 5054. John Charles Fremont: Trail Marker of the Old West (1955)
>> 5055. Ouray the Arrow (1953)
> Butler, Hal
>> 5056. Stormin' Norman Cash (1968)
>> 5057. The Bob Allison Story (1967)
>> 5058. The Willie Horton Story (1970)
> Caldwell, Cy
>> 5059. Henry Ford (1947)
> Coe, Douglas
>> 5060. Marconi: Pioneer of Radio (1943)
> Cooke, David C.
>> 5061. Tecumseh: Destiny's Warrior (1959)
> Crane, William
>> 5062. Discoverer of Oxygen: Joseph Priestley (1962)
>> 5063. Patriotic Rebel: John C. Calhoun (1972)
>> 5064. Prophet with Honor: Doctor William Welch (1966)
>> 5065. The Man Who Transformed the World: James Watt (1963)
> Cranston, Paul
>> 5066. To Heaven on Horseback: The Romantic Story of Narcissa
>>> Whitman (1952)
> Crawford, Deborah
>> 5067. King's Astronomer: William Herschel (1968)
> Denzel, Justin
>> 5068. Champion of Liberty: Henry Knox (1969)
>> 5069. Genius with a Scalpel: Harvey Cushing (1971)
> Deutsch, Babette
>> 5070. Walt Whitman: Builder for America (1941)
> Douty, Esther
>> 5071. America's First Woman Chemist: Ellen Richards (1961)
> Elkon, Juliette
>> 5072. Edith Cavell: Heroic Nurse (1956)

MESSNER BIOGRAPHIES (cont'd)
  Emery, Guy
    5073. Robert E. Lee (1951)
  Epstein, Beryl
    5074. Lillian Wald: Angel of Henry Street (1948)
    5075. Pioneer Oceanographer: Alexander Agassis (1963)
    5076. Plant Explorer: David Fairchild (1961)
    5077. The Great Houdini: Magician Extraordinary (1950)
    5078. William Crawford Gorgas (1953)
  Epstein, Samuel, and Beryl Epstein
    5079. Francis Marion: Swamp Fox of the Revolution (1956)
  Esterer, Arnulf
    5080. Discoverer of X-Ray: Wilhelm Conrad Rontgen (1968)
    5081. Sun Yat Sen: China's Great Champion (1950)
  Esterer, Arnulf, and Louise Esterer
    5082. Prophet of the Atomic Age: Leo Szilard (1972)
  Faber, Doris
    5083. Printer's Devil to Publisher: Adolph S. Ochs (1963)
  Farnsworth, Frances
    5084. Winged Moccasins: The Story of Sacajawea (1953)
  Fast, Howard
    5085. Goethals and the Panama Canal (1942)
    5086. Haym Solomon: Son of Liberty (1941)
  Feuerlicht, Roberta
    5087. In Search of Peace: The Story of Four Americans Who Won the
          Nobel Peace Prize (1970)
  Garbedian, H. Gordon
    5088. Thomas Alva Edison: Builder of Civilization (1947)
  Garst, Shannon
    5089. Amelia Earhart: Heroine of the Skies (1947)
    5090. Big Foot Wallace of the Texas Rangers (1951)
    5091. Buffalo Bill (1948)
    5092. Chief Joseph of the Nez Perces (1953)
    5093. Cowboy Artist: Charles M. Russell (1960)
    5094. Custer: Fighter of the Plains (1944)
    5095. Frontier Hero: Simon Kenton (1963)
    5096. Jack London: Magnet for Adventure (1944)
    5097. James Bowie: His Famous Knife (1944)
    5098. Kit Carson: Trail Blazer (1942)
    5099. Sitting Bull: Champion of His People (1946)
    5100. Three Conquistadors (1947)
    5101. Wild Bill Hickok (1952)
    5102. Will Rogers: Immortal Cowboy (1950)
    5103. William Bent and His Adobe Empire (1957)
  Garst, Shannon, and Warren Garst
    5104. Ernest Thompson Seton: Naturalist (1959)
  Gladych, Michael
    5105. Admiral Byrd of Antarctica (1960)
  Goettel, Elinor
    5106. Eagle of the Philippines: President Manuel Quezon (1960)
  Graham, Shirley
    5107. Booker T. Washington (1955)
    5108. Jean Baptiste Pointe du Sable: Founder of Chicago (1953)
    5109. Paul Robeson: Citizen of the World (1971)

5110. The Story of Phillis Wheatley: Poetess of the American Revolution (1969)

5111. There Once Was a Slave: The Heroic Story of Frederick Douglass (1947)

5112. Your Most Humble Servant: The Story of Benjamin Banneker (1949)

Graham, Shirley, and George Lipscomb

5113. Doctor George Washington Carver: Scientist (1944)

Green, Margaret

5114. Defender of the Constitution: Andrew Johnson (1962)

5115. Paul Revere: The Man behind the Legend (1964)

5116. President of the Confederacy: Jefferson Davis (1963)

5117. Radical of the Revolution: Samuel Adams (1971)

Griffiths, Ann

5118. Black Patriot and Martyr: Toussaint of Haiti (1970)

Halacy, Dan

5119. Father of Supersonic Flight: Theodor von Karmen (1964)

Harlow, Alvin

5120. Andrew Carnegie (1953)

5121. Bret Harte of the Old West (1943)

5122. Joel Chandler Harris: Plantation Storyteller (1941)

5123. The Ringlings: Wizards of the Circus (1951)

5124. Theodore Roosevelt: Strenuous American (1943)

Hatch, Alden

5125. George Patton: General in Spurs (1950)

Haycraft, Howard

5126. Queen Victoria (1956)

Heller, Deane

5127. Hero of Modern Turkey: Ataturk (1972)

Herron, Edward

5128. First Scientist of Alaska: William Healey Dall (1958)

Hoehling, Mary

5129. Girl Soldier and Spy: Sarah Emma Edmundson (1959)

5130. The Real Sherlock Holmes (1965)

5131. Yankee in the White House: John Quincy Adams (1963)

Hoyt, Edwin

5132. He Freed the Minds of Men: Rene Descartes (1969)

Johnson, Enid

5133. Cochise: Great Apache Chief (1953)

Joseph, Joan

5134. Peter the Great (1968)

5135. South African Statesman: Jan Christiaan Smuts (1969)

Komroff, Manuel

5136. Charlemagne (1964)

5137. Disraeli (1963)

5138. Julius Caesar (1955)

5139. Marco Polo (1952)

5140. Napoleon (1954)

5141. Talleyrand (1965)

5142. Thomas Jefferson (1961)

Komroff, Manuel, and Odette Komroff

5143. Marie Antoinette (1967)

MESSNER BIOGRAPHIES   (cont'd)
   Kosner, Alice
      5144. Voice of the People: William Jennings Bryan (1970)
   Kugelmass, J. Alvin
      5145. J. Robert Oppenheimer: Atomic Story (1953)
      5146. Louis Pasteur (1948)
      5147. Ralph J. Bunche: Fighter for Peace (1963)
      5148. Roald Amundsen: A Saga of the Polar Seas (1955)
   Levine, I. E.
      5149. Behind the Silken Curtain: The Story of Townsend Harris (1961)
      5150. Champion of World Peace: Dag Hammarskjold (1962)
      5151. Conqueror of Smallpox: Doctor Edward Jenner (1960)
      5152. Electronics Pioneer: Lee DeForest (1964)
      5153. Inventive Wizard: George Westinghouse (1962)
      5154. Lenin: The Man Who Made a Revolution (1969)
      5155. Miracle Man of Printing: Ottmar Mergenthaler (1963)
      5156. Oliver Cromwell (1966)
      5157. Spokesman for the Free World: Adlai E. Stevenson (1967)
      5158. The Discoverer of Insulin: Doctor Frederick G. Banting (1959)
      5159. Young Man in the White House: John Fitzgerald Kennedy (1954)
   Levinger, Elma
      5160. Albert Einstein (1949)
      5161. Galileo (1952)
      5162. Leonardo da Vinci (1954)
   Libby, Bill
      5163. Rocky: The Story of a Champion (1971)
   Lichello, Robert
      5164. Pioneer in Blood Plasma: Dr. Charles R. Drew (1968)
   McKown, Robin
      5165. Giant of the Atom: Ernest Rutherford (1962)
      5166. Mendeleyev and His Periodic Table (1965)
      5167. She Lived for Science: Irene Joliet-Curie (1961)
   Malvern, Gladys
      5168. Curtain Going Up: The Story of Katharine Cornell (1943)
      5169. Dancing Star: The Story of Anna Pavlova (1942)
   Mantel, S. G.
      5170. Explorer with a Dream: John Ledyard (1969)
   Mardus, Elaine
      5171. Man with a Microscope: Eli Metchnikoff (1968)
   Martin, Ralph
      5172. President from Missouri: Harry S. Truman (1964)
   Miner, Lewis
      5173. Industrial Genius: Samuel Slater (1958)
      5174. King of the Hawaiian Islands: Kamehameha I (1963)
   Mudra, Marie
      5175. David Farragut: Sea Fighter (1953)
   Myers, Elisabeth
      5176. Angel of Appalachia (1968)
      5177. Madame Secretary: Frances Perkins (1972)
      5178. South America's Yankee Genius: Henry Meiggs (1969)
   Noble, Iris
      5179. Clarence Darrow: Defense Attorney (1958)
      5180. Egypt's Queen: Cleopatra (1963)
      5181. Emmeline and Her Daughters: The Pankhurst Suffragettes (1971)

143

5182. Empress of All Russia: Catherine the Great (1966)
5183. First Woman Ambulance Surgeon: Emily Barringer (1962)
5184. Great Lady of the Theatre: Sarah Bernhardt (1960)
5185. Honor of Balboa (1970)
5186. Israel's Golda Meir: Pioneer to Prime Minister (1972)
5187. Joseph Pulitzer: Front Page Pioneer (1957)
5188. Labor's Advocate: Eugene V. Debs (1966)
5189. Master Surgeon: John Hunter (1971)
5190. Nellie Bly: First Woman Reporter (1956)
5191. Nurse around the World: Alice Fitzgerald (1964)
5192. Physician to the Children: Doctor Bela Schick (1963)
5193. Rivals in Parliament: William Pitt and Charles Fox (1970)
5194. Spain's Golden Queen Isabella (1969)
5195. The Doctor Who Dared: William Osler (1959)
5196. William Shakespeare (1961)

Nolan, Jeanette
5197. Abraham Lincoln (1953)
5198. Andrew Jackson (1949)
5199. Belle Boyd: Secret Agent (1967)
5200. Benedict Arnold: Traitor to His Country (1956)
5201. Dolly Madison (1958)
5202. Florence Nightingale (1946)
5203. George Rogers Clark: Soldier and Hero (1954)
5204. John Brown (1950)
5205. LaSalle and the Grand Enterprise (1951)
5206. Little Giant: Stephen A. Douglas (1964)
5207. O. Henry: The Story of William Sydney Porter (1943)
5208. Soldier, Statesman, and Defendant: Aaron Burr (1972)
5209. Spy for the Confederacy: Rose O'Neal Greenhow (1960)
5210. The Gay Poet: The Story of Eugene Field (1940)
5211. The Story of Clara Barton of the Red Cross (1941)
5212. Yankee Spy: Elizabeth Van Lew (1970)

Norman, Charles
5213. John Muir: Father of Our National Parks (1957)

Orrmont, Arthur
5214. Amazing Alexander Hamilton (1964)
5215. Fearless Adventurer: Sir Richard Burton (1969)
5216. Fighter against Slavery: Jehudi Ashmun (1966)
5217. Master Detective: Allan Pinkerton (1965)
5218. Mister Lincoln's Master Spy: Lafayette Baker (1966)

Polatnick, Florence, and Alberta Saletan
5219. Zambia's President: Kenneth Kaunda (1972)

Proudfit, Isabel
5220. Noah Webster: Father of the Dictionary (1942)
5221. River Boy: The Story of Mark Twain (1940)
5222. The Treasure Hunter: The Story of Robert Louis Stevenson (1939)

Purdy, Claire
5223. Antonin Dvorak: Composer from Bohemia (1950)
5224. Gilbert and Sullivan: Masters of Mirth and Melody (1946)
5225. He Heard America Sing: The Story of Stephen Foster (1940)
5226. Song of the North: The Story of Edvard Grieg (1941)
5227. Stormy Victory: The Story of Tchaikowsky (1942)

MESSNER BIOGRAPHIES (cont'd)
    Regli, Adolph
      5228. The Mayos: Pioneers in Medicine (1942)
    Rink, Paul
      5229. Soldier of the Andes: Jose de San Martin (1971)
    Schoor, Gene
      5230. Jim Thorpe: America's Great Athlete (1951)
      5231. The Story of Ty Cobb: Baseball's Greatest Player (1952)
    Shafter, Toby
      5232. Edna St. Vincent Millay: America's Best-Loved Poet (1957)
    Shapiro, Irwin
      5233. Yankee Thunder: The Legendary Life of Davy Crockett (1944)
    Shapiro, Milton
      5234. Jackie Robinson of the Brooklyn Dodgers (1957)
    Sootin, Harry
      5235. Michael Faraday: From Errand Boy to Master Physicist (1954)
    Sootin, Laura
      5236. Isaac Newton (1955)
    Stern, Madeleine
      5237. So Much in a Lifetime: The Story of Doctor Isabel Borrows
          (1964)
    Stevenson, O. J.
      5238. Talking Wire: The Story of Alexander Graham Bell (1947)
    Stone, Adrienne
      5239. Hawaii's Queen: Liliuokalani (1947)
    Suhl, Yuri
      5240. Eloquent Crusader: Ernestine Rose (1970)
    Sutton, Felix
      5241. Big Game Hunter: Carl Akeley (1960)
      5242. Valiant Virginian: Stonewall Jackson (1961)
    Terzian, James
      5243. Defender of Human Rights: Carl Schurz (1965)
      5244. The Many Worlds of Herbert Hoover (1966)
    Thomas, Henry
      5245. Copernicus (1960)
    Weingast, David
      5246. Franklin D. Roosevelt: Man of Destiny (1952)
    Westervelt, Virginia
      5247. Incredible Man of Science: Irving Langmuir (1968)
      5248. The World Was His Laboratory: Doctor Willis H. Whitney (1964)
    White, Dale
      5249. Bat Masterson (1960)
    Wilkie, Katharine
      5250. John Sevier: Son of Tennessee (1958)
      5251. The Man Who Wouldn't Give Up: Henry Clay (1961)
    Wilke, Katharine, and Elizabeth Moseley
      5252. Father of the Constitution: James Madison (1963)
      5253. Frontier Nurse: Mary Breckinridge (1969)
      5254. Teacher of the Blind: Samuel Gridley Howe (1965)
    Wood, Laura
      5255. Raymond L. Ditmars: His Exciting Career with Reptiles,
          Animals, and Insects (1944)
      5256. Walter Reed, Doctor in Uniform (1943)

MESSNER BIOGRAPHIES (cont'd)
>   Young, Bob, and Jan Young
>   5257. Frontier Scientist: Clarence King (1968)
>   5258. Old Rough and Ready: Zachary Taylor (1970)
>   5259. Plant Detective: David Douglas (1966)
>   5260. Reluctant Warrior: Ulysses S. Grant (1971)
>   5261. Seven Faces West (1969)
>   Zanger, Jack
>   5262. The Brooks Robinson Story (1967)

This huge series of biographies is quite good. Although readers will find some standard biographees represented, the strong point here lies in the many biographies of little-known people. For grades 5 on up.

MESSNER CAREERS BOOKS SERIES
>   Bleich, Alan
>   5263. Your Career in Medicine (1964)
>   Boyd, Waldo
>   5264. Your Career in Oceanology (1968)
>   5265. Your Career in the Aerospace Industry (1966)
>   Darby, Patricia
>   5266. Your Career in Physical Therapy (1969)
>   Donohue, Jody
>   5267. Your Career in Public Relations (1967)
>   Dowdell, Dorothy, and Joseph Dowdell
>   5268. Careers in the Horticultural Sciences (1969)
>   5269. Your Career in Teaching (1969)
>   5270. Your Career in the World of Travel (1971)
>   Doyle, Robert
>   5271. Your Career in Interior Design (1969)
>   Duckat, Walter
>   5272. A Guide to Professional Careers (1970)
>   Esterer, Arnulf
>   5273. Your Career in Chemistry (1964)
>   Gay, Kathlyn
>   5274. Careers in Social Service (1969)
>   Gordon, George, and Irving Falk
>   5275. Your Career in Film Making (1969)
>   5276. Your Career in T.V. and Radio (1966)
>   Heal, Edith
>   5277. Beauty as a Career (1969)
>   5278. Fashion as a Career (1966)
>   Hirschfeld, Burt
>   5279. Stagestruck: Your Career in Theater (1963)
>   Johnson, George
>   5280. Your Career in Advertising (1966)
>   Lee, Essie
>   5281. Careers in the Health Field (1972)
>   Liston, Robert
>   5282. On the Job Training and Where to Get It (1967)
>   5283. Your Career in Civil Service (1966)
>   5284. Your Career in Law Enforcement (1965)
>   5285. Your Career in Selling (1967)
>   5286. Your Career in Transportation (1966)

MESSNER CAREERS BOOKS SERIES (cont'd)
      McCall, Virginia, and Joseph McCall
          5287. Your Career in Parks and Recreation (1970)
      McDonnell, Virginia
          5288. Careers in Hotel Management (1971)
      Neal, Harry
          5289. Disease Detectives (1968)
          5290. Engineers Unlimited (1968)
          5291. Skyblazers (1958)
          5292. Your Career in Foreign Service (1965)
      Oakes, Vanya
          5293. Challenging Careers in the Library World (1970)
      Sarnoff, Paul
          5294. Careers in Biological Science (1969)
          5295. Careers in the Legal Profession (1970)
      Searight, Mary
          5296. Your Career in Nursing (1970)
      Seligsohn, I. J.
          5297. Your Career in Computer Programming (1967)
      Spencer, Lila
          5298. Exciting Careers for Home Economists (1967)
      Splaver, Sarah
          5299. Paraprofessions: Careers of the Future and Present (1972)
          5300. Your Career—If You're Not Going to College (1971)
          5301. Your College Education—How to Pay for It (1968)
      Stein, M. L.
          5302. Your Career in Journalism (1965)
In addition to information on the different aspects of each career, this career book series also lists places to train and makes suggestions for further reading. Unlike other career series, however, this one is written in a chatty style that may prove more interesting to the junior high and high school age groups.

MESSNER SPORTS BOOKS
      Bell, Joseph
          5303. Olympic Thrills (1965)
          5304. World Series Thrills (1962)
      Bell, Joseph, and David Bell
          5305. Play-Off Thrills (1967)
      Berger, Phil
          5306. Great Moments in Pro Football (1969)
      Butler, Hal
          5307. Baseball All-Star Game Thrills (1968)
          5308. Stormin' Norman Cash (1968)
          5309. The Bob Allison Story (1967)
          5310. The Harmon Killebrew Story (1966)
          5311. The Roar of the Road (1969)
          5312. The Willie Horton Story (1970)
          5313. There's Nothing New in Sports (1967)
          5314. Underdogs of Sport (1969)
      Coan, Howard
          5315. Great Pass Catchers in Pro Football (1971)
      Darby, Ray
          5316. The Space Age Sport (1964)

MESSNER SPORTS BOOKS (cont'd)
>
>Libby, Bill
>>5317. Rocky (1971)
>>5318. Rookie Goalie (1970)
>>5319. The Dick Bass Story (1969)
>
>Lichello, Robert
>>5320. Ju-Jitsu: Self-Defense for Teenagers (1961)
>
>Schoor, Gene
>>5321. Christy Mathewson (1953)
>>5322. The Jim Thorpe Story (1951)
>>5323. The Story of Ty Cobb (1952)
>
>Shapiro, Milton
>>5324. A Beginner's Book of Sporting Guns and Hunting (1961)
>>5325. All-Stars of the Outfield (1970)
>>5326. Baseball's Greatest Pitchers (1969)
>>5327. Champions of the Bat (1967)
>>5328. Heroes behind the Mask (1968)
>>5329. Heroes of the Bullpen (1967)
>>5330. Jackie Robinson of the Brooklyn Dodgers (1966)
>>5331. Laughs from the Dugout (1966)
>>5332. The Day They Made the Record Book (1968)
>>5333. The Pro Quarterbacks (1971)
>>5334. The Year They Won the Most Valuable Player Award (1966)
>>5335. Treasury of Sports Humor (1972)

Like most sports series, these books recount famous events and the lives of famous players in different sports. Features of interest are the good photographs and the listings of players' lifetime records.

MILESTONES IN HISTORY SERIES —Messner
>
>Alderman, Clifford
>>5336. Blood-Red the Roses: The Story of the Wars of the Roses (1971)
>>5337. Death to the King: The Story of the English Civil War (1968)
>>5338. Flame of Freedom: The Peasants' Revolt of 1381 (1969)
>>5339. Gathering Storm: The Story of the Green Mountain Boys (1970)
>>5340. Golden Century: England under the Tudors (1972)
>>5341. Great Invasion: The Norman Conquest of 1066 (1969)
>>5342. Liberty, Equality, Fraternity (1965)
>>5343. That Man Shall Be Free (1964)
>>5344. The Devil's Shadow (1967)
>
>Archer, Jules
>>5345. 1968: Year of Crisis (1971)
>>5346. The Congo: The Birth of a New Nation (1970)
>
>Dolan, Edward
>>5347. The Disaster of 1906 (1967)
>
>Gerson, Noel
>>5348. Mr. Madison's War (1966)
>>5349. Passage to the West: The Great Voyages of Henry Hudson (1968)
>>5350. Rock of Freedom (1964)
>>5351. Survival: Jamestown (1967)
>
>Hirschfeld, Burt
>>5352. A Cloud over Hiroshima (1967)
>>5353. A State Is Born (1967)
>>5354. After the Alamo (1966)
>>5355. Fifty-Five Days of Terror (1964)

MILESTONES IN HISTORY SERIES —Messner (cont'd)
    5356. Four Cents an Acre (1966)
    5357. Freedom in Jeopardy: The Story of the McCarthy Years (1969)
    5358. The Vital Link: The Story of the Suez Canal (1968)
Hoehling, Mary, and Betty Randall
    5359. For Life and Liberty (1969)
Johnson, Enid
    5360. Rails across the Continent (1962)
Nolan, Jeanette
    5361. The Shot Heard Round the World (1963)
Rink, Paul
    5362. In Defense of Freedom: The Story of the Monroe Doctrine (1968)
    5363. Land Divided, the World United (1963)
    5364. Quest for Freedom: Bolivar and the South American Revolution
        (1969)
Roberts, John
    5365. Black Ships and Rising Sun (1971)
Severn, Bill
    5366. Free But Not Equal (1967)
    5367. The End of the Roaring Twenties (1969)
Teall, Kay
    5368. From Tsars to Commissars (1966)
Werstein, Irving
    5369. A Nation Fights Back (1963)
    5370. I Accuse: The Story of the Dreyfus Case (1967)
    5371. The Cruel Years: The Story of the Spanish Civil War (1969)
    5372. The Franco-Prussian War (1965)
    5373. Turning Point for America (1964)
Wilhelm, Maria
    5374. For the Glory of France (1968)
Young, Bob, and Jan Young
    5375. 54-40 or Fight (1967)
    5376. Forged in Silver (1968)
    5377. Gusher: The Search for Oil in America (1971)
    5378. Pike's Peak or Bust (1970)
    5379. The Forty-Niners (1966)
    5380. The Last Emperor (1969)
These various important events in history, which could easily stand on their own as intriguing tales, have been put in story form for this series. Although the authors provide bibliographies and indices, the fictionalization makes the books virtually useless for history and social science requirements.

MILITARY HISTORIES SERIES —Watts
Dupuy, Trevor
    5381. The Military History of Civil War Land Battles (1960)
    5382. The Military History of Civil War Naval Actions (1960)
    5383. The Military History of Revolutionary War Land Battles (1970)
    5384. The Military History of Revolutionary War Naval Battles (1970)
    5385. The Military History of the Chinese Civil War (1971)
Mr. Dupuy discusses the events preceding each battle, the battle itself, and its subsequent impact. These volumes are excellent supplementary material.

MILITARY HISTORY OF WORLD WAR I —Watts
      Dupuy, Trevor
            5386. Campaigns in Southern Europe (1967)
            5387. Campaigns on the Turkish Front (1967)
            5388. Naval and Overseas War, 1914-1915 (1967)
            5389. Naval and Overseas War, 1916-1918 (1967)
            5390. 1918: Decision in the West (1967)
            5391. 1918: The German Offensive (1967)
            5392. 1914: The Battles in the East (1967)
            5393. 1914: The Battles in the West (1967)
            5394. Stalemate in the Trenches, November 1914–March 1918 (1967)
            5395. Triumphs and Tragedies in the East, 1915-1917 (1967)
            5396. War in the Air (1965)
This series follows the same approach as Mr. Dupuy's other excellent military series. He manages to portray quite ably the futility of most of the efforts of World War I. Photos and maps add interest.

MILITARY HISTORY OF WORLD WAR II —Watts
      Dupuy, Trevor
            5397. Asian and Axis Resistance Movements (1965)
            5398. Asiatic Land Battles: Allied Victories in China and Burma (1963)
            5399. Asiatic Land Battles: Expansion of Japan in Asia (1963)
            5400. Asiatic Land Battles: Japanese Ambitions in the Pacific (1963)
            5401. Chronological Survey of World War II (1967)
            5402. Combat Leaders of World War II (1965)
            5403. European Land Battles: 1944-1945 (1962)
            5404. European Land Battles: 1939-1943 (1962)
            5405. European Resistance Movements (1965)
            5406. Land Battles: North Africa, Sicily, and Italy (1962)
            5407. The Air War in the Pacific: Air Power Leads the Way (1964)
            5408. The Air War in the Pacific: Victory in the Air (1964)
            5409. The Air War in the West: June 1941–April 1945 (1963)
            5410. The Air War in the West: September 1939–May 1941 (1963)
            5411. The Naval War in the Pacific: On to Tokyo (1964)
            5412. The Naval War in the Pacific: Rising Sun of Nippon (1964)
            5413. The Naval War in the West: The Raiders (1963)
            5414. The Naval War in the West: The Wolf Packs (1963)
In the same format as his other series, Mr. Dupuy covers various battles and events quite clearly and in detail. There are many photographs and an index.

MILITARY LIVES SERIES —Watts
      Dupuy, Trevor
            5415. The Military Life of Abraham Lincoln (1969)
            5416. The Military Life of Adolf Hitler (1969)
            5417. The Military Life of Alexander the Great of Macedon (1969)
            5418. The Military Life of Frederick the Great of Prussia (1969)
            5419. The Military Life of Genghis Khan, Khan of Khans (1969)
            5420. The Military Life of George Washington, American Soldier (1969)
            5421. The Military Life of Gustavus Adolphus, Father of Modern
                 War (1969)
            5422. The Military Life of Hannibal, Father of Strategy (1969)
            5423. The Military Life of Hindenburg and Ludendorff of Imperial
                 Germany (1969)
            5424. The Military Life of Winston Churchill of Britain (1969)

MILITARY LIVES SERIES —Watts (cont'd)
A biographical series with a twist—it deals strictly with the military aspect of the
lives of these famous people. Military historian Dupuy follows all campaigns in
detail, discussing their good and their bad points. Maps and photographs are
provided, as well as an index.

MIRSKY, REBA —Follett
        5425. Beethoven (1957)
        5426. Brahms (1966)
        5427. Haydn (1963)
        5428. Johann Sebastian Bach (1965)
        5429. Mozart (1960)
Credibility suffers in this series because the author fictionalizes conversations,
attitudes, and certain events. There are no bibliographies, no indices, and no
suggestions for listening to accompany the books. The illustrations—cute, rather
than realistic—are also a disappointment.

MODERN AMERICA SERIES —Watts
    Lindop,.Edmund
        5430. The Dazzling Twenties (1970)
        5431. The Turbulent Thirties (1970)
As social histories of important periods in modern American history, these are
excellent books. The author discusses politics, sports, entertainment, and the
social life of different segments of society during these times. The many photographs add interest. For grade 6 on up.

MODERN TIMES SERIES —McGraw-Hill
    Bayne-Jardine, C. C.
        5432. Mussolini and Italy (1968)
    Elliott, B. J.
        5433. Hitler and Germany (1963)
    Feuerlicht, Roberta
        5434. The Desperate Act: The Assassination of Franz Ferdinand at
            Sarajevo (1968)
    Robottom, John
        5435. China in Revolution (1970)
        5436. Modern Russia (1971)
    Snellgrove, L. E.
        5437. Franco and the Spanish Civil War (1968)
    Williams, Barry
        5438. Emerging Japan (1969)
Important events are discussed in detail in this outstanding series. The authors
examine the causes of our wars and political upheavals, as well as the growing
pains of emerging nations. For social studies and history classes, grades 7 on up.

MYTHS AND LEGENDS SERIES —Walck
    Arnott, Kathleen
        5439. African Myths and Legends (1963)
    Birch, Cyril
        5440. Chinese Myths and Fantasies (1961)
    Downing, Charles
        5441. Russian Tales and Legends (1957)
    Gray, John
        5442. India's Tales and Legends (1961)

MYTHS AND LEGENDS SERIES —Walck (cont'd)
    Jones, Gwyn
        5443. Scandinavian Legends and Folk Tales (1956)
    McAlpine, Helen, and William McAlpine
        5444. Japanese Tales and Legends (1959)
    Muller-Guggenbühl, Fritz
        5445. Swiss-Alpine Folk Tales (1958)
    O'Faolain, Eileen
        5446. Irish Sagas and Folk Tales (1954)
    Picard, Barbara Leonie
        5447. French Legends, Tales, and Fairy Stories (1955)
        5448. German Hero-Sagas and Folk Tales (1958)
    Prodanovic, Nada
        5449. Yugoslav Folk Tales (1957)
    Reeves, James
        5450. English Fables and Fairy Stories (1954)
    Sherlock, Philip
        5451. West Indian Folk-Tales (1966)
    Wilson, Barbara Ker
        5452. Scottish Folk Tales and Legends (1954)
While these books provide interesting folk tales adapted by the authors, the small print and the limited number of illustrations may hamper the enjoyment of all but the aficionados and the storytellers.

MYTHS, TALES AND LEGENDS SERIES —Garrard
    Watson, Jane
        5453. Castles in Spain (1971)
        5454. Rama of the Golden Age (1971)
    White, Anne Terry
        5455. Ali Baba and the Forth Thieves; Abu Kir and Abu Sir (1968)
        5456. Csar of the Water; The Little Humpbacked Horse (1968)
        5457. Knights of the Table Round (1970)
        5458. Of Beasts, Birds, and Man (1970)
        5459. Sinbad the Seaman; The Ebony Horse (1969)
        5460. Six Russian Tales (1969)
These are adaptations and, in some cases, translations of stories from other lands. Intended for grades 5 through 7. The color illustrations are appealing.

NATIONS OF THE MODERN WORLD SERIES —Praeger
    Alisky, Marvin
        5461. Uruguay: A Contemporary Survey (1969)
    Avery, Peter
        5462. Modern Iran (1965)
    Balfour, Michael
        5463. West Germany (1968)
    Benes, Vaclav, and Norman Pounds
        5464. Poland (1970)
    Bowle, John
        5465. England: A Portrait (1966)
    Campbell, John, and Philip Sherrard
        5466. Modern Greece (1968)
    Childs, David
        5467. East Germany (1969)

Cohen, Mark, and Lorna Hahn
    5468. Morocco: Old Land, New Nation (1956)
Cope, John
    5469. South Africa (1967)
Dening, Esler
    5470. Japan (1961)
Donnison, F. S. V.
    5471. Burma (1970)
Ferns, H. S.
    5472. Argentina (1969)
Gindrod, Muriel
    5473. Italy (1968)
Griffiths, Percival
    5474. Modern Iran (1965)
Gullick, J. M.
    5475. Malaysia (1969)
Heppell, Muriel, and Frank Singleton
    5476. Yugoslavia (1961)
Hills, George
    5477. Spain (1970)
Ignotus, Paul
    5478. Hungary (1972)
Jones, Glyn
    5479. Denmark (1970)
Koutaissoff, Elizabeth
    5480. Soviet Union (1971)
Lewis, Geoffrey
    5481. Turkey (1965)
Little, Tom
    5482. Modern Egypt (1967)
MacPhee, Marshall
    5483. Kenya (1968)
Mallinson, Vernon
    5484. Belgium (1970)
Marett, Robert
    5485. Peru (1969)
Mead, W. R.
    5486. Finland (1968)
Niven, Rex
    5487. Nigeria (1967)
Pakeman, S. A.
    5488. Ceylon (1964)
Pavlowitch, Stevan
    5489. Yugoslavia (1971)
Purcell, H. D.
    5490. Cyprus (1969)
Rowe, James, and Margaret Rowe
    5491. New Zealand (1968)
Southern, Richard
    5492. Chile (1972)
Spate, O. H. K.
    5493. Australia (1971)

NATIONS OF THE MODERN WORLD SERIES   —Praeger (cont'd)
        Stephens, Ian
            5494. Pakistan (1969)
        Wright, John
            5495. Libya (1969)
Although this series is intended for older readers than the Portraits of the Nations and the Lands and Peoples series, it nevertheless contains much of the same information—on geography, economy, politics, social structure, and culture. The authors discuss not only history but also the general trends that the history of these countries has taken.

NATIONS TODAY BOOKS   —Macmillan
        Barry, Joseph
            5496. France (1965)
        Carew, Dorothy
            5497. Portugal (1969)
            5498. The Netherlands (1965)
        Comay, Joan
            5499. Israel (1964)
        Fellows, Lawrence
            5500. East Africa (1972)
        Gerson, Noel
            5501. Belgium (1964)
        Goldston, Robert
            5502. Spain (1968)
        Graham, Frank
            5503. Austria (1964)
        Halsell, Grace
            5504. Peru (1969)
        Hancock, Ralph
            5505. Mexico (1964)
        Lamb, Beatrice
            5506. India (1965)
        Marsh, Ngaio
            5507. New Zealand (1964)
        Matthews, Hubert
            5508. Cuba (1964)
        Middleton, Drew
            5509. England (1964)
        Quigley, Lillian
            5510. Ireland (1964)
        Ritchie, P.
            5511. Australia (1968)
        Roland, A.
            5512. The Philippines (1968)
        Salisbury, Harrison
            5513. Russia (1965)
        Steinberg, Rafael
            5514. Japan (1969)
Similar to other series on foreign countries, this one does present more material on the social lives and customs of peoples in these lands than is found in the other series. Bibliographies and indices are provided. For grades 5 through 9.

NATURAL SCIENCE PICTURE BOOKS   —McGraw-Hill
    Bentley, Linnd
       5515. Plants That Eat Animals (1968)
    Blough, Glen
       5516. Discovering Dinosaurs (1960)
    Cloudsley-Thompson, J. L.
       5517. Animals of the Desert (1971)
    Crowcroft, Peter
       5518. Australian Marsupials (1972)
    Knight, Maxwell
       5519. Small Water Mammals (1968)
    Leutscher, Alfred
       5520. The Curious World of Snakes (1965)
    Morris, Desmond
       5521. Apes and Monkeys (1965)
       5522. Big Cats (1965)
    Ommanney, F. D.
       5523. Animal Life in the Antarctic (1971)
    Ronan, Colin
       5524. Stars (1966)
    Vevers, Gwynne
       5525. Animals of the Arctic (1965)
       5526. Ants and Termites (1966)
       5527. Life in the Sea (1965)

The illustrations are large, in this excellent series, and new words are presented in heavy type. Although there is no index, the authors give the scientific names of the animals or plants involved and often list botanical gardens and zoos that readers might visit.

NATURE AND SCIENCE LIBRARY SERIES   —Doubleday
    Anderson, M. D.
       5528. Through the Microscope (1968)
    Burland, Cottie
       5529. Men without Machines (1969)
    Carthy, J. D.
       5530. Animals and Their Ways (1969)
    Chandler, T. J.
       5531. The Air around Us (1969)
    Clark, William
       5532. Explorers of the World (1970)
    Clayton, Keith
       5533. The Crust of the Earth (1968)
    Edlin, H. L.
       5534. Plants and Man (1969)
    Fisher, James
       5535. Zoos of the World (1971)
    Garnett, Henry
       5536. Treasures of Yesterday (1967)
    Joffe, Joyce
       5537. Conservation (1970)
    Kind, Stuart, and Michael Overman
       5538. Science against Crime (1972)
    Lauwerys, J. A.
       5539. Man's Impact on Nature (1970)

NATURE AND SCIENCE LIBRARY SERIES —Doubleday (cont'd)
    McCulloch, Gordon
        5540. Man and His Body (1967)
    Newman, Leonard H.
        5541. Man and Insects (1965)
    Reid, Keith
        5542. Nature's Network (1970)
    Ronan, Colin
        5543. Man Probes the Universe (1968)
    Russell, W. M. S.
        5544. Man, Nature, and History (1969)
    Sterland, E. G.
        5545. Energy into Power (1970)
Natural science subjects are discussed in greater detail in this series than in most similar series. There are illustrations and photographs on every page, and the volumes are indexed. For grades 5 to 9.

NATURE BOOKS FOR YOUNG PEOPLE SERIES —Doubleday
    Bevans, Michael
        5546. The Book of Reptiles and Amphibians (1967)
        5547. The Book of Sea Shells (1961)
    Echard, Margaret
        5548. Hoofs, Claws, and Antlers (1968)
    Hoffman, Melita
        5549. The Book of Big Birds (1965)
    Pettit, Ted
        5550. Animal Signs and Signals (1965)
    Shuttlesworth, Dorothy
        5551. The Age of Reptiles (1958)
        5552. The Story of Ants (1964)
        5553. The Story of Cats (1962)
        5554. The Story of Dogs (1961)
        5555. The Story of Flies (1970)
        5556. The Story of Horses (1959)
        5557. The Story of Rocks (1966)
        5558. The Story of Spiders (1962)
    Swain, SuZan
        5559. Insects in Their World (1965)
    Webb, Addison
        5560. Birds in Their Homes (1960)
Large color drawings amplify the basic text of these slender volumes. They are good bets for collections because of the eye appeal and the pictorial information; additionally, all the books are indexed.

NATURE OF MAN SERIES —Macrae Smith
    Halacy, Dan
        5561. Feast and Famine: Man and the Food-Life Chain (1971)
        5562. Habitat: Man's Universe and Ecology (1970)
        5563. Man Alive: Life and Man's Physical Nature (1970)
        5564. Social Man: The Relationship of Humankind (1972)
The detailed treatment of these various subjects often makes difficult reading. The books present excellent background material on ecological problems today. For grades 6 through 12.

NEVINS, ALBERT J. —Dodd
    5565. Away to Central America (1967)
    5566. Away to the Lands of the Andes (1962)
    5567. Away to Venezuela (1970)
In addition to the usual information on foreign lands, these books also present information on history, religion, tourism, and fiestas. They are very well done and can be used in connection with school work and travel interests. For ages 12 to 14.

NEW CONSERVATION SERIES —Coward
    Heindl, L. A.
    5568. The Water We Live By: How to Manage It Wisely (1969)
    Marshall, James
    5569. Going to Waste: Where Will All the Garbage Go? (1971)
    5570. The Air We Live In: Air Pollution, What We Must Do about It
        (1968)
    Perry, William
    5571. Our Threatened Wildlife: An Ecological Study (1969)
    Vosburgh, John
    5572. Land Management: Restoring Our Most Valuable Resource (1970)
    5573. The Land We Live On (1971)
    Worth, Jean
    5574. Man, Earth, and Change: The Principles and History of Con-
        servation (1969)
Each book presents a detailed analysis of an aspect of our ecological situation today. The authors are all highly qualified to write on their subjects, and the photographs and drawings help to explain the subject. For grades 5 through 12.

NEW WORLD OF . . . SERIES —Dodd
    Delear, Frank
    5575. The New World of Helicopters (1967)
    Eberle, Irmengarde
    5576. The New World of Fabrics (1964)
    5577. The New World of Paper (1969)
    5578. The New World of Rubber (1966)
    Hill, Frank
    5579. The New World of Wood (1965)
    Lewis, Alfred
    5580. The New World of Computers (1965)
    5581. The New World of Food (1968)
    5582. The New World of Petroleum (1966)
    5583. The New World of Plastics (1963)
    O'Toole, Edward
    5584. The New World of Banking (1965)
    Sullivan, George
    5585. The New World of Communications (1969)
    5586. The New World of Construction Engineering (1968)
    Tracy, Edward
    5587. The New World of Aluminum (1967)
    5588. The New World of Copper (1964)
    5589. The New World of Iron and Steel (1971)
    Woodbury, David
    5590. The New World of the Atom (1965)

NEW WORLD OF . . . SERIES —Dodd (cont'd)
Concise but excellent treatment of various modern products. The format is
not only clear and easy to read, but it is also attractive. Each book is indexed.
For grades 4 through 8.

NICKELSBURG, JANET —Coward
        5591. California's Climates (1964)
        5592. California's Mountains (1964)
        5593. California's Natural Resources (1964)
        5594. California's Water and Land (1964)
Each aspect of California's natural history is treated in detail. Since California is
a state of such varying characteristics, these books will be of interest to natural
history students throughout the entire country.

NORTH STAR BOOKS SERIES —Houghton Mifflin
    Bakeless, John
        5595. The Adventures of Lewis and Clark (1962)
    Chase, Mary Ellen
        5596. Donald McKay and the Clipper Ships (1959)
        5597. Fishing Fleets of New England (1961)
        5598. Sailing the Seven Seas (1967)
    Clapesattle, J.
        5599. The Mayo Brothers (1962)
    Daniels, Jonathan
        5600. Robert E. Lee (1960)
    DosPassos, John
        5601. Thomas Jefferson: The Making of a President (1964)
    Douglas, William O.
        5602. Muir of the Mountains (1961)
    Hahn, Emily
        5603. Around the World with Nellie Bly (1959)
    Higgins, Marguerite
        5604. Jessie Benton Fremont (1962)
    Hough, Henry
        5605. Great Days of Whaling (1958)
        5606. Melville in the South Pacific (1960)
    Johnson, William
        5607. The Birth of Texas (1960)
    Kielty, Bernardine
        5608. Jenny Lind Sang Here (1959)
    Lancaster, Bruce
        5609. Ticonderoga: The Story of a Fort (1959)
    Lavender, David
        5610. The Trail to Santa Fe (1958)
    Mason, F. VanWyck
        5611. The Battle for New Orleans (1962)
        5612. The Battle of Lake Erie (1960)
    Maurois, Andre
        5613. Lafayette in America (1960)
    Montross, Lynn
        5614. The U.S. Marines (1962)
        5615. Washington and the Revolution (1969)
    Moody, Ralph
        5616. American Horses (1962)

NORTH STAR BOOKS SERIES   —Houghton Mifflin   (cont'd)
      5617. Riders of the Pony Express (1958)
North, Sterling
      5618. Captured by the Mohawks (1960)
      5619. First Steamboat on the Mississippi (1962)
      5620. Mark Twain and the River (1961)
      5621. Thoreau of Walden Pond (1959)
      5622. Young Thomas Edison (1958)
O'Meara, Walter
      5623. The First Northwest Passage (1960)
Papashivily, Helen
      5624. Louisa May Alcott (1965)
Pei, Mario
      5625. Our National Heritage (1960)
Seton, Anya
      5626. Washington Irving (1960)
Ullman, James
      5627. Down the Colorado with Major Powell (1960)
Wellman, Paul
      5628. Gold in California (1958)
      5629. The Greatest Cattle Drive (1964)
      5630. The Race to the Golden Spike (1961)
Very similar to the Landmark Series in the low quality of binding, paper, and illustrations. While Landmark at least provides information on some unusual subjects and events in American history, this series covers only commonplace ones. Even these well-qualified authors pale under the strain.

OAKESHOTT, R. EWART   —Dufour
      5631. A Knight and His Armour (1963)
      5632. A Knight and His Castle (1964)
      5633. A Knight and His Horse (1963)
      5634. A Knight and His Weapons (1963)
Through presentations of the various phases of a knight's training, these books portray his life and life in the manor during the Middle Ages: customs, dress, and entertainment. For grades 5 through 9.

OF BLACK AMERICANS SERIES   —McGraw-Hill
      Lindenmeyer, Otto
      5635. Black and Brave: The Black Soldier in America (1969)
      Liston, Robert
      5636. Slavery in America: Volume I, The Background of Slavery
                1619-1865 (1970)
      5637. Slavery in America: Volume II, The Heritage of Slavery 1865-
                1969 (1970)
The books in this series were based on materials used in researching a CBS-TV presentation of the same name. Their aim is to provide a thorough examination of the black man's condition in America both present and past. Excellent for use in black culture and history studies.

ONE DAY IN . . . SERIES   —Harcourt Brace Jovanovich
      Kirtland, G. B.
      5638. One Day in Ancient Rome (1961)
      5639. One Day in Aztec Mexico (1963)
      5640. One Day in Elizabethan England (1962)

ONE DAY IN . . . SERIES —Harcourt Brace Jovanovich (cont'd)
Fictionalized accounts of life in these various civilizations. The author focuses on
the reader as the central character of the events depicted. The books include
glossaries and interesting line drawings. While use for social studies is limited,
the books could nevertheless be fun for beginning students of ancient history.

OPEN DOOR SERIES —Childrens Press
        Chaffin, Lillie
           5641. A World of Books (1970)
        Cobe, Al
           5642. Great Spirit (1970)
        Coleman, James
           5643. Whatever You Can't Have (1970)
        Davis, Charles
           5644. On My Own (1970)
        Daylie, Daddie-O
           5645. You're On the Air (1970)
        Deer, Ada
           5646. Speaking Out (1970)
        Diaz, Paul
           5647. Up from El Paso (1970)
        Dunham, John
           5648. Someday I'm Going to Be Somebody (1970)
        Ellis, James
           5649. Run for Your Life (1970)
        Gibson, Truman
           5650. The Lord Is My Shepherd (1970)
        Glary, Chuck
           5651. What I'm about Is People (1970)
        Hannahs, Herb
           5652. People Are My Profession (1970)
        Hardin, Gail
           5653. The Road from West Virginia (1970)
        Hoard, Edison
           5654. Curse Not the Darkness (1970)
        Jones, Mallory
           5655. So Many Detours (1970)
        Leak, Zenolia
           5656. Mission Possible (1970)
        Lopez, J.
           5657. El Rancho de Muchachos (1970)
        McCalip, William
           5658. Call It Fate (1970)
        Mack, John
           5659. Nobody Promised Me (1970)
        Martinez, Jose
           5660. A Foot in Two Worlds (1970)
        Melendez, Carmello
           5661. A Long Time Growing (1970)
        Patterson, Betty
           5662. I Reached for the Sky (1970)
        Robinson, Emmett
           5663. Where There's Smoke (1970)

OPEN DOOR SERIES —Childrens Press (cont'd)
    Sagora, Petter
        5664. Written on Film (1970)
    Sims, William
        5665. West Side Cop (1970)
    Sinc, Jerry
        5666. Son of This Land (1970)
    Stallworth, Dave
        5667. Look to the Light Side (1970)
    Standerford, Betty
        5668. No Hablo Ingles (1970)
    Stovall, Emmett
        5669. In the Face of the Sun (1970)
    Thompson, Chester
        5670. New Fields (1970)
    Travis, Dempsey
        5671. Don't Stop Me Now (1970)
    Vasquez, Joseph
        5672. My Tribe (1970)
    Washington, Adolphus
        5673. Hey, Taxi (1970)
    Williams, Billy
        5674. Iron Man (1970)
    Williams, Joe
        5675. Enterprise (1970)
    Yokley, Joseph
        5676. Meigs Tower (1970)
Men and women from various minority groups, who have been successful in their lives and their careers, discuss how they overcame the difficulties forced on them by their backgrounds. At the end of each book is a career section dealing with aspects of the author's career and discussing opportunities in the field. Especially good for use with inner-city readers. Grades 7 and up.

OPERA STORIES FOR YOUNG PEOPLE SERIES —Putnam
    Johnston, Johanna
        5677. The Barber of Seville (1966)
    Moreton, John
        5678. Love for Three Oranges (1966)
    Orgel, Doris
        5679. Lohengrin (1966)
    Spender, Stephen
        5680. The Magic Flute (1966)
    Stevenson, Florence
        5681. Aida (1965)
    Weil, Lisl
        5682. The Bartered Bride (1967)
The brightly colored illustrations of these picture-books should appeal to children from pre-school age through grade 6.

OTHER PEOPLE, OTHER PLACES SERIES —Messner
    Feuerlicht, Roberta
        5683. Zhivko of Yugoslavia (1971)
    Lippman, Ingeborg
        5684. Fisherboy of Portugal (1971)

OTHER PEOPLE, OTHER PLACES SERIES —Messner (cont'd)
    Liss, Howard
        5685. Asgeir of Iceland (1970)
    Spiegelman, Judith
        5686. Ali of Turkey (1969)
        5687. Dayapala of Ceylon (1970)
        5688. Galong, River Boy of Thailand (1970)
        5689. Ketut, Boy Woodcarver of Bali (1971)
        5690. Shaer of Afghanistan (1969)
    Spiegelman, Judith, and Jack Ling
        5691. Two Brothers of Peru (1969)
    Stein, Mimi
        5692. Majola, a Zulu Boy (1969)
        5693. Puleng of Lesotho (1969)
Another series to feature the events in the life of a foreign child. The usable information here is minimal, but the photographs are many. For the casual reader only.

OUR NATIONAL PARKS SERIES —Follett
    Wood, Frances
        5694. Grand Canyon, Zion, Bryce Canyon (1963)
        5695. Great Smoky Mountains, Everglades, Mammoth Cave (1964)
        5696. Mount Rainier, Mount McKinley, Olympic (1964)
        5697. Rocky Mountains, Mesa Verde, Carlsbad Cavern (1963)
        5698. Yellowstone, Glacier, Grand Teton (1963)
        5699. Yosemite, Sequoia and Kings Canyon, Hawaii (1963)
This is the only series devoted to American national parks. The author provides information on the origins of the parks, as well as on the wildlife to be found in each. There are many color photos and maps, in addition to descriptions of the area. A good bet for use with geography classes or for travelers.

OUR WORLD SERIES —Messner
    Burt, Olive
        5700. Our World: Bulgaria (1970)
    Golann, Cecil
        5701. Our World: The Taming of Israel's Negev (1970)
    Werner, Vivian
        5702. Our World: France (1971)
    Witton, Dorothy
        5703. Our World: Mexico (1969)
An excellent series, which covers the usual aspects of foreign countries, but in more detail than will be found in other series of this nature. For grades 5 to 9.

PACESETTER BOOKS —Holt
    Bova, Ben
        5704. Escape! (1970)
        5705. Out of the Sun (1968)
    Chaber, M. E.
        5706. Fix (1970)
        5707. The Acid Nightmare (1967)
    Corbett, Scott
        5708. Diamonds Are More Trouble (1969)
        5709. Diamonds Are Trouble (1967)
    Devaney, John
        5710. Baseball's Youngest Big Leaguers (1969)

PACESETTER BOOKS —Holt (cont'd)
Ellis, Mel
     5711. The Sad Song of the Coyote (1967)
Higdon, Hal
     5712. Electronic Olympics (1971)
     5713. The Horse That Played Center Field (1969)
Hill, Elizabeth
     5714. Master Mike and the Miracle Maid (1967)
     5715. Pardon My Fangs (1969)
Place, Marian
     5716. The Frontiersman: The True Story of Billy Dixon (1967)
Rogers, James
     5717. Four Tough Cases of the F.B.I. (1969)
Silverberg, Robert
     5718. Planet of Death (1967)
     5719. Three Survived (1969)
Waller, Leslie
     5720. New Sound (1969)
     5721. Overdrive (1967)
Exciting and timely stories intended for the reluctant reader. Although the format
gives the books an adult appearance, the vocabulary is at the fifth grade level. Good
for grades 5 through high school.

PAGEANT SERIES —McKay
Diets, M.
     5722. The Pageant of Japanese History (1969)
Peck, Anne
     5723. The Pageant of Canadian History (1963)
     5724. The Pageant of Middle American History (1947)
     5725. The Pageant of South American History (1962)
Seeger, Elizabeth
     5726. The Pageant of Chinese History (1962)
     5727. The Pageant of Russian History (1950)
Sen, G. E.
     5728. The Pageant of India's History (1964)
Not only the history but often pre-historical myths and legends of each nation's
folklore are presented in these books. In some cases the authors provide a pronunciation key, and all the authors examine the history of art and literature of the
countries. Beacuse of the small print and lack of illustrations, the series would be
more useful for grades 6 and up.

PATHFINDER BIOGRAPHIES SERIES —Praeger
Bird, Anthony
     5729. Gottlieb Daimler (1962)
Blancke, Wendell
     5730. Juarez of Mexico (1971)
Cartwright, Frederick
     5731. Joseph Lister (1963)
Chasan, Will
     5732. Samuel Gompers: Leader of American Labor (1971)
Cowie, Leonard
     5733. Martin Luther: Leader of the Reformation (1969)

PATHFINDER BIOGRAPHIES SERIES —Praeger (cont'd)
    Farrington, Benjamin
        5734. Aristotle: Founder of Scientific Philosophy (1970)
        5735. Francis Bacon: Pioneer of Planned Science (1969)
    Gunston, David
        5736. Michael Faraday (1962)
    Ivimey, Alan
        5737. Marie Curie: Pioneer of the Atomic Age (1969)
    McGlashan, Agnes, and Christopher Reeve
        5738. Sigmund Freud: Founder of Psychoanalysis (1970)
    Mellersh, H. E. L.
        5739. Charles Darwin: Pioneer in the Theory of Evolution (1969)
    Pike, E. Royston
        5740. Mohammed: Prophet of the Religion of Islam (1969)
    Reines, Bernard
        5741. A People's Hero: Rizal of the Philippines (1971)
    Rowland, John
        5742. Ernest Rutherford (1964)
These biographees are individuals who have profoundly influenced society and its
way of thinking. The books are well written, clear, and concise. For grades 5 and up.

PATHS OF PROGRESS SERIES —Putnam
    Carter, Samuel
        5743. Lightning beneath the Sea (1969)
    Howard, Robert
        5744. The South Pass Story (1968)
    Lens, Sidney
        5745. Unions and What They Do (1968)
    Sullivan, George
        5746. The Seven Wonders of the Modern World (1968)
An attempt to examine the events that have led up to improvements in the social,
physical, and economic environment. The presentations are generally clear, with
illustrations and indices.

PEARE, CATHERINE —Holt
        5747. Aaron Copland: His Life (1969)
        5748. Albert Einstein: A Biography for Young People (1949)
        5749. Charles Dickens: His Life (1959)
        5750. Henry Wadsworth Longfellow: His Life (1953)
        5751. Jules Verne: His Life (1956)
        5752. Louisa May Alcott: Her Life (1954)
        5753. Mark Twain: His Life (1954)
        5754. Painter of Patriots: Charles Willson Peale (1964)
        5755. Robert Louis Stevenson: His Life (1955)
        5756. Rosa Bonheur: Her Life (1956)
        5757. Stephen Foster: His Life (1952)
        5758. Washington Irving: His Life (1957)
        5759. William Penn (1958)
Like Ms. Mirsky, Ms. Peare fictionalizes the lives of her subjects. There is no index,
and no attempt is made to illustrate the books realistically. The only redeeming feature
is the frequent use of quotes from the individuals' works, plus the suggestion of
books or poems of the biographees for further reading.

PEDRO BOOKS SERIES —Putnam
>Boys Life, Editors
>>5760. Ahead of Their Time (1968)
>>5761. Baseball As We Played It (1969)
>>5762. Best Jokes from "Boys Life" (1970)
>>5763. Best of "Boys Life I" (1968)
>>5764. Great True Adventures (1968)
>>5765. Pedro's Tall Tales (1967)
>Hynd, Alan
>>5766. Great Crime Busters (1967)
>Keith, Donald
>>5767. Time Machine to the Rescue (1967)
>Wingert, Dick
>>5768. The Cub Book (1967)

Like the "Boy's Life" series, this one presents various popular articles and stories that have appeared in the magazine. The binding and general format of these are superior to those of the "Boy's Life" series.

PEOPLE AND EVENTS SERIES —Putnam
>Farrell, Alan
>>5769. Winston Churchill (1965)
>Footman, David
>>5770. Russian Revolutions (1964)
>Paradis, Adrian
>>5771. The Problem Solvers (1964)
>Ross, Sutherland
>>5772. The English Civil War (1966)
>Silverberg, Robert
>>5773. The Dawn of Medicine (1967)
>>5774. The Great Doctors (1964)
>>5775. The Men Who Mastered the Atom (1965)

An examination of the people and occurrences surrounding a great event. The circumstances leading up to an event are presented, as well as its influence on the future. All books have an index, glossary, and bibliography.

PEOPLE OF DESTINY SERIES —Childrens Press
>Oldfield, Ruth
>>5776. Albert Einstein (1969)
>Reidy, John, and Kenneth Richards
>>5777. John F. Kennedy (1967)
>>5778. Leonard Bernstein (1967)
>>5779. Louis Armstrong (1967)
>>5780. Pope John XXIII (1968)
>>5781. Robert Frost (1968)
>>5782. Sir Winston Churchill (1968)
>>5783. Will Rogers (1968)
>Richards, Kenneth
>>5784. Albert Schweitzer (1968)
>>5785. Babe Ruth (1967)
>>5786. Charles Lindbergh (1968)
>>5787. Dag Hammarskjold (1969)
>>5788. Douglas MacArthur (1967)
>>5789. Eleanor Roosevelt (1969)
>>5790. Ernest Hemingway (1968)

PEOPLE OF DESTINY SERIES —Childrens Press (cont'd)
      5791. Frank Lloyd Wright (1968)
      5792. Harry S. Truman (1968)
      5793. Helen Keller (1968)
      5794. Henry Ford (1967)
   Torgersen, Don
      5795. Gandhi (1969)
Most of the individuals under discussion here have been written about many times before. The chief selling point is the publisher's claim that each book has been read and approved by the subject himself or by someone close to him. For grades 6 and up.

PERSPECTIVE BOOKS —Doubleday
   Gayle, Addison
      5796. Oak and Ivy: A Biography of Paul Laurence Dunbar (1971)
   Killens, John
      5797. Great Gittin' Up Morning (1972)
   Sterling, Dorothy
      5798. The Making of an Afro-American: Martin Robinson Delany (1971)
The three men covered in this new series of biographies of blacks have not been the subjects of biographies before this—a fact which makes these books a must for libraries. All the books are very readable, with good illustrations and with indices.

PICTURE AIDS TO WORLD GEOGRAPHY —John Day
   Brooks, Anita
      5799. The Picture Book of Fisheries (1961)
      5800. The Picture Book of Grains (1962)
      5801. The Picture Book of Metals (1971)
      5802. The Picture Book of Oil (1965)
      5803. The Picture Book of Salt (1964)
      5804. The Picture Book of Tea and Coffee (1961)
      5805. The Picture Book of Timber (1967)
In picturebook format, these works present a photograph with one paragraph of explanation under each picture. The books are indexed, but they remain purely supplementary because of the lack of extensive textual treatment.

PICTURE ALBUMS SERIES —Watts
   Ingraham, Leonard
      5806. An Album of Colonial America (1969)
      5807. An Album of the American Revolution (1971)
   Malone, John
      5808. An Album of the American Cowboy (1971)
   Miller, Donald
      5809. An Album of Black Americans in the Armed Forces (1969)
   Rowe, Jeanne
      5810. An Album of Martin Luther King, Jr. (1970)
      5811. An Album of the Presidents (1959)
   Suhl, Yuri
      5812. An Album of the Jew in America (1972)
   Yellow Robe, Rosebud
      5813. An Album of the American Indian (1969)
Like the previous series, this one features photographs with only one paragraph of text under each. The pictures here, however, are often more useful for classwork and

PICTURE ALBUMS SERIES —Watts (cont'd)
informational purposes than the Picture Aids to World Geography series. The lack
of an index is a handicap, however, since it is difficult for the reader to find the
exact picture or information that he is seeking.

PICTURE MAP GEOGRAPHY SERIES —Lippincott
      Hall, Elvajean, and Calvin Criner
          5814. Picture Map Geography of Eastern Europe (1968)
      Nazaroff, Alexander
          5815. Picture Map Geography of the U.S.S.R. (1969)
      Quinn, Vernon
          5816. Picture Map Geography of Africa (1964)
          5817. Picture Map Geography of Asia (1962)
          5818. Picture Map Geography of Canada and Alaska (1960)
          5819. Picture Map Geography of Mexico, Central America and the
               the West Indies (1964)
          5820. Picture Map Geography of South America (1959)
          5821. Picture Map Geography of the Pacific Islands (1964)
          5822. Picture Map Geography of the United States (1959)
      Wohlrabe, Raymond
          5823. Picture Map Geography of Western Europe (1967)
After several chapters of background material on each country or area, the authors
then discuss divisions such as industrial areas, agricultural areas, and cities. Along
with each discussion are maps picturing the products that each region is known for.
Each book is indexed. Good supplementary material for social studies and geography courses.

PILOT BOOKS SERIES —Whitman
      Bannon, Laura
          5824. Who Walks in the Attic? (1962)
      Carper, Jean, and Grace Dickerson
          5825. Little Turtle (1959)
      Chandler, Edna
          5826. Almost Brothers (1971)
          5827. Popcorn Patch (1969)
      Heide, Florence, and Sylvia VanClief
          5828. The Mystery of the Missing Suitcase (1972)
          5829. The Mystery of the Silver Tag (1972)
      Jenkins, Emyl
          5830. Greg Walker, News Photographer (1969)
      Johnston, Louisa
          5831. Mystery Hotel (1964)
      Johnston, Louisa, and Mabel Bristle
          5832. Monkey in the Family (1972)
      Mahon, Julia
          5833. The Mystery at Old Sturbridge Village (1964)
      Neigoff, Mike
          5834. Best in Camp (1969)
          5835. Dive In (1965)
          5836. Free Throw (1968)
          5837. Goal to Go (1970)
          5838. Hal, Tennis Champ (1971)
          5839. Nine Makes a Team (1963)
          5840. Ski Run (1972)

PILOT BOOKS SERIES —Whitman (cont'd)
      5841. Smiley Sherman, Substitute (1964)
      5842. Two on First (1967)
      5843. Up Sails (1966)
    Sankey, Alice
      5844. Basketballs for Breakfast (1963)
      5845. Judo Yell (1971)
      5846. Music by the Got-Rocks (1969)
      5847. Three-in-One Car (1967)
    Taylor, Florence
      5848. Jim Long-Knife (1959)
The publisher uses sports and mysteries to appeal to reluctant readers. With its short sentences and simple vocabulary, this series does not try to present as adult a format as the Pacesetter Books.

PIPER BOOKS SERIES —Houghton Mifflin
    Bailey, Bernardine
      5849. Abraham Lincoln: Man of Courage (1960)
      5850. Christopher Columbus: Sailor and Dreamer (1960)
    Edwards, Cecile
      5851. Horace Mann: Sower of Learning (1954)
      5852. John Alden: Steadfast Pilgrim (1961)
      5853. King Phillip: Loyal Indian (1962)
    Garst, Shannon
      5854. Hans Christian Andersen: Fairy Tale Author (1963)
    Gilbert, Miriam
      5855. Henry Ford: Maker of the Model T (1962)
    Hays, Wilma Pitchford
      5856. Pontiac: Lion in the Forest (1965)
    Humphreville, Frances
      5857. Harriet Tubman: Flame of Freedom (1964)
    Jones, William Percival
      5858. Patrick Henry: Voice of Liberty (1961)
    Kelly, Regina
      5859. Abigail Adams: The President's Lady (1962)
      5860. Henry Clay: Statesman and Patriot (1960)
      5861. James Madison: Statesman and President (1966)
      5862. Paul Revere: Colonial Craftsman (1963)
    Mason, Miriam
      5863. John Smith: Man of Adventure (1959)
    Olgin, Joseph
      5864. Sam Houston: Friend of the Indians (1963)
      5865. Thomas Jefferson: Champion of the People (1961)
    Place, Marian
      5866. John Wesley Powell: Canyon's Conqueror (1964)
    Ripley, Sheldon
      5867. Ethan Allen: Green Mountain Hero (1959)
      5868. Matthew Henson: Arctic Hero (1966)
    Seibert, Jerry
      5869. Amelia Earhart: First Lady of the Air (1962)
    Snow, Dorothea
      5870. Henry Hudson: Explorer of the North (1961)
    Tottle, John
      5871. Benjamin Franklin: First Great American (1960)

    Wilkie, Katharine
        5872. Ferdinand Magellan: Noble Captain (1963)
        5873. Robert Louis Stevenson: Storyteller and Adventurer (1964)
    Worcester, Donald
        5874. John Paul Jones: Soldier of the Sea (1962)
        5875. Kit Carson: Mountain Scout (1962)
Rather than concentrating on the adult lives of most of these biographees, the authors dwell more on their childhoods and the traits formed at that time which led to the subsequent achievements. In spite of this approach, the series seems superfluous because all of these subjects have been written about so many times before.

POEMS OF THE WORLD SERIES —Crowell
    Aldan, Daisy
        5876. Poems from India (1959)
    Cole, William
        5877. Poems from Ireland (1972)
    DiGiovanni, Norman
        5878. Poems from Spanish America (announced)
    Mezcy, Robert
        5879. Poems from the Hebrew (announced)
    Plotz, Helen
        5880. Poems from the German (1967)
    Smith, W. J.
        5881. Poems from France (1967)
        5882. Poems from Italy (1972)
Excellent collections of past and present poetry from different European countries. There are well-thought-out prefaces, brief biographical sketches of each poet, and indices (first line, title, and poet). Even better, some of the volumes offer a bilingual format, with original poem and translation on alternating pages. An excellent series for grades 7 and up.

PORTRAITS OF THE NATIONS SERIES —Lippincott
    Barnouw, Adriaan
        5883. The Land and People of Holland (1972)
    Berry, Erick
        5884. The Land and People of Finland (1972)
        5885. The Land and People of Iceland (1972)
    Blunden, Godfrey
        5886. The Land and People of Australia (1972)
    Bowen, J. David
        5887. The Land and People of Chile (1966)
        5888. The Land and People of Peru (1963)
        5889. The Land and People of Puerto Rico (1968)
    Bragdon, Lillian
        5890. The Land and People of France (1972)
        5891. The Land and People of Switzerland (1961)
    Brown, Rose
        5892. The Land and People of Brazil (1972)
    Buchanan, Freda
        5893. The Land and People of Scotland (1958)
    Chandler, David
        5894. The Land and People of Cambodia (1972)

Clifford, Mary
  5895. The Land and People of Afghanistan (1962)
  5896. The Land and People of Liberia (1971)
  5897. The Land and People of Malaysia (1968)
Copeland, Paul
  5898. The Land and People of Jordan (1972)
  5899. The Land and People of Libya (1972)
  5900. The Land and People of Syria (1972)
Crane, Louise
  5901. The Land and People of the Congo (1971)
Dobler, Lavinia
  5902. The Land and People of Uruguay (1972)
Fletcher, Alan
  5903. The Land and People of the Guianas (1972)
Gianakoulis, Theodore
  5904. The Land and People of Greece (1972)
Hale, Julian
  5905. The Land and People of Romania (1972)
Hall, Elvajean
  5906. The Land and People of Argentina (1972)
  5907. The Land and People of Czechoslovakia (1972)
  5908. The Land and People of Norway (1963)
Harrison, Brenda, and Lee Forman
  5909. The Land and People of Nigeria (1972)
Hinckley, Helen
  5910. The Land and People of Iran (1972)
Hoffman, Gail
  5911. The Land and People of Israel (1972)
Karen, Ruth
  5912. The Land and People of Central America (1972)
Kaula, Edna
  5913. The Land and People of Ethiopia (1972)
  5914. The Land and People of Kenya (1968)
  5915. The Land and People of New Zealand (1972)
  5916. The Land and People of Rhodesia (1967)
  5917. The Land and People of Tanganyika (1972)
  5918. The Land and People of Tanzania (1972)
Kelly, Eric
  5919. The Land and People of Poland (1972)
Kostich, Dragos D.
  5920. The Land and People of the Balkans (1962)
Landry, Lionel
  5921. The Land and People of Burma (1968)
  5922. The Land and People of Colombia (1970)
Lang, Robert
  5923. The Land and People of Pakistan (1968)
Larralde, Elsa
  5924. The Land and People of Mexico (1964)
Lengyel, Emil
  5925. The Land and People of Hungary (1972)
Loder, Dorothy
  5926. The Land and People of Belgium (1957)
  5927. The Land and People of Spain (1972)

PORTRAITS OF THE NATIONS SERIES —Lippincott (cont'd)
 Lovejoy, Bahija
  5928. The Land and People of Iraq (1964)
 Mahmoud, Zaki
  5929. The Land and People of Egypt (1972)
 Matthew, Eunice
  5930. The Land and People of Thailand (1964)
 Modak, Manorama
  5931. The Land and People of India (1960)
 Nano, Frederic
  5932. The Land and People of Sweden (1949)
 Nazaroff, Alexander
  5933. The Land and People of Russia (1972)
 O'Brien, Elinor
  5934. The Land and People of Ireland (1972)
 Paton, Alan
  5935. The Land and People of South Africa (1972)
 Ross, Frances
  5936. The Land and People of Canada (1960)
 Sale, J. Kirk
  5937. The Land and People of Ghana (1972)
 Sherlock, Philip
  5938. The Land and People of the West Indies (1967)
 Smith, Bradford
  5939. The Land and People of the Islands of Hawaii (1967)
 Smith, Datus
  5940. The Land and People of Indonesia (1972)
 Smith, Frances
  5941. The Land and People of the Arctic (1960)
 Solberg, S. E.
  5942. The Land and People of Korea (1966)
 Spencer, Cornelia
  5943. The Land and People of China (1972)
 Spencer, William
  5944. The Land and People of Algeria (1969)
  5945. The Land and People of Morocco (1965)
  5946. The Land and People of Tunisia (1972)
  5947. The Land and People of Turkey (1972)
 Street, Alicia
  5948. The Land and People of England (1969)
 Vaughan, Josephine
  5949. The Land and People of Japan (1972)
  5950. The Land and People of the Philippines (1960)
 Wilber, Donald
  5951. The Land and People of Ceylon (1972)
 Winder, Viola
  5952. The Land and People of Lebanon (1965)
 Winwar, Frances
  5953. The Land of the Italian People (1961)
 Wohlrabe, Raymond
  5954. The Land and People of Denmark (1972)
  5955. The Land and People of Portugal (1960)
  5956. The Land and People of Venezuela (1959)

PORTRAITS OF THE NATIONS SERIES —Lippincott (cont'd)
      Wohlrabe, Raymond, and Werner Krusch
          5957. The Land and People of Austria (1972)
          5958. The Land and People of Germany (1972)
Of all the books on foreign countries, this series ranks among the most comprehensive. Volumes are illustrated with photographs and are indexed. Many of the titles are currently being revised or are scheduled for revision. Fortunately, the revisions are generally complete and not just nominal. A must for grades 5 through 9.

PRENTICE-HALL JUNIOR RESEARCH BOOKS
      Alexander, Arthur
          5959. The Hidden You: Psychology in Your Life (1962)
          5960. The Magic of Words (1962)
      Carona, Philip
          5961. Magic Mixtures: Alloys and Plastics (1962)
          5962. Things That Measure (1962)
      Comfort, Iris
          5963. Earth Treasures: Rocks and Minerals (1964)
      David, Eugene
          5964. Electricity in Your Life (1963)
          5965. Spiders and How They Live (1964)
          5966. Television and How It Works (1962)
      Dean, Elizabeth
          5967. Printing: Tool of Freedom (1964)
      Faber, Doris
          5968. Horace Greeley: The People's Editor (1964)
          5969. Robert Frost: America's Poet (1964)
          5970. The Life of Pocahontas (1963)
      Farr, Muriel
          5971. Children in Medicine (1964)
      Friendly, Natalie
          5972. Wildlife Teams (1963)
      Goldstein, Rhoda
          5973. Tools of the Scientist (1963)
      Hellman, Hal
          5974. Navigation: Land, Sea and Sky (1966)
      Jonas, Arthur
          5975. Archimedes and His Wonderful Discoveries (1963)
          5976. More Ways in Math (1964)
          5977. New Ways in Math (1962)
      Jupo, Frank
          5978. The Story of the Three R's (1970)
          5979. The Story of Things (1971)
      Kohn, Bernice
          5980. Computers at Your Service (1962)
          5981. Fireflies (1966)
          5982. Light You Cannot See (1965)
          5983. Marvelous Mammals: Monotremes and Marsupials (1964)
          5984. Our Tiny Servants: Molds and Yeasts (1962)
          5985. Secret Codes and Ciphers (1968)
          5986. The Peaceful Atom (1963)
          5987. The Scientific Method (1964)
      Kohn, Eugene
          5988. Photography: A Manual for Shutterbugs (1965)

PRENTICE-HALL JUNIOR RESEARCH BOOKS (cont'd)
    Kovalik, Vladimar, and Nada Kovalik
        5989. The Undersea World of Tomorrow (1969)
    Larson, Joan
        5990. Visit with Us in Japan (1964)
    Lerner, Marguerite
        5991. Who Do You Think You Are? The Story of Heredity (1963)
    McCarthy, Agnes
        5992. Creatures of the Deep (1963)
        5993. Giant Animals of Long Ago (1963)
    Manchel, Frank
        5994. Movies and How They Are Made (1968)
    Mawson, Colin
        5995. The Story of Radioactivity (1969)
    Morgan, Elizabeth
        5996. In the Deep Blue Sea (1962)
    Nespojohn, Katherine
        5997. Animal Eyes (1965)
    Olney, Ross
        5998. Sounds All Around (1967)
        5999. The Story of Traffic Control (1968)
    Sander, Lenore
        6000. Animals That Work for Man (1963)
        6001. The Curious World of Crystals (1964)
    Sarasy, Phyllis
        6002. Winter Sleepers (1962)
    Saxon, Gladys
        6003. Secrets in Animal Names (1964)
    Schere, Monroe
        6004. The Story of Maps (1969)
        6005. Your Changing City (1969)
    Shor, Pekay
        6006. Libraries and You (1964)
    Stone, A. Harris
        6007. The Chemistry of a Lemon (1966)
    Sullivan, Navin
        6008. Animal Timekeepers (1966)
    Vanderboom, Mae
        6009. Miracle Salt (1965)
    Verral, Charles
        6010. Go! The Story of Outer Space (1962)
        6011. Jets (1962)
        6012. Robert Goddard: Father of the Space Age (1963)
    Webb, Nancy
        6013. Aguk of Alaska (1968)
        6014. Makima of the Rain Forest (1964)
    Welty, Susan
        6015. Birds with Bracelets: The Story of Bird-Banding (1965)
    Windle, Eric
        6016. Sounds You Cannot Hear (1963)
The volumes of this series really have no common denominator, since the series covers social sciences, natural sciences, and recreational materials. All of the books are by qualified authors, and all feature clear drawings. For grades 3 to 6.

PRESERVE OUR WILDLIFE SERIES   —Hastings House
     Adrian, Mary
         6017. The American Alligator (1967)
         6018. The American Eagle (1963)
         6019. The American Mustang (1964)
         6020. The American Prairie Chicken (1968)
         6021. The North American Bighorn Sheep (1966)
Long before the current interest in endangered species, this series began examining each species that is gradually dying out. The illustrations and photographs are plentiful, and the text is appealing and timely.

PRICE, CHRISTINE   —Dutton
         6022. Made in Ancient Egypt (1970)
         6023. Made in Ancient Greece (1967)
         6024. Made in the Middle Ages (1961)
         6025. Made in the Renaissance (1963)
Using a rather different approach, Ms. Price studies these ancient people through their art and artifacts. Each book is handsomely designed and includes many drawings and illustrations of things made during the period. A first-rate addition to any collection.

PRO BASKETBALL SERIES   —Random House
     Berger, Phil
         6026. Heroes of Pro Basketball (1968)
     Burns, Bill, and Dave Wolf
         6027. Great Moments in Pro Basketball (1968)
     Hollander, Zander
         6028. Great Rookies of Pro Basketball (1969)
     Liss, Howard
         6029. Strange But True Basketball Stories (1972)
     Sabin, Lou
         6030. Great Teams of Pro Basketball (1971)
     Sabin, Lou, and Dave Sendler
         6031. Stars of Pro Basketball (1970)
Like other series of major professional sports, this series provides information on outstanding incidents or events in basketball, plus biographies of outstanding players. Good for reluctant readers.

PRO HOCKEY SERIES   —Random House
     Fischler, Stan
         6032. Heroes of Pro Hockey (1971)
     Libby, Bill
         6033. Great Stanley Cup Playoffs (1972)
     Liss, Howard
         6034. Strange But True Hockey Stories (1972)
     Orr, Frank
         6035. The Story of Hockey (1971)
Like the preceding series, this one deals with events and players in hockey. Since little has been written thus far about hockey, these books might be given extra consideration; hockey is an up-and-coming sport.

PROGRESS IN AMERICA SERIES   —Putnam
     Howard, Robert
         6036. The Boatmen (1967)

PROGRESS IN AMERICA SERIES —Putnam   (cont'd)
        6037. The Wagonmen (1964)
        Lens, Sidney
        6038. Workingmen: The Story of Labor (1960)
        Loening, Grover
        6039. Takeoff into Greatness (1968)
        McCaig, Robert
        6040. Electric Power in America (1970)
        Roseberry, C. R.
        6041. Steamboats and Steamboat Men (1966)
        Sobel, Robert, and Paul Sarnoff
        6042. Automobile Makers (1969)
The birth, development, and decline of various facets of American society and
industry are examined in this series. Authors provide technical information, anecdotes, and folk tales and legends surrounding each subject. A good addition to any
library.

PUNT, PASS AND KICK LIBRARY   —Random House
        Anderson, Dave
        6043. Great Defenseive Players of the N.F.L. (1967)
        6044. Great Pass Receivers of the N.F.L. (1966)
        6045. Great Quarterbacks of the N.F.L. (1965)
        Berger, Phil
        6046. Championship Teams of the N.F.L. (1968)
        Devaney, John
        6047. Star Pass Receivers of the N.F.L. (1972)
        Hand, Jack
        6048. Great Running Backs of the N.F.L. (1966)
        6049. Heroes of the N.F.L. (1965)
        Hollander, Zander
        6050. Great Moments in Pro Football (1969)
        6051. Strange But True Football Stories (1967)
        Kaplan, Richard
        6052. Great Linebackers of the N.F.L. (1970)
        6053. Great Upsets of the N.F.L. (1972)
        Libby, Bill
        6054. Star Quarterbacks of the N.F.L. (1970)
        6055. Star Running Backs of the N.F.L. (1971)
        Liss, Howard
        6056. The Making of a Rookie (1968)
        Pickens, Richard
        6057. How to Punt, Pass and Kick (1965)
        Rosenthal, Harold
        6058. The Big Play (1965)
Any boy and most reluctant readers should be attracted to this popular series,
with its numerous photographs. Both stars and lesser-known lights in football are
written about.

PUTNAM DOCUMENTARY HISTORY SERIES
        Cowie, L. W.
        6059. Plague and Fire (1970)
        6060. The Reformation of the Sixteenth Century (1970)
        Kendall, Alan
        6061. Medieval Pilgrims (1970)

175

PUTNAM DOCUMENTARY HISTORY SERIES (cont'd)
        Parkinson, Roger
                6062. The Origins of World War I (1970)
                6063. The Origins of World War II (1970)
        Rooke, Patrick
                6064. The Age of Dickens (1970)
Primary sources are used to give a picture of life during the eras under discussion.
Illustrations are taken from contemporary photographs and paintings of the time.
Diaries, letters, articles, and books written during the time are the basic sources.
Excellent material for grades 7 and up.

PUTNAM NATURAL FIELD BOOKS
        Alexander, W. B.
                6065. Birds of the Ocean (1963)
        Cochran, Doris, and Coleman Goin
                6066. The New Field Book of Reptiles and Amphibians (1970)
        Durand, Herbert
                6067. The Field Book of Common Ferns (1949)
        Hausman, Leon
                6068. The Field Book of Eastern Birds (1946)
        Hillcourt, William
                6069. The Field Book of Nature Activities and Conservation (1961)
                6070. The New Field Book of Nature Activities and Conservation (1970)
        Loomis, Frederic
                6071. The Field Book of Common Rocks and Minerals (1948)
        Mathews, F. Schuyler
                6072. The Field Book of American Trees and Shrubs (1915)
                6073. The Field Book of American Wild Flowers (1966)
        Mayall, R., Margaret Mayall, and William Olcott
                6074. The Field Book of the Skies (1954)
        Miner, Roy
                6075. The Field Book of Seashore Life (1950)
        Morgan, Ann
                6076. The Field Book of Ponds and Streams (1930)
        Rickett, Harold
                6077. The New Field Book of American Wildflowers (1963)
        Schmidt, Karl, and Dwight Davis
                6078. The Field Book of Snakes of the U.S. and Canada (1941)
        Thomas, William
                6079. The Field Book of Common Mushrooms (1948)
        Verill, A. Hyatt
                6080. Shell Collector's Handbook (1950)
Like the Golden Nature Series, this one is intended primarily as an identification
source. Each book provides drawings of plants and animals and a brief description
of them, along with their scientific names.

PUTNAM PICTORIAL SOURCES
        Crone, G. R.
                6081. The Voyages of Discovery (1970)
        Ellis, Keith
                6082. The American Civil War (1971)
        Fox, Levi
                6083. Shakespeare's England (1970)

PUTNAM PICTORIAL SOURCES (cont'd)
>   Hindley, Geoffrey
>   6084. The Medieval Establishment 1200-1500 (1970)
>   6085. The Medieval Warfare (1971)
>   Johnson, Douglas
>   6086. The French Revolution (1970)
>   Kochan, Lionel
>   6087. The Russian Revolution (1971)
>   Megan, Vincent, and Rhys Jones
>   6088. The Dawn of Man (1971)
>   Parkinson, Roger
>   6089. The American Revolution (1971)
>   Robottom, John
>   6090. Twentieth Century China (1970)

The social and historical themes that were important during a given period are illustrated by means of paintings, drawings, and artifacts from museums. Good supplementary material for grades 6 on up.

PUTNAM SPORTS SHELF
>   Allen, Lee
>   6091. Babe Ruth: His Story in Baseball (1956)
>   6092. Dizzy Dean (1967)
>   Ashford, Jeffrey
>   6093. See Fiction Series
>   Cepeda, Orlando, and Charles Einstein
>   6094. My Ups and Downs in Baseball (1968)
>   Crossetti, Frank
>   6095. Secrets of Baserunning and Infield Play (1966)
>   Daley, Arthur
>   6096. All the Home Run Kings (1972)
>   6097. Kings of the Home Run (1962)
>   Devaney, John
>   6098. Bob Cousy (1965)
>   6099. Great Olympic Champions (1967)
>   6100. Juan Marichal: Mr. Strike (1970)
>   6101. Pro Quarterbacks (1966)
>   6102. The Greatest Cardinals of Them All (1968)
>   Douglas, James McM.
>   6103. See Fiction Series
>   Einstein, Charles
>   6104. Willie Mays: Coast to Coast Giant (1963)
>   Gelman, Steve
>   6105. The Greatest Dodgers of Them All (1968)
>   Gibson, Althea, and Richard Curtis
>   6106. So Much to Live For (1968)
>   Gibson, Michael
>   6107. LeMans: Twice around the Clock (1964)
>   Graham, Frank
>   6108. Lou Gehrig: A Quiet Hero (1942)
>   Greene, Lee
>   6109. The Johnny Unitas Story (1962)
>   Hano, Arnold
>   6110. Roberto Clemente: Batting King (1968)
>   6111. Sandy Koufax: Strikeout King (1964)

    6112. The Greatest Giants of Them All (1967)
Hegan, Jim
    6113. Secrets of Catching (1968)
Higdon, Hal
    6114. Thirty Days in May: The Indy 500 (1971)
Hirshberg, Al
    6115. Baseball's Greatest Catchers (1966)
    6116. Basketball's Greatest Stars (1963)
    6117. Basketball's Greatest Teams (1966)
    6118. Glory Runners (1967)
    6119. Henry Aaron: Quiet Superstar (1969)
    6120. The Greatest American Leaguers (1970)
Johnson, Chuck
    6121. The Greatest Packers of Them All (1968)
Klein, Larry
    6122. Jim Brown: The Running Back (1965)
Kramer, George
    6123. Kid Battery (1968)
    6124. The Left Hander (1964)
Lardner, Rex
    6125. Great Golfers (1970)
Lent, Henry
    6126. The "X" Cars: Detroit's One-of-a-Kind Autos (1971)
Libby, Bill
    6127. Ernie Banks: Mr. Cub (1971)
    6128. Fran Tarkenton (1970)
    6129. Johnny Bench: The Little General (1972)
    6130. Pete Rose: They Call Him Charlie Hustle (1972)
Lipman, David
    6131. Joe Namath: A Football Legend (1968)
    6132. Ken Boyer (1967)
    6133. Mr. Baseball: The Story of Branch Rickey (1966)
Lovelace, Delos
    6134. Rockne of Notre Dame (1957)
McCormick, Wilfred
    6135. Rookie on First (1967)
MacPherson, Tom
    6136. Dragging and Driving (1960)
    6137. Dragging, Driving and Basic Customizing (1972)
Mays, Willie, and Charles Einstein
    6138. Learn to Play Ball (1965)
Newcombe, Jack
    6139. The Fireballers: Baseball's Fastest Pitchers (1964)
Nolan, William
    6140. Steve McQueen: Star on Wheels (1972)
Olney, Ross
    6141. Great Dragging Wagons (1970)
    6142. Kings of Motor Speed (1970)
    6143. Kings of the Drag Strip (1969)
Olney, Ross, and Richard Graham
    6144. Kings of the Surf (1970)
Orr, Frank
    6145. Hockey's Greatest Stars (1970)

PUTNAM SPORTS SHELF   (cont'd)
>Owens, Jesse, and Paul Neimark
>>6146. The Jesse Owens Story (1970)
>Robinson, Ray
>>6147. Baseball's Most Colorful Managers (1969)
>>6148. Speed Kings of the Base Paths (1964)
>>6149. Stan Musial: Baseball's Durable Man (1963)
>>6150. Ted Williams (1962)
>>6151. The Greatest Yankees of Them All (1969)
>Rubin, Robert
>>6152. Tony Conigliaro: Up from Despair (1971)
>Schoor, Gene
>>6153. Mickey Mantle of the Yankees (1959)
>>6154. Roy Campanella: A Man of Courage (1959)
>>6155. Willie Mays: Modest Champion (1960)
>Silverman, Al
>>6156. Heroes of the World Series (1964)
>>6157. Mickey Mantle: Mr. Yankee (1963)
>>6158. More Sports Titans of the Twentieth Century (1969)
>>6159. Sports Titans of the Twentieth Century (1968)
>Stambler, Irwin
>>6160. Great Moments in Stock Car Racing (1971)
>Storey, Edward
>>6161. Secrets of Kicking the Football (1971)
>Sullivan, George
>>6162. Bart Starr: Cool Quarterback (1970)
>>6163. Pro Football's Unforgettable Games (1967)
>>6164. Tom Seaver of the Mets (1971)
>Turley, Bob
>>6165. Secrets of Pitching (1965)
>Wells, Bob
>>6166. The Saga of Shorty Gone (1969)
>>6167. See Fiction Series

Biographies, famous incidents in sports history, and instructional books are combined in this sports series. Photographs are not plentiful, but many lesser-known sports figures are included among the biographees. For grades 5 through 9.

RAINBOW CLASSICS SERIES   —World
>Alcott, Louisa May
>>6168. Eight Cousins (1948)
>>6169. Jack and Jill (1948)
>>6170. Jo's Boys (1957)
>>6171. Little Women (1969)
>>6172. Old-Fashioned Girl (1947)
>Andersen, Hans Christian
>>6173. Andersen's Fairy Tales (1946)
>Becker, May
>>6174. The Book of Bible Stories (1948)
>>6175. The Rainbow Mother Goose (1947)
>Bronte, Charlotte
>>6176. Jane Eyre (1946)
>Bronte, Emily
>>6177. Wuthering Heights (1947)

RAINBOW CLASSICS SERIES —World (cont'd)
>Carroll, Lewis
>>6178. Alice's Adventures in Wonderland and Through the Looking
>>>Glass (1946)
>Collodi, Carlo
>>6179. Pinocchio (1946)
>Cooper, James Fenimore
>>6180. The Last of the Mohicans (1957)
>Defoe, Daniel
>>6181. Robinson Crusoe (1946)
>Dickens, Charles
>>6182. Christmas Stories (1946)
>Dodge, Mary Mapes
>>6183. Hans Brinker or The Silver Skates (1945)
>Grimm, Jacob, and Wilhelm Grimm
>>6184. Grimm's Fairy Tales (1947)
>MacLeod, Mary
>>6185. King Arthur and His Knights (1950)
>Mulock, Dinah Maria
>>6186. The Little Lame Prince (1948)
>Ruskin, John
>>6187. King of the Golden River (1946)
>Sidney, Margaret
>>6188. Five Little Peppers (1950)
>Spyri, Johanna
>>6189. Heidi (1972)
>Stevenson, Robert Louis
>>6190. Kidnapped (1947)
>>6191. Treasure Island (1972)
>Swift, Jonathan
>>6192. Gulliver's Travels (1947)
>Twain, Mark
>>6193. The Adventures of Huckleberry Finn (1947)
>>6194. The Adventures of Tom Sawyer (1972)
>>6195. The Prince and the Pauper (1948)
>Verne, Jules
>>6196. Mysterious Island (1947)
>>6197. 20,000 Leagues under the Sea (1972)
>Wyss, Johann
>>6198. Swiss Family Robinson (1972)

Although this series of children's classics features an introduction to each volume and illustrations throughout the books, the format is not as appealing as that of Macmillan's similar series.

RAINBOW GIANTS SERIES —World
>Craven, Thomas
>>6199. The Rainbow Book of Art (1956)
>Gwynne, J. Harold
>>6200. The Rainbow Book of Bible Stories (1956)
>Leach, Maria
>>6201. The Rainbow Book of American Folktales and Legends (1958)
>Mead, Margaret
>>6202. People and Places (1959)

RAINBOW GIANTS SERIES —World (cont'd)
>   Miers, Earl Schenck
>   6203. The Rainbow Book of American History (1958)
>   Peattie, Donald
>   6204. The Rainbow Book of Nature (1957)
>   Wright, Wendell
>   6205. The Rainbow Dictionary (1972)

These oversized books, with lavish illustrations, are indexed so that they can be used with school work as well as for pleasure reading. An attractive addition to any collection.

RANDALL, RUTH —Lippincott
>   6206. I Elizabeth: A Biography of the Girl Who Married General George Armstrong Custer (1966)
>   6207. I Jessie: A Biography of the Girl Who Married John Charles Fremont (1963)
>   6208. I Mary: A Biography of the Girl Who Married Abraham Lincoln (1959)
>   6209. I Ruth: The Autobiography of a Marriage (1968)
>   6210. I Varina: A Biography of the Girl Who Married Jefferson Davis (1962)

Concentrating primarily on the adult married life of the women involved, these books generally begin with the meeting of the future couple and then turn their attention to the marriage. There is no fictionalization here, and the author uses many quotes from the writing of the subjects themselves. All books are indexed. Excellent additions to a collection.

RANDOM HOUSE SCIENCE LIBRARY
>   Dietz, David
>   6211. Stars and the Universe (1968)
>   Freeman, Ira
>   6212. Light and Radiation (1968)
>   6213. Sound and Ultrasonics (1968)
>   Freeman, Ira, and A. Rae Patton
>   6214. The Science of Chemistry (1968)
>   Lauber, Patricia
>   6215. The Planets (1968)
>   6216. This Restless Earth (1970)
>   Patton, A. Rae
>   6217. The Chemistry of Life (1970)
>   Simon, Seymour
>   6218. Weather and Climate (1969)

Detailed explanations and extensive illustrations are the features of these good basic texts. Important new terms are printed in boldface type. For grades 4 through 6.

RANDOM HOUSE SPORTS LIBRARY
>   Gibson, Jerry
>   6219. Big League Batboy (1970)
>   Lake, John
>   6220. Jim Ryun: Master of the Mile (1968)
>   Orr, Frank
>   6221. The World's Great Race Drivers (1972)

RANDOM HOUSE SPORTS LIBRARY (cont'd)
The same general format as the other Random House sports series. The subjects of these books, however, are more unusual than the others.

READ ABOUT SERIES —Watts
        Klagsbrun, Francine
                6222. Read about the Librarian (1970)
                6223. Read about the Parkman (1971)
                6224. Read about the Sanitation Man (1972)
                6225. Read about the Teacher (1970)
        Slobodkin, Louis
                6226. Read about the Busman (1967)
                6227. Read about the Fireman (1967)
                6228. Read about the Policeman (1966)
                6229. Read about the Postman (1966)
The authors discuss the history of these civil service jobs, what the jobs are like today, and career possibilities. Print is large and illustrations are plentiful, and the books present considerably more detail than is usually found in books of this sort for beginning readers. The series can be used with reluctant readers as well as with children from grades 3 and 4.

REAL WORLD SERIES —Lerner
        Jones, Claire
                6230. Pollution: The Air We Breathe (1971)
                6231. Pollution: The Balance of Nature (1972)
                6232. Pollution: The Dangerous Atom (1972)
                6233. Pollution: The Food We Eat (1972)
                6234. Pollution: The Land We Live On (1971)
                6235. Pollution: The Noise We Hear (1971)
                6236. Pollution: The Population Explosion (1972)
                6237. Pollution: The Waters of the Earth (1971)
A truly outstanding series on all aspects of pollution, more comprehensive than any other. Illustrations are plentiful, and the books are full of information. All volumes are indexed. A must.

REASON WHY BOOKS —John Day
        Adler, Irving, and Ruth Adler
                6238. Air (1972)
                6239. Atomic Energy (1971)
                6240. Atoms and Molecules (1966)
                6241. Coal (1965)
                6242. Communications (1967)
                6243. Directions and Angles (1969)
                6244. Energy (1970)
                6245. Evolution (1965)
                6246. Fibers (1964)
                6247. Heat (1964)
                6248. Houses: From Cave to Skyscraper (1965)
                6249. Insects and Plants (1962)
                6250. Integers: Positive and Negative (1972)
                6251. Irrigation (1964)
                6252. Language and Man (1970)
                6253. Learning about Steel (1961)
                6254. Machines (1964)

REASON WHY BOOKS —John Day (cont'd)
   6255. Magnets (1966)
   6256. Numbers Old and New (1960)
   6257. Numerals (1964)
   6258. Oceans (1962)
   6259. Rivers (1961)
   6260. Sets (1967)
   6261. Shadows (1968)
   6262. Storms (1963)
   6263. Taste, Touch and Smell (1966)
   6264. The Calendar (1967)
   6265. The Earth's Crust (1963)
   6266. Things That Spin (1960)
   6267. Tree Products (1966)
   6268. Why, a Book of Reasons (1961)
   6269. Why and How? (1963)
   6270. Your Ears (1963)
   6271. Your Eyes (1963)

Although these volumes are slender, the text is not exceptionally simple, so the series would have limited use with reluctant readers. The drawings are clear and the authors do provide a guide to pronunciation, but there is no index. For grades 3 to 6.

REGIONAL AMERICAN STORIES SERIES —Garrard
  Bradford, Lois
   6272. Here Come the Racing Ducks (1972)
  Hall, Lynn
   6273. The Famous Battle of Bravery Creek (1972)
  Nesbitt, Rosemary
   6274. Colonel Meacham's Mountains: The Journey of Five Black
      Children (1972)

At the time of publication, this series has not yet appeared, so judgment will have to be suspended here.

REVOLUTIONS OF OUR TIME SERIES —Praeger
  Barclay, Glen
   6275. Twentieth Century Nationalism (1972)
  Vaizey, John
   6276. Capitalism (1972)
   6277. Social Democracy (1972)

Important political movements during our time are the subjects of these books. Lavish illustrations help to picture the violence and upheaval involved. For grades 7 on up.

RICHES OF THE EARTH SERIES —Messner
  Esterer, Arnulf, and Louise Esterer
   6278. Food (1969)
  Harrison, C. William
   6279. Forests (1969)
   6280. Rivers (1967)
   6281. Wildlife (1970)
  Neal, Harry
   6282. Oil (1970)

RICHES OF THE EARTH SERIES —Messner (cont'd)
While emphasizing conservation, these books also provide information on various
aspects of natural history and natural products. Each book investigates the history
of the topic, its use in the past and in the present, and its future use and abuse.
For grades 5 through 9.

RIPLEY, ELIZABETH
      6283. Botticelli (Lippincott, 1960)
      6284. Copley (Lippincott, 1967)
      6285. Durer (Lippincott, 1958)
      6286. Gainsborough (Lippincott, 1964)
      6287. Goya (Walck, 1956)
      6288. Hokusai (Lippincott, 1968)
      6289. Leonardo da Vinci (Walck, 1952)
      6290. Michelangelo (Walck, 1963)
      6291. Picasso (Lippincott, 1959)
      6292. Raphael (Lippincott, 1961)
      6293. Rembrandt (Walck, 1955)
      6294. Rodin (Lippincott, 1966)
      6295. Rubens (Walck, 1957)
      6296. Titian (Lippincott, 1962)
      6297. Velasquez (Lippincott, 1965)
      6298. Vincent Van Gogh (Walck, 1954)
      6299. Winslow Homer (Lippincott, 1963)
A page of text alternates with a reproduction of one of the artist's works. Although
the books are primarily biographies, some information is also given on the style
of painting, philosophy, and the paintings reproduced in the book. There are
bibliographies and indices in each book.

RIVER SERIES —McGraw-Hill
    Davenport, William
      6300. The Seine: From Its Source to Paris, to the Sea (1968)
    Komroff, Manuel
      6301. The Hudson: From Lake Tear of the Clouds to New York
           Harbor (1969)
    McKown, Robin
      6302. The Congo: River of Mystery (1968)
    Malkus, Alida
      6303. The Amazon: River of Promise (1970)
    Solomon, Louis
      6304. The Mississippi: America's Mainstream (1971)
    Warren, Ruth
      6305. The Nile: The Story of Pharoahs, Farmers, and Explorers (1968)
This series discusses the historical origins of each of these major rivers, as well as the
geography surrounding them, the people who live on their banks, famous events
that occurred on them, customs, legends, and beliefs that surround them. For
grades 7 on up.

RIVERS OF THE WORLD SERIES —Garrard
    Carmer, Elizabeth, and Carl Carmer
      6306. The Susquehanna: From New York to the Chesapeake (1964)
    Crosby, Alexander
      6307. The Colorado: Mover of Mountains (1961)
      6308. The Rimac: River of Peru (1966)

RIVERS OF THE WORLD SERIES —Garrard (cont'd)
    6309. The Rio Grande: Life for the Desert (1966)
Epstein, Samuel, and Beryl Epstein
    6310. The Sacramento: Golden River of California (1968)
Lambie, Beatrice
    6311. The Mackenzie: River to the Top of the World (1967)
Latham, Jean
    6312. The Chagres: Power of the Panama Canal (1964)
    6313. The Columbia: Powerhouse of North America (1967)
Lauber, Patricia
    6314. The Congo: River into Central Africa (1964)
    6315. The Mississippi: Giant at Work (1961)
McNeer, May
    6316. The Hudson: River of History (1962)
Nowlan, Nora
    6317. The Shannon: River of Loughs and Legends (1965)
    6318. The Tiber: The Roman River (1967)
Spencer, Cornelia
    6319. The Yangtze: China's River Highway (1963)
Sperry, Armstrong
    6320. The Amazon: River Sea of Brazil (1961)
Streatfeild, Noel
    6321. The Thames: London's River (1964)
VonMaltitz, Frances
    6322. The Rhone: River of Contrasts (1965)
Watson, Jane
    6323. The Indus: South Asia's Highway of History (1970)
    6324. The Niger: Africa's River of Mystery (1971)
Weingarten, Violet
    6325. The Ganges: Sacred River of India (1969)
    6326. The Jordan: River of the Promised Land (1967)
    6327. The Nile: Lifeline of Egypt (1964)
White, Anne Terry
    6328. The St. Lawrence: Seaway of North America (1961)
Wilson, Hazel
    6329. The Seine: River of Paris (1962)
Like the preceding series, this one presents information on all facets of these rivers.
Many photographs, old prints, and maps enhance the appeal of the books. For
grades 4 through 7.

ROCKWELL, ANNE —Atheneum
    6330. Filippo's Dome (1967)
    6331. Glass, Stones and Crown (1968)
    6332. Temple on a Hill (1969)
Three architectural triumphs are the subjects of these books: 1) Brunelleschi and
the Dome of St. Mary of the Flowers in Florence; 2) Abbe Suger and the development of the Gothic arch; 3) the Parthenon. Fine supplemental material with good
clear illustrations.

SAGAS OF THE WEST SERIES —Putnam
    Casewit, Curtis
    6333. The Adventures of Snowshoe Thompson (1970)
    Chester, Michael
    6334. First Wagons to California (1965)

SAGAS OF THE WEST SERIES —Putnam (cont'd)
   6335. Forts of Old California (1967)
   6336. Joseph Strauss: Builder of the Golden Gate Bridge (1965)
  Lauritzen, Jonreed
   6337. Colonel Anza's Impossible Journey (1966)
   6338. The Battle of San Pasqual (1968)
  Miller, Helen Markley
   6339. The San Francisco Earthquake and Fire (1970)
  Muir, Jean
   6340. The Adventures of Grizzly Adams (1970)
True stories of the West told in narrative fashion. While their use in school courses
might be limited, they will nevertheless provide interesting, exciting, and stimulating
reading for grades 5 through 7.

SCHLOAT, G. WARREN —Knopf
   6341. Conchita and Juan, a Girl and Boy of Mexico (1964)
   6342. Duee, a Boy of Liberia (1962)
   6343. Fay Gow, a Boy of Hong Kong (1964)
   6344. Fernando and Marta, a Boy and Girl of Spain (1970)
   6345. Johnnyshah, a Boy of Iran (1963)
   6346. Junichi, a Boy of Japan (1964)
   6347. Kwaku, a Boy of Ghana (1962)
   6348. Maria and Ramon, a Girl and Boy of Puerto Rico (1966)
   6349. Naim, a Boy of Turkey (1963)
   6350. Prapan, a Boy of Thailand (1963)
   6351. Uttam, a Boy of India (1963)
These photo stories about children from different lands generally supply only one
sentence of explanation under each picture. The information conveyed is obviously
minimal.

SCIENCE DISCOVERY SERIES —Childrens Press
  Challand, Helen J., and Elizabeth Brandt
   6352. Science Activities from A to Z (1963)
  National College of Education
   6353. Young People's Science Dictionary (1964)
  Neal, Charles
   6354. Exploring Light and Color (1964)
   6355. Safe and Simple Projects with Electricity (1965)
  Pacilio, James
   6356. Discovering Aerospace (1965)
  Podendorf, Illa
   6357. Discovering Science on Your Own (1962)
   6358. 101 Science Experiments (1960)
These experiments have easy-to-follow directions and use equipment that is either
already in the home or classroom or very easily obtainable. Good for grades 3 to 6.

SCIENCE EXPERIENCES SERIES —Watts
  Bendick, Jeanne
   6359. Adaptation (1971)
   6360. Heat and Temperature (1972)
   6361. Living Things (1969)
   6362. Measuring (1971)
   6363. Motion and Gravity (1972)
   6364. Names, Sets and Numbers (1971)

SCIENCE EXPERIENCES SERIES —Watts (cont'd)
>6365. Shapes (1968)
>6366. Space and Time (1968)
>6367. The Human Senses (1968)
>Simon, Seymour
>>6368. Science at Work (1971)

The large illustrations and simple format of this series will attract beginning and reluctant readers. Many of these books duplicate subjects in the Reason Why series, but the information here is not as detailed so it may have more appeal to younger and reluctant readers. The series is indexed.

SCIENCE EXPLORER SERIES —Putnam
>Frimmer, Steven
>>6369. Finding the Forgotten (1971)
>>6370. The Stone That Spoke (1969)
>Golding, Morton
>>6371. Bridges (1967)
>Hapgood, Charles
>>6372. Great Mysteries of the Earth (1960)
>Scharff, Robert
>>6373. Rays and Radiation (1960)
>Smith, George
>>6374. Mathematics: The Language of Science (1961)
>Wolfe, Louis
>>6375. The Deepest Hole in the World: The Story of the Project Mohole (1963)

The aim of these books is to provide a basic introduction to various facets of science on the level of fourth to sixth grade. Unfortunately, drawings and illustrations are not very plentiful (and in some cases not very clear), and not all volumes of the series are indexed.

SCIENCE IN ACTION SERIES —Putnam
>Bergaust, Erik
>>6376. Aircraft Carriers in Action (1967)
>>6377. Convertiplanes in Action (1969)
>Bergaust, Erik, and William O. Foss
>>6378. Coast Guard in Action (1962)
>>6379. Helicopters in Action (1962)
>>6380. Oceanographers in Action (1968)
>>6381. Skin Divers in Action (1965)

All aspects of a given subject are examined, from building or training to the various jobs that are performed. The treatment is extensive and the photographs are plentiful. Excellent for use with social studies assignments.

SCIENCE IN THE CITY SERIES —McGraw-Hill
>Tannenbaum, Beulah, and Myra Stillman
>>6382. City Traffic (1972)
>>6383. Feeding the City (1971)

This new series examines the various modern manufacturing and scientific achievements that ensure the smooth running of major cities. Many photos and an index increase the usability for classes in civics and social studies.

SCIENCE INQUIRY PROJECT SERIES —Prentice-Hall
    Stone, A. Harris, and Dale Ingmanson
        6384. Crystals from the Sea: A Look at Salt (1969)
        6385. Drop by Drop: A Look at Water (1969)
        6386. Rocks and Rills: A Look at Geology (1967)
    Stone, A. Harris, and Irving Leskowitz
        6387. Animals Are Like This (1968)
        6388. Microbes Are Something Else (1969)
        6389. Plants Are Like That (1969)
    Stone, A. Harris, and Bertram Siegel
        6390. Have a Ball (1969)
        6391. Puttering with Paper (1968)
        6392. Take a Balloon (1967)
        6393. The Chemistry of a Lemon (1966)
        6394. The Chemistry of Soap (1968)
        6395. The Heat's On (1970)
        6396. Turned On: A Look at Electricity (1970)
    Stone, A. Harris, and Herbert Spiegel
        6397. The Winds of Weather (1969)
The texts in this series ask questions and then set up experiments to answer them.
There is little actual information provided on each subject, since the approach is
for readers to learn by experiment rather than by being told. No index is provided,
but there is a glossary of terms for each volume.

SCIENCE PARADE SERIES —Harvey
    Dean, Anabel
        6398. Men under the Sea (1972)
    Elting, Mary
        6399. Water Come, Water Go (1964)
    Elting, Mary, and Michael Folsom
        6400. The Secret Story of Pueblo Bonito (1963)
    Georgiou, Constantine
        6401. Wait and See (1962)
        6402. Whitey and Whiskers and Food (1964)
    Greene, Carla
        6403. Let's Meet the Chemist (1966)
        6404. Where Does a Letter Go? (1966)
    Harvey, Fran
        6405. Why Does It Rain? (1969)
    Hendrickson, Walter
        6406. Apollo 11: Men to the Moon (1970)
        6407. What's Going on in Space (1969)
        6408. Wild Wings (1969)
    Klein, Lenore
        6409. How Old Is Old? (1967)
        6410. Just a Minute: A Book about Time (1969)
        6411. What Is an Inch? (1966)
    Lee, Joan
        6412. Watch for the Clouds (1966)
    Mitchell, Arthur
        6413. First Aid for Insects and Much More (1964)
    Rosenfeld, Sam
        6414. A Drop of Water (1970)

SCIENCE PARADE SERIES —Harvey (cont'd)
>   Ruchlis, Hy
>   >   6415. Thank You, Mr. Sun (1957)
>   >   6416. What Makes Me Tick (1957)
>   >   6417. Your Changing Earth (1963)
>   VanGelder, Richard
>   >   6418. The Professor and the Mysterious Box (1964)
>   >   6419. The Professor and the Vanishing Flags (1965)
>   Waters, John
>   >   6420. Saltmarshes and Shifting Dunes (1970)
>   Wood, F. Dorothy
>   >   6421. The Bear Family (1966)
>   >   6422. The Cat Family (1968)
>   >   6423. The Deer Family (1969)

Simplified explanations of various aspects of science, sometimes in narrative form, typify these books. The illustrations are drawings rather than photographs; in some cases, photographs would have been far more effective. The books are indexed. For grades 3 to 5.

SCIENCE SURVEY SERIES —Putnam
>   Baldwin, Gordon
>   >   6424. America's Buried Past: The Story of North American Archaeology (1962)
>   >   6425. How the Indians Really Lived (1967)
>   >   6426. Race against Time: The Story of Salvage Archaeology (1966)
>   >   6427. The World of Prehistory: The Story of Man's Beginnings (1963)
>   Becker, Beril
>   >   6428. Mechanical Man (1959)
>   Black, Archibald
>   >   6429. Engineering (1965)
>   Boyd, Waldo
>   >   6430. The World of Cryogenics (1968)
>   Chester, Michael
>   >   6431. Robots in Space (1965)
>   Chester, Michael, and David McClinton
>   >   6432. The Moon (1963)
>   Faber, Doris
>   >   6433. Captive Rivers: The Story of Big Dams (1966)
>   >   6434. The Miracle of Vitamins (1964)
>   Friedman, Estelle
>   >   6435. Digging into Yesterday (1958)
>   >   6536. Man in the Making (1960)
>   Hellman, Hal
>   >   6437. The Right Size: Why Some Creatures Survive and Others Are Extinct (1968)
>   Ludovici, L. J.
>   >   6438. Great Tree of Life: Natural History of Living Creatures (1963)
>   >   6439. Links of Life: The Story of Heredity (1961)
>   >   6440. Origins of Language (1965)
>   >   6441. Seeing Near and Seeing Far: The Story of Microscopes and Telescopes (1967)
>   >   6442. The World of the Microscope (1958)
>   McNeel, John
>   >   6443. The Brain of Man (1968)

SCIENCE SURVEY SERIES —Putnam (cont'd)
    Newcomb, Ellsworth, and Hugh Kenny
        6444. Alchemy to Atoms (1961)
        6445. Miracle Fabrics (1957)
        6446. Miracle Glass (1968)
        6447. Miracle Metals (1962)
        6448. Miracle Plastics (1965)
    Place, Marian
        6449. Our Earth: The Story of Geology (1961)
    Silverberg, Robert
        6450. Four Men Who Changed the Universe (1968)
    Stephens, William
        6451. Science beneath the Sea: The Story of Oceanography (1966)
    Winchester, James
        6452. Hurricanes, Storms, Tornadoes (1968)
    Woodburn, John
        6453. Know Your Skin (1967)
Although this is a very readable series, the lack of illustrations decreases the eye-appeal, especially for poorer readers. On the other hand, the authors provide a bibliography, a glossary, and an index, as well as information on subjects such as cryogenics, not found in other series. For grades 5 through 9.

SCIENTISTS AT WORK SERIES —John Day
    Berger, Melvin
        6454. Animal Hospital (1972)
        6455. Oceanography Lab (1972)
        6456. South Pole Station (1971)
        6457. The National Weather Service (1971)
The work taking place in various important laboratories is examined in these clear, concise accounts. The books cover both the everyday activities and the research activities of the scientists. For grades 8 through 10.

SCRIBNER ILLUSTRATED CLASSICS
    Baldwin, James
        6458. The Story of Roland (1930)
        6459. The Story of Siegfried (1931)
    Boyd, James
        6460. Drums (1928)
    Burnett, Frances Hodgson
        6461. A Little Princess (1938)
    Cooper, James Fenimore
        6462. The Deerslayer (1953)
        6463. The Last of the Mohicans (1947)
    Creswick, Paul
        6464. Robin Hood (1957)
    Defoe, Daniel
        6465. Robinson Crusoe (1957)
    Dodge, Mary Mapes
        6466. Hans Brinker (1943)
    Field, Eugene
        6467. Poems of Childhood (1904)
    Grimm, Jacob, and Wilhelm Grimm
        6468. Grimm's Fairy Tales (1948)

SCRIBNER ILLUSTRATED CLASSICS (cont'd)
>James, Will
>>6469. Smoky (1929)
>Kingsley, Charles
>>6470. Westward, Ho! (1948)
>Lanier, Sidney
>>6471. The Boy's King Arthur (1952)
>Marryat, Captain
>>6472. The Children of the New Forest (1927)
>Porter, Jane
>>6473. The Scottish Chiefs (1921)
>Rawlings, Marjorie Kinnan
>>6474. The Yearling (1967)
>Scott, Walter
>>6475. Quentin Durward (1923)
>Sherman, Henry, and Charles Kent
>>6476. The Children's Bible (1922)
>Spyri, Johanna
>>6477. Heidi (1958)
>Stevenson, Robert Louis
>>6478. A Child's Garden of Verses (1905)
>>6479. David Balfour (1952)
>>6480. Kidnapped (1941)
>>6481. The Black Arrow (1944)
>>6482. Treasure Island (1939)
>Verne, Jules
>>6483. Michael Strogoff (1927)
>>6484. Mysterious Island (1946)
>>6485. Twenty Thousand Leagues under the Sea (1953)
>Wiggin, Kate Douglas
>>6486. The Arabian Nights (1909)

Perhaps the oldest classic series in print, this is still one of the best. The print is large, and the illustrations, by such well-known artists as N. C. Wyeth, are excellent. Some of the titles in this series are not available in the others.

SEE-AND-READ BIOGRAPHIES —Putnam
>Dines, Glen
>>6487. Crazy Horse (1966)
>Graves, Charles
>>6488. Mark Twain (1972)
>Martin, Patricia Miles
>>6489. Abraham Lincoln (1964)
>>6490. Andrew Jackson (1966)
>>6491. Daniel Boone (1965)
>>6492. Dolly Madison (1967)
>>6493. Jacqueline Kennedy Onassis (1969)
>>6494. James Madison (1970)
>>6495. Jefferson Davis (1966)
>>6496. John Fitzgerald Kennedy (1964)
>>6497. Pocahontas (1964)
>>6498. Thomas Edison (1971)
>>6499. Zachary Taylor (1969)
>Olds, Helen
>>6500. Christopher Columbus (1964)

SEE-AND-READ BIOGRAPHIES —Putnam (cont'd)
  6501. Lyndon Baines Johnson (1965)
  6502. Richard Nixon (1970)
Paradis, Adrian
  6503. Henry Ford (1968)
Thompson, Vivian
  6504. George Washington (1964)
Voight, Virginia
  6505. Nathan Hale (1965)
  6506. Sacajawea (1967)
Wise, William
  6507. Booker T. Washington (1968)
  6508. Franklin Delano Roosevelt (1967)
While these biographies have a second-grade vocabulary, the content is still mature enough to interest reluctant readers through grade 4. The only difficulty with the series is the use of vague illustrations rather than photographs or more detailed drawings.

SIGNATURE BOOKS —Grosset
Baker, Nina
  6509. The Story of Abraham Lincoln (1952)
  6510. The Story of Christopher Columbus (1952)
Beckhard, Arthur
  6511. The Story of Dwight D. Eisenhower (1956)
Bontemps, Arna
  6512. The Story of George Washington Carver (1954)
Collier, Edmund
  6513. The Story of Annie Oakley (1956)
  6514. The Story of Buffalo Bill (1953)
DeLeeuw, Adele
  6515. The Story of Amelia Earhart (1955)
Douty, Esther
  6516. The Story of Stephen Foster (1954)
Graham, Shirley
  6517. The Story of Pocahontas (1953)
Hickok, Lorena
  6518. The Story of Eleanor Roosevelt (1959)
  6519. The Story of Franklin D. Roosevelt (1956)
  6520. The Story of Helen Keller (1958)
Howard, James
  6521. The Story of John J. Audubon (1954)
  6522. The Story of Louisa May Alcott (1955)
  6523. The Story of Mark Twain (1953)
  6524. The Story of Robert Louis Stevenson (1958)
Kaufman, Helen
  6525. The Story of Beethoven (1958)
  6526. The Story of Haydn (1962)
  6527. The Story of Mozart (1955)
Kjelgaard, Jim
  6528. The Story of Geronimo (1958)
Leighton, Margaret
  6529. The Story of Florence Nightingale (1952)
  6530. The Story of General Custer (1954)

SIGNATURE BOOKS —Grosset (cont'd)
    Malkus, Alida
        6531. The Story of Louis Pasteur (1952)
        6532. The Story of Winston Churchill (1957)
    Meadowcroft, Enid
        6533. The Story of Andrew Jackson (1953)
        6534. The Story of Benjamin Franklin (1952)
        6535. The Story of Crazy Horse (1954)
        6536. The Story of George Washington (1952)
        6537. The Story of Thomas Alva Edison (1952)
    Miers, Earl Schenck
        6538. The Story of Thomas Jefferson (1955)
    Neilson, Winthrop
        6539. The Story of Theodore Roosevelt (1953)
    Nolan, Jeanette
        6540. The Story of Joan of Arc (1953)
        6541. The Story of Martha Washington (1954)
        6542. The Story of Ulysses S. Grant (1952)
    Price, Olive
        6543. The Story of Clara Barton (1954)
        6544. The Story of Marco Polo (1953)
    Steele, William O.
        6545. The Story of Daniel Boone (1953)
    Thorne, Alice
        6546. The Story of Madame Curie (1959)
    Vinton, Iris
        6547. The Story of Edith Cavell (1959)
        6548. The Story of John Paul Jones (1953)
        6549. The Story of President Kennedy (1964)
        6550. The Story of Robert E. Lee (1952)
    Webb, Robert
        6551. The Story of Dan Beard (1958)
    Wilson, Hazel
        6552. The Story of Lafayette (1952)
        6553. The Story of Mad Anthony Wayne (1953)
This biography series is not recommended. The quality of paper and binding is poor and the life stories are fictionalized. The authors provide no index or bibliography.

SPACESHIP EARTH SERIES —World
    Hunter, Mel
        6554. How Man Began (1972)
        6555. How Plants Began (1972)
        6556. How the Earth Began (1972)
        6557. How the Fishes Began (1972)
At the time of publication, the volumes of this series were still to be published. For this reason, judgment must be suspended.

SPEED SPORTS SERIES —Lippincott
    Gladstone, Gary
        6558. Dune Buggies (1972)
    Halacy, Dan
        6559. Soaring (1972)

SPEED SPORTS SERIES —Lippincott (cont'd)
>   Klein, H. Arthur
>   > 6560. Surf-Riding (1972)
>   Morgan, Julie
>   > 6561. Drag Racing (1971)
>   > 6562. Model Airplane Racing (1972)
>   > 6563. Snowmobiles (1971)
>   > 6564. Speedboat Racing (1972)
>   Seaver, David-Linn
>   > 6565. Mini-Bike Racing (1972)
>   > 6566. Moto-Cross Racing (1972)

These slender volumes consist mainly of photographs with a paragraph of information beneath them. At best, this series will arouse interest in youngters for various speed sports. It has little value beyond that.

SPICER, DOROTHY —Coward
>   > 6567. Thirteen Devils (1967)
>   > 6568. Thirteen Ghosts (1965)
>   > 6569. Thirteen Giants (1966)
>   > 6570. Thirteen Goblins (1969)
>   > 6571. Thirteen Jolly Saints (1970)
>   > 6572. Thirteen Monsters (1964)
>   > 6573. Thirteen Rascals (1971)
>   > 6574. Thirteen Witches—Two Wizards, the Devil and a Pack of
>   > > Goblins (1963)

Ms. Spicer collected these tales during her travels in foreign countries, and she later adapted them into this series. Both legends and folktales are included. A good bet for the storyteller.

SPIES OF THE WORLD SERIES —Putnam
>   DeLeeuw, Adele
>   > 6575. Edith Cavell: Nurse, Spy, Heroine (1968)
>   DeLeeuw, Cateau
>   > 6576. Benedict Arnold: Hero and Traitor (1970)
>   Duncan, Lois
>   > 6577. Major Andre: Brave Enemy (1969)
>   Faber, Doris
>   > 6578. Rose Greenhow: Spy for the Confederacy (1968)
>   Talmadge, Marion, and Iris Gilmore
>   > 6579. Emma Edmonds: Nurse and Spy (1970)

These well-written accounts pull no punches about the hardships involved in the lives of these famous spies. The authors maintain an objective view and use only documented quotations from their subjects. This could prove a painless way to teach history to students.

SPORTS HEROES SERIES —Putnam
>   Burchard, Sue, and Marshall Burchard
>   > 6580. Sports Hero: Brooks Robinson (1972)
>   > 6581. Sports Hero: Joe Namath (1971)
>   > 6582. Sports Hero: Johnny Bench (1972)
>   > 6583. Sports Hero: Kareem Abdul-Jabbar, the Story of Lew Alcindor
>   > > (1972)

The first easy-to-read sports series to present biographical information on current sports heroes, with lots of photographs. For grades 2 to 4 and reluctant readers.

SPOTLIGHT ON HISTORY SERIES   —Time-Life
        Freeman, Fred
                6584. Duel of the Ironclads (1969)
        Phelan, Joseph
                6585. The Whale Hunters (1969)
        Sallison, Ken
                6586. When Zeppelins Flew (1969)
        Time-Life, Editors
                6587. The Warrior Knights (1969)
Well-documented and detailed information is presented in these attractive books.
The illustrations—both color and black-and-white—add verve, and the index is
good.

STATES OF THE NATION SERIES   —Coward
        Baker, Betty
                6588. Arizona (1969)
        Bell, Thelma, and Corydon Bell
                6589. North Carolina (1970)
        Coit, Margaret
                6590. Massachusetts (1967)
        Corbett, Scott
                6591. Rhode Island (1969)
        Derleth, August
                6592. Wisconsin (1967)
        Douglas, Emily
                6593. Illinois (1971)
        Edwards, Sally
                6594. South Carolina (1968)
        Frome, Michael
                6595. Virginia (1966)
        Laxalt, Robert
                6596. Nevada (1971)
        Noble, Iris
                6597. Oregon (1966)
        Nolan, Jeanette
                6598. Indiana (1969)
        Nye, Russell
                6599. Michigan (1966)
        Pedersen, Elsa
                6600. Alaska (1968)
        Pellegrini, Angelo
                6601. Washington (1967)
        Renick, Marion
                6602. Ohio (1970)
        Robertson, Keith
                6603. New Jersey (1968)
        Schaefer, Jack
                6604. New Mexico (1967)
        Smith, Mike
                6605. Florida (1970)
        Steele. William O., and Allerton Steele
                6606. Tennessee (1971)
        Sutton, Felix
                6607. West Virginia (1968)

STATES OF THE NATION SERIES —Coward (cont'd)
        Veglahn, Nancy
            6608. South Dakota (1970)
        Yates, Elizabeth
            6609. New Hampshire (1969)
This series will eventually have a volume on each of the United States. The photos
and maps are excellent, and the authors provide a quick reference section in the
back, as well as a pronunciation guide. The books are strong on history and are
intended for an older reader than the Enchantment of America series.

STEP-UP BOOKS SERIES —Random House
        Barrett, Marvin
            6610. Meet Thomas Jefferson (1967)
        Cary, Barbara
            6611. Meet Abraham Lincoln (1965)
        DeKay, James
            6612. Meet Martin Luther King (1969)
        DeKay, Ormonde
            6613. Meet Andrew Jackson (1967)
            6614. Meet Christopher Columbus (1968)
            6615. Meet Theodore Roosevelt (1967)
            6616. The Adventures of Lewis and Clark (1968)
        Dyment, John
            6617. Meet the Men Who Sailed the Seven Seas (1966)
        Heilbroner, Joan
            6618. Meet George Washington (1965)
        Hornblow, Leonora, and Arthur Hornblow
            6619. Animals Do the Strangest Things (1965)
            6620. Birds Do the Strangest Things (1965)
            6621. Fish Do the Strangest Things (1966)
            6622. Insects Do the Strangest Things (1968)
            6623. Reptiles Do the Strangest Things (1970)
        Paris, John
            6624. The First Christmas (1970)
        Payne, Elizabeth
            6625. Meet the North American Indian (1965)
            6626. Meet the Pilgrim Fathers (1966)
        Scarf, Maggi
            6627. Meet Benjamin Franklin (1968)
        Settle, Mary Lee
            6628. The Story of Flight (1967)
        Trow, George
            6629. Meet Robert E. Lee (1969)
        White, Nancy
            6630. Meet John F. Kennedy (1965)
An easy-to-read biography series with large print and plenty of photographs to
attract the younger reader (from age 7 to 11) or reluctant readers.

STERLING NATURE SERIES —Sterling
        Doering, Harald
            6631. A Bee Is Born (1962)
        Doering, Harald, and Jo McCormick
            6632. An Ant Is Born (1964)

STERLING NATURE SERIES —Sterling (cont'd)
>   Eeckhoudt, Jean
>   6633. A Butterfly Is Born (1959)
>   6634. The Secret Life of Small Animals (1972)
>   Guilcher, J. M., and E. Bosiger
>   6635. A Bird Is Born (1963)
>   Guilcher, J. M., and R. H. Noailles
>   6636. A Fern Is Born (1971)
>   6637. A Fruit Is Born (1960)
>   6638. A Tree Grows Up (1972)
>   6639. A Tree Is Born (1960)
>   6640. The Hidden Life of the Flowers (1971)
>   Stepp, Ann
>   6641. A Silkworm Is Born (1972)
>   White, William
>   6642. A Frog Is Born (1972)

From general information on the growth and development of the species, these books proceed to a discussion of the characteristics of individual birds or flowers, etc., in the species. There is no index, but the table of contents is generally clear enough to give reference to specific animals and the photographs are plentiful.

STORY OF BRITAIN SERIES —Coward
>   Hodges, C. Walter
>   6643. Magna Carta (1966)
>   6644. The Norman Conquest (1966)
>   6645. The Puritan Revolution (1972)
>   6646. The Spanish Armada (1968)

A well-known author-illustrator presents small incidents of English history, with bright colorful illustrations. The books should be fine supplemental material to any collection, clarifying the importance of the incidents for readers not well acquainted with English history.

STORY OF SCIENCE SERIES —Harvey
>   Adler, Irving
>   6647. The Story of Light (1971)
>   Arnold, Oren
>   6648. The Story of Cattle Ranching (1968)
>   6649. The Story of Man against Winter (1966)
>   Brown, Stanley, and Barbara Brown
>   6650. The Story of Dinosaurs and the Age of Reptiles (1958)
>   Cahn, William, and Rhoda Cahn
>   6651. The Story of Writing (1963)
>   Elting, Mary, and Michael Folsom
>   6652. The Story of Archaeology in the Americas (1960)
>   Farb, Peter
>   6653. The Story of Butterflies and Other Insects (1959)
>   6654. The Story of Dams (1961)
>   6655. The Story of Life (1962)
>   Johnson, Gaylord
>   6656. The Story of Animals (1965)
>   6657. The Story of Planets, Space and Stars (1959)
>   Martin, Curtis
>   6658. The Story of Shells and Life within Them (1956)

STORY OF SCIENCE SERIES —Harvey (cont'd)
    Matthews, William
        6659. The Story of the Earth (1968)
        6660. The Story of Volcanoes (1969)
    Meadow, Charles
        6661. The Story of Computers (1970)
    Pough, Frederick
        6662. The Story of Gems and Semi-Precious Stones (1967)
    Rappaport, Uriel
        6663. The Story of the Dead Sea Scrolls (1967)
    Rosenfeld, Sam
        6664. The Story of Coins (1968)
    Ruchlis, Hy, and Jack Engelhardt
        6665. The Story of Mathematics (1958)
    Seeman, Bernard
        6666. The Story of Electricity and Magnetism (1967)
        6667. The Story of Rocks and Minerals (1966)
    Simon, Irving
        6668. The Story of Printing (1965)
    Stephens, Peter
        6669. The Story of Fire Fighting (1966)
    Stepp, Ann
        6670. The Story of Radioactivity (1971)
    Wheeler, Ruth
        6671. The Story of the Birds of North America (1965)
These qualified authors present information on how each item or subject originated, how it works, how it had been used in the past and is used today. The illustrations are clear, and the authors provide bibliographies, glossaries, and indices. For ages 10 to 14.

SURVEYOR BOOKS SERIES —Crowell
    Anderson, Poul
        6672. The Infinite Voyage: Man's Future in Space (1969)
    Babern, Edward
        6673. The Varieties of Man (1969)
    Barbour, John
        6674. In the Wake of the Whale (1969)
    Berry, James
        6675. Exploring Crystals (1969)
    Bova, Ben
        6676. In Quest of Quasars (1970)
The first part of each book in this series is an explanation of the principles involved, while the second part presents experiments which prove these principles. Illustrations are clear and the experiments should stimulate interest among teenage readers as it adds to their knowledge.

SYSTEMS OF THE BODY SERIES —Prentice-Hall
    Silverstein, Alvin, and Virginia Silverstein
        6677. Cells: Building Blocks of Life (1969)
        6678. The Circulatory System (1970)
        6679. The Digestive System (1970)
        6680. The Endocrine System (1971)
        6681. The Excretory System (1972)
        6682. The Muscular System (1972)

SYSTEMS OF THE BODY SERIES   —Prentice-Hall (cont'd)
>   6683. The Nervous System (1970)
>   6684. The Reproductive System (1971)
>   6685. The Respiratory System (1969)
>   6686. The Sense Organs (1971)
>   6687. The Skeletal System (1972)
>   6688. The Skin (1972)

Each of the systems of the body is analyzed simply, yet in detail. The illustrations are quite clear, and new terms are not only printed in italics but are provided with pronunciation guides. The books are indexed. Good for use with health and science courses for grades 3 through 6.

TELL ME WHY SERIES   —Grosset
>   Leokum, Arkady
>   6689. Lots More Tell Me Why (1972)
>   6690. More Tell Me Why (1967)
>   6691. Still More Tell Me Why (1968)
>   6692. Tell Me Why (1969)

Subjects from the human body to natural science, from history to arts and crafts are covered in this series. The writing style is lively as well as factual, and the illustrations are not only interesting but informative.

THESE MADE HISTORY SERIES   —Putnam
>   Cooke, David C.
>   6693. Bomber Planes That Made History (1959)
>   6694. Dirigibles That Made History (1962)
>   6695. Fighter Planes That Made History (1958)
>   6696. Flights That Made History (1961)
>   6697. Helicopters That Made History (1963)
>   6698. Inventions That Made History (1969)
>   6699. Racing Cars That Made History (1960)
>   6700. Racing Planes That Made History (1960)
>   6701. Seaplanes That Made History (1963)
>   6702. Transport Planes That Made History (1959)

In format, this series is much like the Colby Books: a full-page photograph alternates with a page of text. However, there are more details in this series than in the Colby Books. No index is provided.

THEY KNEW SERIES   —McGraw-Hill
>   Pine, Tillie, and Joseph Levine
>   6703. The Chinese Knew (1958)
>   6704. The Egyptians Knew (1964)
>   6705. The Eskimos Knew (1962)
>   6706. The Incas Knew (1968)
>   6707. The Mayans Knew (1971)
>   6708. The Pilgrims Knew (1957)

These books are poetically written narratives of scientific innovations of these ancient civilizations. The authors attempt to show what was discovered by these cultures and how it affects us still today. No indexes are provided, and, because of the style of presentation, these books would have only marginal use in school libraries.

THEY LIVED LIKE THIS SERIES —Watts
　　　　Neurath, Marie
　　　　　　6709. They Lived Like This in Ancient Africa (1967)
　　　　　　6710. They Lived Like This in Ancient Britain (1969)
　　　　　　6711. They Lived Like This in Ancient China (1967)
　　　　　　6712. They Lived Like This in Ancient Crete (1965)
　　　　　　6713. They Lived Like This in Ancient Egypt (1965)
　　　　　　6714. They Lived Like This in Ancient Greece (1968)
　　　　　　6715. They Lived Like This in Ancient India (1967)
　　　　　　6716. They Lived Like This in Ancient Mesopotamia (1965)
　　　　　　6717. They Lived Like This in Ancient Palestine (1965)
　　　　　　6718. They Lived Like This in Ancient Persia (1970)
　　　　　　6719. They Lived Like This in Ancient Peru (1967)
　　　　　　6720. They Lived Like This in Ancient Rome (1969)
　　　　　　6721. They Lived Like This in Chaucer's England (1967)
　　　　　　6722. They Lived Like This in Old Japan (1966)
　　　　　　6723. They Lived Like This in Shakespeare's England (1968)
　　　　　　6724. They Lived Like This in the Old Stone Age (1971)
　　　　　　6725. They Lived Like This in the Roman Empire (1970)
　　　　　　6726. They Lived Like This: The Ancient Maya (1966)
　　　　　　6727. They Lived Like This: The Vikings (1971)
　　　　Neurath, Marie, and John Ellis
　　　　　　6728. They Lived Like This in Ancient Mexico (1971)
Simple text and drawings will capture the interest of the beginning and reluctant
readers. There is no index, and the books do not have chapter divisions, which
makes them somewhat difficult to use. For ages 9 to 11.

THINGS TO MAKE AND DO SERIES —World
　　　　Williams, Peter
　　　　　　6729. Making Things Is Fun (1972)
　　　　　　6730. Making Things That Move (1972)
　　　　　　6731. Making Your Own Musical Instruments (1972)
　　　　　　6732. Seasonal Activities (1972)
　　　　　　6733. Using Things around the House (1972)
At the time of printing, this series had not yet appeared for review, so judgment
will be suspended temporarily.

THIRTEEN MOONS SERIES —Crowell
　　　　George, Jean Craighead
　　　　　　6734. Moon of the Alligators (1969)
　　　　　　6735. Moon of the Bears (1967)
　　　　　　6736. Moon of the Chickarees (1968)
　　　　　　6737. Moon of the Deer (1969)
　　　　　　6738. Moon of the Fox Pups (1968)
　　　　　　6739. Moon of the Gray Wolves (1969)
　　　　　　6740. Moon of the Moles (1970)
　　　　　　6741. Moon of the Monarch Butterflies (1968)
　　　　　　6742. Moon of the Mountain Lions (1968)
　　　　　　6743. Moon of the Owls (1967)
　　　　　　6744. Moon of the Salamanders (1967)
　　　　　　6745. Moon of the Wild Pigs (1968)
　　　　　　6746. Moon of the Winter Bird (1969)
The activities of each creature during one night are related in narrative style, with
black-and-white drawings as illustrations. Of marginal use for science courses, but
good for arousing interest.

THIS IS . . . SERIES —Crowell
  Sasek, Miroslav
      6747. This Is Australia (1971)
      6748. This Is Cape Kennedy (1964)
      6749. This Is Edinburgh (1961)
      6750. This Is Greece (1966)
      6751. This Is Hong Kong (1965)
      6752. This Is Ireland (1964)
      6753. This Is Israel (1962)
      6754. This Is London (1959)
      6755. This Is Munich (1961)
      6756. This Is New York (1960)
      6757. This Is Paris (1959)
      6758. This Is Rome (1960)
      6759. This Is San Francisco (1962)
      6760. This Is Texas (1967)
      6761. This Is the United Nations (1968)
      6762. This Is Venice (1961)
      6763. This Is Washington, D.C. (1969)
Colored cartoon-like illustrations of travel around different cities and countries
are the features of these oversized volumes. The series constitutes a picture-book
introduction to some of the famous sites of these places.

THRUSHWOOD BOOKS SERIES —Grosset
  Barrie, James M.
      6764. Peter Pan (1958)
  Bennett, Arnold
      6765. Master Skylark (1924)
  Crane, Stephen
      6766. The Red Badge of Courage (1971)
  Fisher, Dorothy
      6767. Understood Betsy (1917)
  Fox, John, Jr.
      6768. The Little Shepherd of Kingdom Come (1970)
  Gates, Eleanor
      6769. Poor Little Rich Girl (1970)
  Harris, Joel Chandler
      6770. Uncle Remus (1921)
  Kipling, Rudyard
      6771. Captains Courageous (1889)
  Rice, Alice
      6772. Mrs. Wiggs of the Cabbage Patch (1928)
  Salten, Felix
      6773. Bambi (1929)
  Tarkington, Booth
      6774. Penrod (1914)
      6775. Seventeen (1916)
  Webster, Jean
      6776. Daddy Longlegs (1940)
  Wiggin, Kate Douglas
      6777. Rebecca of Sunnybrook Farm (1917)
In some cases, these are the only in-print editions of these books. Although the
print is only medium-sized and the illustrations are not very plentiful, the titles
still remain good additions to a collection.

TOMORROW'S WORLD SERIES —Messner
>   Hey, Nigel
>   6778. How Will We Feed the Hungry Billions? (1971)
>   McLeod, Sterling
>   6779. How Will We Move All the People? Transportation for Tomorrow's
>   World (1971)
>   Michelsohn, David
>   6780. The Oceans in Tomorrow's World (1972)
>   Millard, Reed
>   6781. Clean Air—Clean Water for Tomorrow's World (1971)
>   6782. How Will We Meet the Energy Crisis? (1971)
>   6783. Natural Resources—Will We Have Enough for Tomorrow's
>   World? (1972)

Aimed at grades 5 through 9, this series examines current problems, discusses their implications for the future, and postulates solutions. A timely choice for the collection.

TOWARD FREEDOM SERIES —Garrard
>   McCague, James
>   6784. The Long Bondage (1972)
>   White, Anne Terry
>   6785. Human Cargo: The Story of the Atlantic Slave Trade (1972)
>   6786. North to Liberty: The Story of the Underground Railroad (1972)

An essential choice for black history and American history courses, this series provides information on different aspects of slavery in America.

TRADE ROUTES SERIES —McGraw-Hill
>   Collins, Robert
>   6787. East to Cathay: The Silk Road (1968)
>   Fanning, Leonard
>   6788. Over Mountains, Prairies, and Seas: The Oil Trade (1968)
>   Honig, Donald
>   6789. Frontiers of Fortune: The Fur Trade (1967)
>   Masselman, George
>   6790. The Money Trees: The Spice Trade (1967)
>   Robinson, M. Gregg
>   6791. Rival Cities: Venice and Genoa (1969)

The influence of trading ventures on the rise and fall of nations is the subject of this series. In many cases trade disputes furnished the reasons for wars. Old prints and drawings add interest to the books. An excellent background for social studies and history courses.

TRUE STORY BIOGRAPHIES —Childrens Press
>   Arnold, Richard
>   6792. The True Story of David Livingstone, Explorer (1957)
>   Booth, Arthur
>   6793. The True Story of Queen Victoria, British Monarch (1964)
>   6794. The True Story of Sir Winston Churchill, British Statesman (1964)
>   Corley, Anthony
>   6795. The True Story of Napoleon, Emperor of France (1964)
>   Gibbs, Peter
>   6796. The True Story of Cecil Rhodes in Africa (1964)
>   Holwood, Will
>   6797. The True Story of Captain Scott at the South Pole (1964)

TRUE STORY BIOGRAPHIES —Childrens Press
     6798. The True Story of Sir Francis Drake, Privateer (1964)
Houghton, Richard
     6799. The True Story of Lord Nelson, Naval Hero (1964)
Merrett, John
     6800. The True Story of Albert Schweitzer, Humanitarian (1964)
Oldfield, Ruth
     6801. The True Story of Albert Einstein, Man of Science (1964)
Reidy, John
     6802. The True Story of John Fitzgerald Kennedy (1967)
Reynolds, Reginald
     6803. The True Story of Gandhi, Man of Peace (1964)
Thomas, John
     6804. The True Story of Lawrence of Arabia (1964)
These works investigate not only the life of the subject but also his country.
The large print and simple style make this series a possibility for use in remedial
reading. For grades 4 to 6.

TUNIS, EDWIN —World
     6805. Colonial Craftsmen (1965)
     6806. Colonial Living (1957)
     6807. Frontier Living (1961)
These excellent oversized books depict the way of life of all segments of society,
various trades, and women and children in colonial and frontier America. The
illustrations are outstanding, particularly those of the various implements and
machines of early America.

TWENTIETH CENTURY AMERICAN WRITERS SERIES —Crowell
Fahey, William
     6808. F. Scott Fitzgerald (announced)
Geismar, Maxwell
     6809. Ring Lardner and the Portrait of Folly (1972)
Gurko, Leo
     6810. Ernest Hemingway and the Pursuit of Heroism (1968)
Kuner, M. C.
     6811. Thornton Wilder: The Bright and the Dark (1972)
Leary, Lewis
     6812. William Faulkner (announced)
Lisca, Peter
     6813. John Steinbeck (announced)
The junior high and high school student engaged in research on American writers
will find this series useful. The books present information on the lives of the authors,
their works, and their philosophy and style of writing. Background information is
provided on the historical and social backgrounds of his works, and there are also
comparisons with other authors of the time. A must.

TWO WORLDS SERIES —M. Evans
Elting, Mary
     6814. The Hopi Way (1969)
Elting, Mary, and Robin McKown
     6815. A Mongo Homecoming (1969)
Hsiao, Ellen
     6816. A Chinese Year (1970)

TWO WORLDS SERIES —M. Evans (cont'd)
      Shetty, Sharat
         6817. A Hindu Boyhood (1970)
      Villicana, Eugenio
         6818. Viva Morelia (1971)
The aim of these books is to give readers an insight into present-day anthropology.
The authors investigate the ways of life in various small villages in India, China, and
on an Indian reservation, among other places. The books should supplement social
studies texts and may help sensitize readers to the ways of others. Grades 4 to 6.

UBELL, EARL —Atheneum
         6819. The World of Candle and Color (1969)
         6820. The World of Push and Pull (1964)
         6821. The World of the Living (1965)
The rules and principles surrounding aspects of natural science are examined by
Mr. Ubell, with discussions of the sources of life, color, energy, and light, as well
as of the effects of each of these on our lives. For grades 2 to 4.

UNITED STATES BOOKS —Whitman
      Bailey, Bernardine
         6822. The Picture Book of Alabama (1966)
         6823. The Picture Book of Alaska (1965)
         6824. The Picture Book of Arizona (1957)
         6825. The Picture Book of Arkansas (1957)
         6826. The Picture Book of California (1966)
         6827. The Picture Book of Colorado (1966)
         6828. The Picture Book of Connecticut (1966)
         6829. The Picture Book of Delaware (1966)
         6830. The Picture Book of Florida (1966)
         6831. The Picture Book of Georgia (1966)
         6832. The Picture Book of Hawaii (1960)
         6833. The Picture Book of Idaho (1967)
         6834. The Picture Book of Illinois (1964)
         6835. The Picture Book of Indiana (1966)
         6836. The Picture Book of Iowa (1966)
         6837. The Picture Book of Kansas (1965)
         6838. The Picture Book of Kentucky (1963)
         6839. The Picture Book of Louisiana (1967)
         6840. The Picture Book of Maine (1957)
         6841. The Picture Book of Maryland (1966)
         6842. The Picture Book of Massachusetts (1965)
         6843. The Picture Book of Michigan (1965)
         6844. The Picture Book of Minnesota (1967)
         6845. The Picture Book of Mississippi (1966)
         6846. The Picture Book of Missouri (1966)
         6847. The Picture Book of Montana (1965)
         6848. The Picture Book of Nebraska (1966)
         6849. The Picture Book of Nevada (1965)
         6850. The Picture Book of New Hampshire (1961)
         6851. The Picture Book of New Jersey (1965)
         6852. The Picture Book of New Mexico (1966)
         6853. The Picture Book of New York (1966)
         6854. The Picture Book of North Carolina (1970)
         6855. The Picture Book of North Dakota (1966)

    6856. The Picture Book of Ohio (1967)
    6857. The Picture Book of Oklahoma (1952)
    6858. The Picture Book of Oregon (1954)
    6859. The Picture Book of Our Nation's Capital, Washington, D.C. (1962)
    6860. The Picture Book of Pennsylvania (1966)
    6861. The Picture Book of Rhode Island (1966)
    6862. The Picture Book of South Carolina (1966)
    6863. The Picture Book of South Dakota (1960)
    6864. The Picture Book of Tennessee (1966)
    6865. The Picture Book of Texas (1964)
    6866. The Picture Book of Utah (1957)
    6867. The Picture Book of Vermont (1965)
    6868. The Picture Book of Virginia (1966)
    6869. The Picture Book of Washington (1966)
    6870. The Picture Book of West Virginia (1965)
    6871. The Picture Book of Wisconsin (1964)
    6872. The Picture Book of Wyoming (1966)

Aimed at a much younger age group than the Carpenter books or the States of the Nation series. The treatment here is far less extensive, but the print is small and the vocabulary is not especially simple, so the actual use with younger and reluctant readers is questionable. The drawings are vague at best.

USEFUL ARTS OF MAN SERIES —Putnam
    Hoag, Edwin
       6873. The Roads of Man (1967)
    Janes, E. C.
       6874. The Story of Knives (1968)
    McMillen, Wheeler
       6875. The Green Frontier: The Story of Chemurgy (1969)

These books illustrate the ability of man to adapt in order to make his life productive, meaningful, and comfortable. The books discuss various important breakthroughs in engineering and in the social history of man. Good supplementary material for social studies. A glossary is appended to each volume.

VISION BOOKS —Farrar
    Beebe, Catherine
       6876. St. Dominic and the Rosary (1956)
       6877. St. John Bosco and the Children's Saint Dominic Savio (1955)
    Bishop, Virginia, and Jim Bishop
       6878. Fighting Father Duffy (1956)
    Boesh, Mark
       6879. The Cross in the West (1956)
    Brown, Evelyn
       6880. Edel Quinn (1967)
       6881. Kateri Tekakwitha, Mohawk Maid (1958)
    Clark, Ann Nolan
       6882. Brother Andre of Montreal (1967)
       6883. Father Knio, Priest to the Pimas (1963)
    Connally, Francis X.
       6884. St. Philip of the Joyous Heart (1967)
    Derleth, August
       6885. Columbus and the New World (1957)

VISION BOOKS —Farrar (cont'd)
      6886. St. Ignatius and the Company of Jesus (1956)
DeWohl, Louis
      6887. Pope Pius XII, the World's Shepherd (1961)
      6888. St. Helena and the True Cross (1958)
Diethelm, Walter
      6889. St. Pius X, the Farm Boy Who Became Pope (1956)
Farley, James, and James Koniff
      6890. Governor Al Smith (1959)
Fitzgerald, Ed
      6891. Champions in Sports and Spirit (1956)
      6892. More Champions in Sports and Spirit (1959)
Gardiner, Harold
      6893. Edmund Campion (1957)
Garnett, Emmeline
      6894. Charles de Foucauld: Adventurer of the Desert (1962)
Genevieve, Sister Mary
      6895. Marguerite Bourgeoys: Pioneer Teacher (1963)
Homan, Helen
      6896. St. Anthony and the Christ Child (1958)
      6897. St. Therese and the Roses (1955)
Hubbard, Margaret
      6898. Dear Philippine: The Mission of Mother Duchesne (1965)
      6899. Mother Barat's Vineyard (1962)
      6900. St. Louis and the Last Crusade (1958)
      6901. Vincent de Paul: Saint of Charity (1960)
Hume, Ruth
      6902. Our Lady Came to Fatima (1957)
      6903. St. Margaret Mary: Apostle of the Sacred Heart (1960)
Ince, Elizabeth
      6904. St. Thomas More of London (1957)
Kane, Harnett
      6905. The Ursulines, Nuns of Adventure (1959)
Keyes, Frances Parkinson
      6906. Mother Cabrini, Missionary to the World (1959)
Larnen, Brendan, and Milton Lomask
      6907. St. Thomas Aquinas and the Preaching Beggars (1957)
Lomask, Milton
      6908. The Cure of Ars (1958)
      6909. John Carroll: Bishop and Patriot (1956)
      6910. St. Augustine and His Search for Faith (1957)
      6911. St. Isaac and the Indians (1956)
Lomask, Milton, and Ray Neville
      6912. The Way We Worship (1961)
McCarthy, Helen
      6913. Lydia Longley: The First American Nun (1958)
Moore, John, and Rosemarian Staudacher
      6914. Modern Crusaders (1957)
Nevins, Albert J.
      6915. St. Francis of the Seven Seas (1965)
Pauli, Hertha
      6916. Bernadette and the Lady (1956)
Power-Waters, Alma
      6917. St. Catherine Laboure and the Miraculous Medal (1962)

VISION BOOKS —Farrar (cont'd)
>   6918. Sarah Peter: The Dream and the Harvest (1965)
Reilly, Robert
>   6919. Irish Saints (1964)
Roos, Ann
>   6920. Peter Claver, Saint among Slaves (1965)
Sanderlin, George
>   6921. St. Gregory the Great, Consul of God (1964)
>   6922. St. Jerome and the Bible (1961)
Sheehan, Elizabeth
>   6923. Good Pope John (1966)
>   6924. John Neumann, the Children's Bishop (1965)
Sheehan, Elizabeth, and Arthur Sheehan
>   6925. Rose Hawthorne (1959)
Staudacher, Rosemarian
>   6926. Catholic Campuses (1958)
>   6927. Chaplains in Action (1962)
>   6928. Children Welcome: Villages for Boys and Girls (1963)
>   6929. In American Vineyards (1966)
Thompson, Blanche
>   6930. Peter and Paul: The Rock and the Sword (1964)
>   6931. St. Elizabeth's Three Crowns (1958)
>   6932. St. Francis de Sales (1965)
>   6933. Saints of the Byzantine World (1961)
Windeatt, Mary
>   6934. St. Benedict, Hero of the Hills (1968)

In spite of an excessive use of the narrative style, this series of religious biographies is well done. Ideal for collections in Catholic churches and schools.

VISUAL GEOGRAPHY SERIES —Sterling
Sterling, Editors
>   6935. Afghanistan in Pictures (1971)
>   6936. Alaska in Pictures (1966)
>   6937. Argentina in Pictures (1967)
>   6938. Australia in Pictures (1966)
>   6939. Austria in Pictures (1964)
>   6940. Belgium and Luxembourg in Pictures (1966)
>   6941. Berlin—East and West—in Pictures (1965)
>   6942. Brazil in Pictures (1967)
>   6943. Bulgaria in Pictures (1970)
>   6944. Canada in Pictures (1970)
>   6945. Ceylon in Pictures (1967)
>   6946. Chile in Pictures (1965)
>   6947. Colombia in Pictures (1968)
>   6948. Czechoslovakia in Pictures (1969)
>   6949. Denmark in Pictures (1961)
>   6950. Ecuador in Pictures (1969)
>   6951. Egypt in Pictures (1972)
>   6952. England in Pictures (1965)
>   6953. Ethiopia in Pictures (1969)
>   6954. Fiji in Pictures (1972)
>   6955. Finland in Pictures (1963)
>   6956. France in Pictures (1965)
>   6957. French Canada in Pictures (1961)

6958. Ghana in Pictures (1966)
6959. Guatemala in Pictures (1966)
6960. Guyana in Pictures (1972)
6961. Hawaii in Pictures (1966)
6962. Holland in Pictures (1963)
6963. Honduras in Pictures (1968)
6964. Hong Kong in Pictures (1966)
6965. Hungary in Pictures (1970)
6966. Iceland in Pictures (1969)
6967. India in Pictures (1969)
6968. Indonesia in Pictures (1960)
6969. Iran in Pictures (1968)
6970. Iraq in Pictures (1969)
6971. Ireland in Pictures (1964)
6972. Israel in Pictures (1965)
6973. Italy in Pictures (1966)
6974. Jamaica in Pictures (1967)
6975. Japan in Pictures (1966)
6976. Kenya in Pictures (1969)
6977. Korea in Pictures (1968)
6978. Kuwait in Pictures (1970)
6979. Lebanon in Pictures (1969)
6980. Liberia in Pictures (1971)
6981. Malaysia and Singapore in Pictures (1966)
6982. Mexico in Pictures (1965)
6983. Morocco in Pictures (1967)
6984. New Zealand in Pictures (1964)
6985. Norway in Pictures (1967)
6986. Pakistan in Pictures (1968)
6987. Panama and the Canal Zone in Pictures (1969)
6988. Peru in Pictures (1965)
6989. Poland in Pictures (1969)
6990. Portugal in Pictures (1966)
6991. Puerto Rico in Pictures (1965)
6992. Rumania in Pictures (1970)
6993. Russia in Pictures (1966)
6994. Scotland in Pictures (1964)
6995. South Africa in Pictures (1968)
6996. Spain in Pictures (1964)
6997. Surinam in Pictures (1971)
6998. Sweden in Pictures (1967)
6999. Switzerland in Pictures (1964)
7000. Tahiti and the French Islands in Pictures (1967)
7001. Taiwan in Pictures (1971)
7002. Thailand in Pictures (1963)
7003. The Caribbean in Pictures (1968)
7004. The Islands of the Mediterranean in Pictures (1971)
7005. The Philippines in Pictures (1966)
7006. Tunisia in Pictures (1972)
7007. Turkey in Pictures (1966)
7008. Venezuela in Pictures (1966)
7009. Wales in Pictures (1966)
7010. West Germany in Pictures (1967)

VISUAL GEOGRAPHY SERIES —Sterling (cont'd)
>7011. Yugoslavia in Pictures (1963)
These are photographic accounts of such varied subjects as the land, the history, and the people of each country. Some of the similar series provide better coverage, and these books are not indexed.

VOICES FROM THE NATIONS SERIES —Praeger
>Cormack, Margaret, and Kiki Skagen
>>7012. Voices from India (1972)
>Hunter, Neale, and Deirdre Hunter
>>7013. We the Chinese: Voices from China (1971)
>Maki, John
>>7014. We the Japanese: Voices from Japan (1969)
>Shulman, Colette
>>7015. We the Russians: Voices from Russia (1971)
>Sully, Francois
>>7016. We the Vietnamese: Voices from Vietnam (1971)
>Trager, Helen
>>7017. We the Burmese: Voices from Burma (1969)
There is no series similar to this one. Each book is a collection of stories, news articles, poems, cartoons, and folk tales, both past and present, written by natives of each country. The books provide excellent materials on the views of people in foreign countries about themselves, their way of life, and the world in general. For grades 7 and up.

WALCK FAIRY TALES WITH HISTORICAL NOTES
>Ardizzone, Edward
>>7018. The Babes in the Woods (1972)
>Grimm, Jacob, and Wilhelm Grimm
>>7019. Hansel and Gretel (1971)
>Jacobs, Joseph
>>7020. Jack the Giant Killer (1971)
>Lines, Kathleen
>>7021. Agib and the Honey Cakes (1972)
The annotations to these classics discuss the sources of the stories, the symbolic meanings involved, and references to historical people. Especially good for literature students.

WE-WERE-THERE- SERIES —Grosset
>Appel, Benjamin
>>7022. We Were There at the Battle of Bataan (1967)
>>7023. We Were There at the Klondike Gold Rush (1956)
>>7024. We Were There with Cortes and Montezuma (1959)
>Cousins, Margaret
>>7025. We Were There at the Battle of the Alamo (1958)
>Holt, Stephen
>>7026. We Were There with the California Forty-Niners (1956)
>Kjelgaard, Jim
>>7027. We Were There at the Oklahoma Land Run (1967)
>Knight, Clayton
>>7028. We Were There at the Battle of Britain (1959)
>>7029. We Were There at the Normandy Invasion (1956)
>>7030. We Were There withthe Lafayette Escadrille (1961)

WE-WERE-THERE SERIES   —Grosset   (cont'd)
    Malkus, Alida
        7031. We Were There at the Opening of the Erie Canal (1958)
    Miers, Earl Schenck
        7032. We Were There When Grant Met Lee at Appomattox (1960)
        7033. We Were There When Washington Won at Yorktown (1958)
        7034. We Were There with Lincoln in the White House (1953)
    Shepherd, David
        7035. We Were There at the Battle of the Bulge (1961)
        7036. We Were There at the Driving of the Golden Spike (1960)
    Steele, William O.
        7037. We Were There on the Oregon Trail (1965)
        7038. We Were There with the Pony Express (1956)
    Strong, Charles
        7039. We Were There with Byrd at the South Pole (1956)
    Sutton, Felix
        7040. We Were There at Pearl Harbor (1957)
        7041. We Were There at the Battle of Lexington and Concord (1958)
        7042. We Were There at the First Airplane Flight (1960)
    Taylor, Ross
        7043. We Were There on the Chisholm Trail (1957)
        7044. We Were There on the Santa Fe Trail (1960)
    Vinton, Iris
        7045. We Were There with Jean Lafitte at New Orleans (1957)
    Webb, Robert
        7046. We Were There at the Boston Tea Party (1956)
        7047. We Were There on the "Nautilus" (1961)
        7048. We Were There with Caesar's Legions (1960)
        7049. We Were There with Ethan Allen and the Green Mountain Boys
            (1956)
        7050. We Were There with Florence Nightingale in the Crimea (1968)
        7051. We Were There with Richard the Lionhearted in the Crusades
            (1957)
        7052. We Were There with the Mayflower Pilgrims (1956)
The aim of this series is to include the reader in various expeditions and important
historical incidents. Because of the poor quality of the paper, however, and the use
of fictionalized narratives, the books will not be of much use.

WEART, EDITH —Coward
        7053. The Story of Your Blood (1960)
        7054. The Story of Your Bones (1966)
        7055. The Story of Your Brain and Nerves (1961)
        7056. The Story of Your Glands (1962)
        7057. The Story of Your Respiratory System (1964)
        7058. The Story of Your Skin (1970)
Although not as complete as the Systems of the Body Series , and not as simplified
as the Elgin Books, this series provides very clear drawings and explanations of
the parts of the body. In addition to discussing anatomy, the books also investigate
the jobs performed by different organs, what happens when they are damaged, and
such things as the use of human bones in archaeology. All books have a glossary
and an index.

WEISS, HARVEY —Scott Foresman
>   7059. Ceramics, from Clay to Kiln (1964)
>   7060. Clay, Wood and Wire (1956)
>   7061. Collage and Construction (1970)
>   7062. Paint, Brush and Palette (1966)
>   7063. Paper, Ink and Roller (1958)
>   7064. Pencil, Pen and Brush (1961)
>   7065. Sticks, Spools and Feathers (1962)

Ideas for practice and projects are included in this well-prepared series, as well as information on the basics of each craft. Illustrations include examples of the craft under discussion as handled by famous artists—e.g., sculpture by Rodin to show the human figure. For grades 4 to 7.

WHAT A . . . DOES SERIES —John Day
>   Hoopes, Roy
>   7066. What a Pro Football Coach Does (1972)
>   7067. What a State Governor Does (1972)
>   7068. What a United States Congressman Does (1971)
>   7069. What a United States Senator Does (1970)
>   7070. What the President Does All Day (1962)
>   Hoopes, Roy, and Spencer Hoopes
>   7071. What a Baseball Manager Does All Day (1970)

There are many photographs in this series, but the information provided is only of temporary use; for example, the lists of current congressmen are out of date in a few years. The books follow one or more famous people through the day to show the various kinds of jobs that they do, but the personalities under examination may no longer be in the public eye within a few years. In general, the books do not provide enough basic information, aside from the picture story, to make a lasting contribution to a collection.

WHAT DOES A . . . DO SERIES —Dodd
>   Busby, Edith
>   7072. What Does a Librarian Do? (1963)
>   Compton, Grant
>   7073. What Does a Coast Guardsman Do? (1968)
>   7074. What Does a Veterinarian Do? (1964)
>   Hyde, Wayne
>   7075. What Does a Cowboy Do? (1963)
>   7076. What Does a Diver Do? (1961)
>   7077. What Does a Forest Ranger Do? (1964)
>   7078. What Does a Parachutist Do? (1960)
>   7079. What Does a Secret Service Agent Do? (1962)
>   Lavine, David
>   7080. What Does a Congressman Do? (1965)
>   7081. What Does a Senator Do? (1967)
>   Lavine, David, and Ira Mandelbaum
>   7082. What Does a Peace Corps Volunteer Do? (1964)
>   Mergandahl, T. E., and Sheldon Ramsdell
>   7083. What Does a Photographer Do? (1965)
>   Pierson, Sherleigh
>   7084. What Does a U.N. Soldier Do? (1964)
>   Ray, E. Ray
>   7085. What Does an Airline Crew Do? (1968)

WHAT DOES A . . . DO SERIES —Dodd (cont'd)
>   Waters, John
>   7086. What Does an Oceanographer Do? (1970)
>   Wells, Robert
>   7087. What Does a Test Pilot Do? (1969)
>   7088. What Does an Astronaut Do? (1961)
>   Wells, Robert, and Harvey Lippman
>   7089. What Does a Jet Pilot Do? (1959)

Far more informative than the previous series, this one provides detailed but readable explanations of the jobs under examination. Photographs are used for illustration, but there is no index.

WHO, WHEN, WHERE SERIES —Grosset
>   Chambers, Bradford
>   7090. The Aztecs of Mexico (1965)
>   Hanff, Helene
>   7091. Early Settlers in America (1965)
>   7092. Good Neighbors (1966)
>   7093. Religious Freedom, the American Story (1966)
>   Holland, Ruth
>   7094. From Famine to Fame: The Irish in America (1967)
>   7095. German Immigrants in America (1968)
>   7096. Oriental Immigrants in America (1969)
>   7097. Vikings of the West: Scandinavian Immigrants in America (1968)
>   Lindsay, Sally
>   7098. This Is Canada (1965)
>   Parish, Peggy
>   7099. The Story of Grains (1965)
>   Sutton, Felix
>   7100. Discoverers of America (1965)
>   Webb, Robert
>   7101. The Magic of Steel and Oil (1965)

Historical aspects of our continent, with an emphasis on immigrants to the United States, provide the basis for this series. Each book presents a history of the emigration of a national group: why they emigrated, what they found in this country, and what they contributed to it. For grades 6 to 8.

WILDERNESS MYSTERIES SERIES —Harvey
>   Folsom, Franklin
>   7102. The Diamond Cave Mystery (1962)
>   7103. The Forest Fire Mystery (1963)
>   7104. The Hidden Ruin Mystery (1966)
>   7105. The Indian Mummy Mystery (1962)
>   7106. The Mystery at Payrock Canyon (1962)
>   7107. The Mystery at Rustler's Fort (1960)
>   7108. The Sand Dune Pony Mystery (1960)

There is a strong emphasis on the importance of wildlife conservation in this series, and a great deal of scientific information is conveyed painlessly. It strongly resembles Mary Adrian's series, but this one is aimed at older readers from grades 5 to 7.

WILLOW LEAF LIBRARY —Scribner
>   Barrie, James M.
>   7109. Peter Pan (1950)

WILLOW LEAF LIBRARY —Scribner (cont'd)
    Burnett, Frances Hodgson
        7110. Little Lord Fauntleroy (1955)
    Dodge, Mary Mapes
        7111. Hans Brinker (1958)
    Grahame, Kenneth
        7112. The Wind in the Willows (1953)
    James, Will
        7113. Smoky (1926)
    Pyle, Howard
        7114. Otto of the Silver Hand (1954)
        7115. Some Merry Adventures of Robin Hood (1954)
    Stockton, Frank
        7116. Ting-a-Ling Tales (1955)
The format of this series of classics and semi-classics is smaller than that of the
Scribner Illustrated Classics series. The black-and-white illustrations are good, the
print is readable, and some of the choices are unusual. A good selection for libraries.

WOMEN OF AMERICA SERIES —Crowell
    Block, Irvin
        7117. Neighbor to the World: The Story of Lillian Wald (1969)
    False, Maxine
        7118. Beauty Millionaire: The Life of Helena Rubinstein (1972)
    Fleming, Alice .
        7119. Ida Tarbell: First of the Muckrakers (1971)
        7120. The Senator from Maine: Margaret Chase Smith (1969)
    Gruber, Ruth
        7121. Felisa Rincon de Gautier: Mayor of San Juan (1972)
    Lader, Lawrence, and Milton Meltzer
        7122. Margaret Sanger: Pioneer of Birth Control (1969)
    McKown, Robin
        7123. The World of Mary Cassatt (1972)
    Meltzer, Milton
        7124. Tongue of Flame: The Life of Lydia Maria Child (1965)
    Moore, Carmen
        7125. Somebody's Angel Child: The Story of Bessie Smith (1970)
    Phelan, Mary Kay
        7126. Probing the Unknown: The Story of Doctor Frances Sabin (1969)
    Shulman, Alix
        7127. To the Barricades: The Anarchist Life of Emma Goldman (1971)
    Sterling, Phillip
        7128. Sea and Earth: The Life of Rachel Carson (1970)
    Stiller, Richard
        7129. Commune on the Frontier: The Story of Frances Wright (1972)
        7130. Queen of Populists: The Story of Mary Elizabeth Lease (1970)
    Werstein, Irving
        7131. Labor's Defiant Lady: The Story of Mother Jones (1969)
In this excellent series on outstanding women, the facts are presented objectively
and there is much emphasis on the difficulties surmounted by these women in
their struggle for acceptance. For ages 10 to 14.

WONDER OF WONDERS: MAN —Garrard
    White, Anne Terry, and Gerald Lietz
        7132. Built to Survive (1966)

WONDER OF WONDERS: MAN —Garrard (cont'd)
       7133. Man the Thinker (1967)
       7134. Secrets of the Heart and Blood (1965)
       7135. When Hunger Calls (1966)
       7136. Windows on the World (1965)
The physiology, psychology, and sociology of man are examined in this series. Areas covered include man's origin, development, and physical, mental, and social structure. Good supplemental material for both science and social studies. For grades 4 through 7.

WONDERFUL WORLD OF . . . SERIES —Doubleday
     Britten, Benjamin, and Imogen Holst
       7137. The Wonderful World of Music (1968)
     Calder, Ritchie
       7138. The Wonderful World of Medicine (1969)
     Fisher, James
       7139. The Wonderful World of Air (1968)
       7140. The Wonderful World of the Sea (1971)
     Haskell, Arnold
       7141. The Wonderful World of Dance (1970)
     Hogben, Lancelot
       7142. The Wonderful World of Communication (1969)
       7143. The Wonderful World of Energy (1965)
       7144. The Wonderful World of Mathematics (1968)
     Huxley, Julian
       7145. The Wonderful World of Life (1969)
     Jackson, David
       7146. The Wonderful World of Engineering (1970)
     Jessup, Ronald
       7147. The Wonderful World of Archaeology (1956)
     Lee, Laurie, and David Lambert
       7148. The Wonderful World of Transportation (1970)
     Orr, John
       7149. The Wonderful World of Food (1958)
     Priestley, J. B.
       7150. The Wonderful World of the Theatre (1969)
     Swinton, William
       7151. The Wonderful World of Prehistoric Animals (1970)
Each of these slender, oversized volumes presents a brief survey of a given subject. Although the text is not detailed, the books are indexed and the color illustrations add to the appeal. The authors are well-known authorities in their fields.

WONDERLAND BOOKS SERIES —Dodd
     Bailey, Bernardine
       7152. Denmark: Wonderland of Work and Play (1966)
     Braithwaite, Max
       7153. Canada: Wonderland of Surprises (1967)
     Brooks, Patricia
       7154. The Philippines: Wonderland of Many Cultures (1968)
     Daly, Maureen
       7155. Spain: Wonderland of Contrasts (1965)
     Erdoes, Richard
       7156. Ireland: Bewitching Wonderland (1968)

WONDERLAND BOOKS SERIES   —Dodd (cont'd)
    Foster, John
        7157. The Mississippi: Ever-Changing Wonderland (1970)
    Helm, Thomas
        7158. The Everglades: Florida Wonderland (1963)
    Johnson, Dorothy
        7159. Greece: Wonderland of the Past and Present (1964)
    Knowlton, William
        7160. Hawaii: Pacific Wonderland (1962)
    Wakeman, Norman
        7161. Southwest Desert Wonderland (1965)
    Wilson, Barbara Ker
        7162. Australia: Wonderland Down Under (1969)
Excellent coverage of all aspects of each country or section of a country. In addition to the usual topics of geography, history, and religion, such subjects as art, poetry, and sports, among others, are also examined. The books are indexed. A good addition to any collection.

WONDERS BOOKS —Dodd
    Antoine, Tex
        7163. Wonders of Weather (1962)
    Arnov, Boris, and Helen Mindlin
        7164. Wonders of the Deep Sea (1959)
    Ault, Phillip
        7165. Wonders of the Mosquito World (1970)
    Berrill, Jacquelyn
        7166. Wonders of Animal Migration (1964)
        7167. Wonders of Animal Nurseries (1968)
        7168. Wonders of Fields and Ponds at Night (1962)
        7169. Wonders of the Antarctic (1958)
        7170. Wonders of the Arctic (1959)
        7171. Wonders of the Monkey World (1967)
        7172. Wonders of the Seashore (1961)
        7173. Wonders of the Woods and Deserts at Night (1963)
        7174. Wonders of the World of Wolves (1970)
    Cosgrove, Margaret
        7175. Wonders inside You (1955)
        7176. Wonders of the Tree World (1953)
        7177. Wonders of Your Senses (1958)
        7178. Wonders under a Microscope (1959)
    Cruickshank, Helen
        7179. Wonders of the Bird World (1956)
        7180. Wonders of the Reptile World (1959)
    Eifert, Virginia
        7181. Wonders of Rivers (1962)
    Feravolo, Rocco
        7182. Wonders beyond the Solar System (1968)
        7183. Wonders of Gravity (1965)
        7184. Wonders of Mathematics (1963)
        7185. Wonders of Sound (1962)
    Heuer, Kenneth
        7186. Wonders of the Heavens (1954)
    Jacobson, Morris, and William Emerson
        7187. Wonders of Shells (1971)

WONDERS BOOKS —Dodd (cont'd)
    Lavine, Sigmund
        7188. Wonders of Animal Architecture (1964)
        7189. Wonders of Animal Disguises (1962)
        7190. Wonders of the Anthill (1960)
        7191. Wonders of the Bat World (1969)
        7192. Wonders of the Beetle World (1962)
        7193. Wonders of the Fly World (1970)
        7194. Wonders of the Hawk World (1972)
        7195. Wonders of the Hive (1958)
        7196. Wonders of the Owl World (1971)
        7197. Wonders of the Spider World (1966)
        7198. Wonders of the Wasp's Nest (1961)
        7199. Wonders of the World of Horses (1972)
    Lieberg, Owen
        7200. Wonders of Heat and Light (1966)
        7201. Wonders of Magnets and Magnetism (1967)
        7202. Wonders of Measurement (1972)
    McFall, Christie
        7203. Wonders of Sand (1966)
        7204. Wonders of Snow and Ice (1964)
        7205. Wonders of Stones (1970)
    Matthews, William
        7206. Wonders of Fossils (1968)
        7207. Wonders of the Dinosaur World (1963)
    Pearl, Richard
        7208. Wonders of Gems (1963)
        7209. Wonders of Rocks and Minerals (1961)
    Simon, Hilda
        7210. Wonders of Hummingbirds (1964)
        7211. Wonders of the Butterfly World (1963)
    Thomson, Peter
        7212. Wonders of Our National Parks (1961)
    Wakeman, Norman
        7213. Wonders of the World between the Tides (1961)
    Wells, Robert
        7214. Wonders of Flight (1962)
Each of these wonders of the scientific or animal world is explained in detail.
The photographs are good, and the text is clearly presented. The authors are all
well qualified to write on their subjects.

WONDERS OF SCIENCE SERIES —Putnam
    Butterworth, William
        7215. Wonders of Astronomy (1964)
        7216. Wonders of Rockets and Missiles (1964)
    Chester, Michael, and William Nephew
        7217. Wonders of Robots (1962)
    Collins, Henry
        7218. Wonders of Geology (1962)
    Martin, Christopher
        7219. Wonders of Prehistoric Man (1964)
Explanations in these books are clear and simple, with each chapter presenting a
specific interest area. New terms are printed in italics, with pronunciation indicated.
Photographs and an index aid the reader.

WORKING WITH SCIENCE SERIES —Whitman
      Catherall, E. A., and P. N. Holt
           7220. Working with Light (1964)
           7221. Working with Magnets (1962)
           7222. Working with Sounds (1964)
           7223. Working with Water (1964)
The principles of each of the scientific phenomena are briefly outlined in these books. The remainder of each book is devoted to simple experiments designed for the younger and less able reader. For grades 4 and up.

WORLD BACKGROUND BOOKS SERIES —Scribner
      Gatti, Ellen, and Attilio Gatti
           7224. The New Africa (1960)
      Leib, Amos
           7225. The Many Islands of Polynesia (1972)
      Meeker, Oden
           7226. Israel Reborn (1964)
      Miller, Helen H.
           7227. Greece (1965)
      Stefansson, Evelyn
           7228. Here Is Alaska (1959)
           7229. Here is the Far North (1957)
      Weston, Christine
           7230. Afghanistan (1962)
The material covered in this series is about the same as that covered in other series on foreign lands, but it is in depth. There are no chapter headings at all, so the reader must depend on the index to find specific subject areas. For grades 5 to 9.

WORLD CRISIS SERIES —Putnam
      Baum, Patricia
           7231. Cuba: Continuing Crisis (1971)
      Garden, Nancy
           7232. Berlin: City Split in Two (1971)
      McKown, Robin
           7233. Crisis in South Africa (1972)
The emphasis of these books is not on the history, geography, or life style of the countries, but rather on their political problems—the history behind them, current problems today, and their effect on the world in general. The authors provide a bibliography and an index. Excellent material for history, civics, and social studies groups in grades 6 and up.

WORLD EXPLORER BOOKS —Garrard
      Berry, Erick
           7234. Fridtjof Nansen (1969)
      Blassingame, Wyatt
           7235. Ponce de Leon (1965)
      Bristow, Jean
           7236. A World Explorer: Robert Falcon Scott (1972)
      DeLeeuw, Adele
           7237. James Cook (1963)
           7238. Roald Amundsen (1965)
           7239. Sir Walter Raleigh (1964)

WORLD EXPLORER BOOKS —Garrard (cont'd)
    Foster, John
      7240. Sir Francis Drake (1967)
    Graff, Stewart
      7241. Hernando Cortez (1970)
    Graves, Charles
      7242. Henry Morton Stanley (1967)
      7243. John Smith (1965)
      7244. Marco Polo (1963)
    Groh, Lynn
      7245. Ferdinand Magellan (1963)
    Kaufman, Mervyn
      7246. Christopher Columbus (1962)
    Knoop, Faith
      7247. Amerigo Vespucci (1966)
      7248. Francisco Coronado (1967)
      7249. Sir Edmund Hillary (1970)
      7250. Vasco Nunez de Balboa (1969)
    Montgomery, Elizabeth
      7251. Hernando de Soto (1964)
      7252. Lewis and Clark (1966)
In addition to information about the lives of these famous explorers, this series also presents much information about the country and time of their origins and explorations. Particular attention is paid to the political environment surrounding each expedition.

WORLD FOCUS SERIES —Watts
    Foster, John
      7253. The Hundred Days (1972)
    Goldston, Robert
      7254. The Fall of the Winter Palace, November 1917 (1971)
      7255. The Long March, 1934-35 (1971)
    Grant, Neil
      7256. Munich, 1938 (1971)
    Liversidge, Douglas
      7257. The Day the Bastille Fell (1972)
    Poole, Peter
      7258. Dien Bien Phu, 1954 (1972)
    Werstein, Irving
      7259. The Boxer Rebellion (1971)
This series focuses on important events in history. In some cases, unfortunately, the authors tend to over-simplify the reasons behind complex issues. On the other hand, these subjects are not covered in other series. For grades 6 through 9.

WORLD NEIGHBORS SERIES —John Day
    Caldwell, John, and Elsie Caldwell
      7260. Our Neighbors in Africa (1968)
      7261. Our Neighbors in Australia and New Zealand (1967)
      7262. Our Neighbors in Brazil (1962)
      7263. Our Neighbors in Central America (1967)
      7264. Our Neighbors in India (1960)
      7265. Our Neighbors in Japan (1960)
      7266. Our Neighbors in Korea (1961)
      7267. Our Neighbors in Peru (1962)

WORLD NEIGHBORS SERIES —John Day (cont'd)
      7268. Our Neighbors in Thailand (1968)
      7269. Our Neighbors in the Philippines (1961)
Intended for younger readers than Caldwell's Let's Visit series or his Enchantment
of Central and South America series. The text of this one uses simple, short sentences, with many photographs. There is a pronunciation guide for each volume, but
the books are not indexed. This series should serve as a good introduction for
grades 3 to 6.

WORLD NEIGHBORS SERIES —Nelson
    Bailey, Bernardine
      7270. Austria and Switzerland (1968)
    Bryce, L. Winifred
      7271. India: Land of Rivers (1966)
    Cartey, Wilfred
      7272. The West Indies: Islands in the Sun (1967)
    Credle, Ellis
      7273. Mexico: Land of Hidden Treasure (1967)
    Dobrin, Arnold
      7274. Ireland: The Edge of Europe (1971)
      7275. Italy: Modern Renaissance (1968)
    Edelman, Lily
      7276. Israel: New People in an Old Land (1968)
    Edwards, Harvey
      7277. Scandinavia: The Challenge of Welfare (1968)
    Folsom, Franklin
      7278. The Soviet Union: A View from Within (1965)
    Harrington, Lyn
      7279. Australia and New Zealand (1969)
      7280. China and the Chinese (1966)
      7281. Greece and the Greeks (1968)
    Henderson, Larry
      7282. Egypt and the Sudan: Countries of the Nile (1971)
      7283. The Arab Middle East (1970)
      7284. Vietnam and the Countries of the Mekong (1972)
    Homze, Alma, and Edward Homze
      7285. Germany: A Divided Nation (1970)
    Hornos, Axel
      7286. Argentina, Paraguay, and Uruguay (1969)
    Kirk, Ruth
      7287. Japan: Crossroads of East and West (1966)
    Kittler, Glenn
      7288. Central Africa: The New World of Tomorrow (1971)
      7289. Mediterranean Africa: Four Muslim Nations (1969)
    Leitch, Adelaide
      7290. Canada: Young Giant of the North (1968)
    Madden, Daniel
      7291. Spain and Portugal: Iberian Portrait (1969)
    May, Charles
      7292. Central America: Lands Seeking Unity (1966)
      7293. Chile: Progress on Trial (1968)
      7294. Peru, Bolivia, Ecuador: The Indian Andes (1969)
    Moore, Marian
      7295. The United Kingdom: A New Britain (1966)

WORLD NEIGHBORS SERIES —Nelson (cont'd)
    Perl, Lila
        7296. Yugoslavia, Romania, Bulgaria (1970)
    Seegers, Kathleen
        7297. Brazil: Awakening Giant (1967)
    Spring, Norma
        7298. Alaska: Pioneer State (1967)
    Volgyes, Ivan, and Mary Volgyes
        7299. Czechoslovakia, Hungary, Poland (1970)
    Wolseley, Roland
        7300. The Low Countries: Gateways to Europe (1969)
Aside from the standard information on geography, culture, history, and economy in each country, the authors of this excellent series cover semi-obscure topics such as the role of women in the society. Occasionally there are also short interviews with natives of each country. The authors are highly qualified to write on their topics. For grades 5 through 9.

WORLD OF . . . SERIES —Scribner
    Foster, Genevieve
        7301. Abraham Lincoln's World (1944)
        7302. Augustus Caesar's World (1949)
        7303. George Washington's World (1941)
        7304. The World of Captain John Smith (1959)
        7305. The World of Columbus and Sons (1955)
In addition to relating the accomplishments of the biographees, the books of this series also place them in perspective with the lives of other famous people and events of the same era. There are some illustrations, and the books are indexed.

WORLD OF NATURE SERIES —World
    DeMichele, Vincenzo
        7306. The World of Minerals (1972)
    Pinna, Giovanni
        7307. The Dawn of Life (1972)
    Torchio, Menico
        7308. Life beneath the Sea (1972)
    Tosco, Uberto
        7309. The Flowering Wilderness (1972)
The newest addition to a large group of natural history series. The volumes of this series have not yet become available for examination, so judgment must be suspended.

WORLD OF ROMANCE SERIES —World
    Hilton, Margery
        7310. A Man without Mercy (1972)
    Mather, Anne
        7311. Moon Witch (1972)
    Winspear, Violet
        7312. Tawny Sands (1972)
This upcoming series is obviously aimed at teenagers and less selective adults. Because the volumes have not yet appeared, it is difficult to judge their quality. However, considering their settings in far-away Arabia and their basic Gothic plot outlines, they would seem to be a less-than-substantial choice.

WORLD OF THE FUTURE SERIES —M. Evans
Hellman, Hal
7313. Biology in the World of the Future (1971)
7314. Communications in the World of the Future (1969)
7315. Feeding the World of the Future (1972)
7316. The City in the World of the Future (1970)
7317. Transportation in the World of the Future (1968)

Based on proposed programs for the future necessitated by today's problems and developments, this excellent series is a must for all those concerned with what the future will hold. Each volume has a bibliography, an index, and many photographs and illustrations.

WORLD PIONEERS SERIES —Putnam
Kerby, Elizabeth
7318. The Conquistadors (1969)
McKown, Robin
7319. Marie Curie (1971)
Wise, Winifred
7320. Benjamin Franklin (1970)

The biographees are people who have had an important impact on the world. The texts are interesting, and no attempts have been made to fictionalize. For grades 4 to 6.

WORLD WILDLIFE CONSERVATION SERIES —Hastings House
Arundel, Jocelyn
7321. The Wildlife of Africa (1965)
Mason, George
7322. The Wildlife of North America (1966)
Shuttlesworth, Dorothy
7323. The Wildlife of Australia and New Zealand (1967)
7324. The Wildlife of South America (1966)

Information on the history of plants and animals of each geographical area is combined with data on land formations. Emphasis is on the importance of wildlife conservation, with a listing of threatened species in each country and a list of parks and preserves. Each book provides a glossary, a bibliography, and an index.

WORLD WE ARE MAKING SERIES —Coward
Chadwick, Lee
7325. Seeds of Plenty: Agriculture in the Scientific Age (1969)
Jenkins, Alan
7326. The Golden Band: Holland's Fight against the Sea (1958)
Pownall, Eve
7327. The Thirsty Land: Harnessing Australia's Water Resources (1968)

The technological developments that are shaping our present-day world are the subjects of these books. The series discusses past techniques in agriculture and industry, examines present techniques, and delves into future possibilities.

YARDSTICKS OF SCIENCE —Coward
Evans, David
7328. Electric Charge (1971)
Fishlock, David
7329. Taking the Temperature (1968)
Johnson, Timothy
7330. River of Time (1968)

YARDSTICKS OF SCIENCE —Coward (cont'd)
      Roberson, Paul
          7331. Feeling the Pressure (1970)
      Wheeler, Fred
          7332. The Sizes of Things (1968)
Intended for the mature reader, this series covers its subjects thoroughly and intensively. The small print should not prove discouraging because the subjects covered (fossils, Carbon 14 dating, and the mystery of Stonehenge) are fascinating. For grades 6 through 9.

YEAR OF . . . SERIES —Scribner
      Foster, Genevieve
          7333. The Year of Columbus 1492 (1969)
          7334. The Year of Independence 1776 (1970)
          7335. The Year of Lincoln 1861 (1970)
          7336. The Year of the Pilgrims 1620 (1969)
As in her World of . . . series, Ms. Foster here discusses the people and events of an important year in world history. There are many drawings, but they are generally vague; portraits and paintings drawn from the period under discussion would have been a better choice as illustrations.

YOU CAN WORK . . . SERIES —John Day
      Dietz, Betty
          7337. You Can Work in Education Services (1968)
          7338. You Can Work in Health Services (1968)
          7339. You Can Work in the Communications Industry (1970)
          7340. You Can Work in the Transportation Industry (1969)
One of the few career series aimed at the younger reader. Ms. Dietz covers all types of jobs available in each area, and discusses future possibilities. Many photographs add to the appeal. Each book has a chapter on suggestions for preparing for future jobs and interviews.

YOUNG . . . SERIES —Dodd
      Buell, Hal
          7341. Young Japan (1961)
      Harris, Leon
          7342. Young France (1964)
          7343. Young Peru (1969)
      Manning, Jack
          7344. Young Brazil (1970)
          7345. Young Ireland (1965)
          7346. Young Puerto Rico (1962)
          7347. Young Spain (1963)
      Norris, Marianna
          7348. Young Germany (1969)
          7349. Young Hungary (1970)
          7350. Young India (1966)
          7351. Young Turkey (1964)
      Pinney, Roy
          7352. Young Israel (1963)
      Vandivurt, Rita
          7353. Young Russia (1960)
Yet another series focusing on the life of children in foreign countries, with the usual

YOUNG . . . SERIES —Dodd (cont'd)
format: many photographs and only a short paragraph of explanation. May have some appeal to the reluctant reader. For grades 4 to 6.

YOUNG ARCHAEOLOGISTS SERIES —Putnam
 Anthony, Ilid
  7354. Roman London (1972)
 Hassall, Mark
  7355. The Romans (1972)
 Jones, John E.
  7356. The Greeks (1971)
 Millard, Anne
  7357. Egypt (1971)
In addition to providing information on what life was like for various ancient civilizations, this series also explains how an archaeological dig is carried out. The authors also discuss important finds that led to further knowledge of each culture. The photographs and illustrations are excellent.

YOUNG CHAMPIONS SERIES —McGraw-Hill
 Antonacci, Robert, and Jene Barr
  7358. Baseball for Young Champions (1956)
  7359. Basketball for Young Champions (1960)
  7360. Football for Young Champions (1958)
  7361. Physical Fitness for Young Champions (1962)
These books provide rules, tips on playing and equipment, diagrams of plays and player positions, and suggestions as to how to keep score and team records. The physical fitness book is particularly well done.

YOUNG HISTORIAN SERIES —John Day
 Addison, John
  7362. Ancient Africa (1971)
 Bull, George
  7363. The Renaissance (1968)
 Burland, Cottie
  7364. The Ancient Maya (1967)
  7365. The Aztecs (1961)
 Colloms, Brenda
  7366. Israel (1971)
 Cowie, Leonard
  7367. The Reformation (1967)
 Fisher, John
  7368. Latin America: From Conquest to Independence (1972)
 Green, Roger Lancelyn
  7369. Ancient Egypt (1964)
  7370. Ancient Greece (1970)
 Hollings, Jill
  7371. African Nationalism (1972)
 Kidder, J. E.
  7372. Ancient Japan (1965)
 Kochan, Lionel
  7373. The Russian Revolution (1970)
 Little, Tom
  7374. The Arab World in the Twentieth Century (1972)

YOUNG HISTORIAN SERIES —John Day (cont'd)
    Mellersh, H. E. L.
      7375. Imperial Rome (1964)
    Pike, E. Royston
      7376. Ancient India (1961)
      7377. Ancient Persia (1961)
      7378. Republican Rome (1966)
    Powell, Brian
      7379. Modern Japan (1969)
    Proctor, George
      7380. Ancient Scandinavia (1965)
    Rooke, Patrick
      7381. The Industrial Revolution (1972)
    Spencer, Cornelia
      7382. Ancient China (1965)
      7383. Modern China (1969)
    Talbot-Rice, Tamara
      7384. Byzantium (1970)
    Wilkins, Frances
      7385. Ancient Crete (1966)
    Wren, Melvin
      7386. Ancient Russia (1965)
Intended for older readers, this series features subject headings in the margin for easy student use. All books contain excellent photographs, bibliographies, and indices. The treatment of each period of time is quite extensive. For grades 7 through 12.

YOUNG NATURALIST SERIES —Macmillan
    Hylander, Clarence
      7387. Animals in Armor (1967)
      7388. Animals in Fur (1956)
      7389. Feathers and Flight (1967)
      7390. Fishes and Their Ways (1964)
      7391. Flowers of Field and Forest (1962)
      7392. Insects on Parade (1967)
      7393. Sea and Shore (1950)
These books provide an introduction to each life science with much interesting information. All books have photographs, and all are indexed. For grades 7 to 9.

YOUNG PEOPLE AND . . . SERIES —John Day
    Cain, Dr. Arthur
      7394. Young People and Crime (1968)
      7395. Young People and Drinking (1963)
      7396. Young People and Drugs (1969)
      7397. Young People and Education (1972)
      7398. Young People and Neurosis (1970)
      7399. Young People and Parents (1971)
      7400. Young People and Religion (1970)
      7401. Young People and Revolution (1970)
      7402. Young People and Sex (1967)
      7403. Young People and Smoking (1965)
      7404. Young People and Work (1971)
    Purdy, Ken
      7405. Young People and Driving (1967)

YOUNG PEOPLE AND . . . SERIES —John Day (cont'd)
Here is a must: a series which deals honestly with all the current problems facing
young people. The authors present the pros and cons of each controversial subject,
and the end of each book is devoted to a symposium of young people discussing
the subject. The authors also provide the addresses of various groups to contact in
relation to each problem. There is no index, but bibliographies are provided.

YOUNG READER'S GUIDE TO MUSIC SERIES —Walck
        Appleby, William, and Frederick Fowler
            7406. The Nutcracker and Swan Lake (1968)
            7407. The Sleeping Beauty and the Firebird (1965)
        Crozier, Eric
            7408. The Magic Flute (1965)
            7409. The Mastersingers of Nuremberg (1964)
        Gibson, Enid
            7410. The Golden Cockerel (1963)
        Gough, Catherine
            7411. Boyhoods of Great Composers, Book I (1965)
            7412. Boyhoods of Great Composers, Book II (1965)
        Hosier, John
            7413. The Sorcerer's Apprentice (1961)
        Hurd, Michael
            7414. Sailors' Songs and Shanties (1965)
            7415. Soldiers' Songs and Marches (1966)
        Young, Patricia
            7416. Great Performers (1967)
This series is intended for older readers than the Opera Stories Series. The author
provides plot outlines, illustrated by black-and-white line drawings. After the plot
description, the authors discuss the music in each work—what its characteristics
are and why it is important. For grades 5 to 9.

YOUNG SCIENTIST . . . SERIES —McGraw-Hill
        Barr, George
            7417. Entertaining with Number Tricks (1971)
            7418. Fun and Tricks for Young Scientists (1968)
            7419. More Research Ideas for Young Scientists (1961)
            7420. Research Adventures for Young Scientists (1964)
            7421. Research Ideas for Young Scientists (1958)
            7422. Show Time for Young Scientists (1965)
            7423. Young Scientist and Sports (1962)
            7424. Young Scientist and the Dentist (1970)
            7425. Young Scientist and the Doctor (1969)
            7426. Young Scientist and the Fire Department (1966)
            7427. Young Scientist and the Police Department (1967)
            7428. Young Scientist Looks at Skyscrapers (1963)
            7429. Young Scientist Takes a Ride (1960)
            7430. Young Scientist Takes a Walk (1959)
Experiments that are easy to understand and easy to try are the basis for these
books. The principles underlying each experiment are clearly explained, and the
illustrations are to the point. For grades 4 through 8.

YOUNG SCIENTISTS SERIES —Putnam
        Coats, Norman
            7431. Energy and Power (1968)

YOUNG SCIENTISTS SERIES —Putnam (cont'd)
    Shepherd, Walter
       7432. Geophysics (1970)
    Udall, D. H.
       7433. The Story of Life (1969)
As an up-to-date, comprehensive introduction to science, this series is more detailed than most introductory texts. The authors provide glossaries, indices, and many tables, diagrams, and photographs. It should benefit readers from grades 5 to 9.

YOUNG TEENS SERIES —McGraw-Hill
    Beery, Mary
       7434. Manners Made Easy (1966)
       7435. Young Teens and Money (1971)
       7436. Young Teens Away from Home (1970)
       7437. Young Teens Plan Dates and Proms (1969)
       7438. Young Teens Talk It Over (1957)
Intended to help the teenager with his social and public life. Unfortunately, the author often seems preachy or goody-goody, and almost always out of touch with the thinking of young people today. The Young People and . . . Series is far more useful.

ZENITH BOOKS —Doubleday
    Bambara, Toni
       7439. Tales and Stories for Black Folks (1971)
    Bearden, Romare, and Harry Henderson
       7440. Six Black Masters of American Art (1972)
    Childress, Alice
       7441. Black Scenes (1971)
    Chu, Daniel
       7442. The Glorious Age in Africa (1965)
       7443. Passage to the Golden Gate (1967)
    Davidson, Basil
       7444. A Guide to African History (1971)
    Dobler, Lavinia
       7445. Great Rulers of the African Past (1965)
       7446. Pioneers and Patriots (1965)
    Henri, Florette
       7447. Bitter Victory (1970)
    Kgotsitsile, Keorapetse
       7448. The World Is Here (1972)
    McCarthy, Agnes
       7449. Worth Fighting For (1965)
    Meltzer, Milton
       7450. Time of Trial, Time of Hope (1966)
    Sterling, Dorothy
       7451. Lift Every Voice (1965)
This series emphasizes important incidents and outstanding people in the Afro-American past. The books, which will be good background material for black history courses, are available in both hardbound and paperback editions.

AUTHOR INDEX

Hammond, Winifred, 3470-73
Hammontree, M., 2106-2109
Hancock, Ralph, 5505
Hand, Jack, 6048-49
Hanff, Helene, 2769, 7091-93
Hannahs, Herb, 5652
Hano, Arnold, 6110-12
Hansen, Harry, 4241
Hapgood, Charles, 6372
Harbison, David, 3169
Hardin, Gail, 5653
Harding, James, 3757
Harley, Ruth, 2110
Harlow, Alvin, 5120-24
Harmer, Mabel, 1450
Harrington, Lyn, 7279-81
Harris, Joanna, 4492
Harris, Joel Chandler, 6770
Harris, Leon, 7342-43
Harris, Miles, 2026, 3619
Harrison, Brenda, 5909
Harrison, C. W., 3134-35, 3252-
  53, 6279-81
Harrison, George, 3254-56
Harrison, Hal, 4786
Hart, Roger, 2899-2901
Hartman, Louis, 3826
Harvey, Fran, 6405
Harvey, Lois, 4809
Harvey, Tad, 3926
Haskell, Arnold, 7141
Hassall, Mark, 7355
Hastings, Evelyn, 1451-52
Hatch, Alden, 5125
Hatch, John, 2514
Haughey, Betty, 1716
Hausman, Ethel, 1801-1802
Hausman, Leon, 1803, 6068
Haverstock, Nathan, 2027
Havighurst, W., 2477, 4242
Haviland, V., 3119-33
Hawes, Gene, 1986
Hawkes, Jacquette, 3841
Hawkinson, John, 2444-48
Hawthorne, N., 2322-23
Haycraft, Howard, 5126
Hayden, Robert, 2605
Hayes, Florence, 3566-67
Hays, Wilma P., 2478-80, 5856
Heal, Edith, 5277-78
Healy, Frederick, 3148
Heavlin, Jay, 2770
Hebb, David, 1606
Hefflinger, Jane, 1453-58
Hegan, Jim, 6113
Heide, Florence, 5828-29
Heilbroner, Joan, 6618
Heimann, Susan, 3229

Heindl, L. A., 5568
Helfman, Harry, 3776-79
Heller, Deane, 5127
Hellman, Hal, 4082, 5974,
  6437, 7313-17
Helm, Everett, 3758
Helm, Thomas, 7158
Henderson, Dion, 3790
Henderson, Harry, 7440
Henderson, Larry, 7282-84
Henderson, Nancy, 2919
Hendrickson, W., 6406-6408
Henri, Florette, 7447
Henry, Joanne, 2111-15
Henry, Marguerite, 1550
Henry, Will, 4243
Heppell, Muriel, 5476
Herbert, Fred, 1987
Herbert, Wally, 4071
Herold, Christopher, 3842
Herrick, Robert, 2591
Herron, Edward, 5128
Herschler, Mildred, 4597
Heuer, Kenneth, 7186
Heuman, William, 3037-40
Hey, Nigel, 6778
Hibbert, Christopher, 3843
Hickok, Lorena, 6518-20
Hiebert, Roslyn, 3413
Hiebert, Ray, 3413
Higdon, Hal, 5712-13, 6114
Higgins, Helen, 2116-20
Higgins, Marguerite, 5604
Highland, Harold, 3878-81
Hill, Elizabeth, 5714-15
Hill, Frank, 3041, 5579
Hill, Ralph, 4244-45
Hillcourt, William, 6069-70
Hills, George, 5477
Hillyer, Clement, 4246
Hilton, Margery, 7310
Hilton, Suzanne, 3918-19
Hinckley, Helen, 5910
Hindley, Geoffrey, 6084-85
Hinds, Shirley, 3191
Hine, Al, 1692
Hinkelbein, Albert, 4072
Hinkle, Thomas, 3096
Hirschfeld, Burt, 5279, 5352-58
Hirshberg, Al, 6115-20
Hitte, Kathryn, 3568
Hoag, Edwin, 6873
Hoard, Edison, 5654
Hoare, Robert, 4114-15
Hodges, C. W., 6643-46
Hodgson, Dennis, 2270
Hoehling, Mary, 5129-31, 5359
Hoff, Rhona, 1505-1509

Hoffman, Ann, 3938
Hoffman, E. T. A., 2624-25
Hoffman, Elaine, 1453-58
Hoffman, Gail, 5911
Hoffman, Melita, 5549
Hoffmeister, Donald, 3709, 3716
Hofsinde, Robert, 3979-91
Hogben, L., 7142-44
Hogeboom, Amy, 3811-21
Hoke, Helen, 3257-63
Hoke, John, 3264-68
Holbrook, Sabra, 2028-29,
  3620-21
Holbrook, Stewart, 4247-51
Holcomb, Hank, 3791
Holden, Raymond, 1551-52
Holland, John, 2606
Holland, Marion, 3569
Holland, Ruth, 7094-97
Hollander, Zander, 4368, 6028,
  6050-51
Hollings, Jill, 7371
Holst, Imogen, 3759-60, 7137
Holt, John, 4780
Holt, P. N., 7220-23
Holt, Stephen, 3097-99, 7026
Holwood, Will, 6797-98
Homan, Helen, 6896-97
Homze, Alma, 7285
Homze, Edward, 7285
Honig, Donald, 6789
Hood, Flora, 4810
Hood, Thomas, 2573
Hoopes, Roy, 7066-71
Hoopes, Spencer, 7071
Hope, Anthony, 2324-25, 4847
Hope-Simpson, Jacynth, 2009
Hopf, Alice, 1892
Hopman, Harry, 1874
Hoppe, H., 4674
Horizon, Editors, 3844
Hornblow, A., 4252, 6619-23
Hornblow, L., 4252, 6619-23
Hornby, John, 1973
Horner, Dave, 1875
Hornos, Axel, 7286
Hosier, John, 7413
Hoss, Norman, 3882
Hough, Henry, 5605-5606
Hough, Richard, 3739-40
Houghton, Richard, 6799
Howard, Cecil, 3845
Howard, James, 6521-24
Howard, R., 3269, 4598, 5744,
  6036-37
Howe, Jane, 2121
Howell, F. Clark, 4645
Hoyt, Edwin, 5132

233

AUTHOR INDEX

Martin, Patricia M., 6489-99
Martin, Ralph, 5172
Martin, Robert, 4978
Martin, Rupert, 4390, 4837-38
Martinez, Jose, 5660
Marx, Richard, 1469
Masin, Herman, 4017-19
Mason, F. V., 3444, 4287, 5611-12
Mason, George, 3116, 4980-92, 7322
Mason, Herbert, 3086
Mason, Miriam, 2131 37, 5863
Masselman, George, 6790
Mather, Anne, 7311
Mathews, F. S., 6072-73
Matley, Ian, 2515
Matschat, Cecile, 1760
Matthew, Eunice, 5930
Matthews, Hubert, 5508
Matthews, W., 2997
Matthews, William, 3322-23, 6659-60, 7206-7207
Matthewson, Robert, 3897-98
Maurois, Andre, 5613
Mauthner, Maria, 2274
Mawson, Colin, 5995
Maxwell-Lefroy, C., 4391-92
May, Charles, 1761, 4035-36, 7292-94
May, J., 1825-26, 3000-3002
Mayall, Margaret, 1804, 6074
Mayall, R., 1804, 6074
Mayer, A. I., 2494
Mayer, Jane, 4288-89
Mayne, William, 2005-2006
Mays, Willie, 6138
Maziere, Francis, 2290-91
Mead, Margaret, 6202
Mead, W. R., 5486
Meadow, Charles, 6661
Meadowcroft, Enid, 3962, 4056, 6533-37
Mearns, Martha, 2628-29
Mee, Charles, 3853
Meek, S. P., 3075, 3107
Meeker, Oden, 7226
Meeks, Esther, 3003-3005
Megan, Vincent, 6088
Meier, Don, 4975
Melegari, Vezio, 4074
Melendez, Carmello, 5661

Melin, Grace, 2138-40
Mellersh, H. E. L., 4630, 5739, 7375
Mellor, William, 4725
Meltzer, Milton, 3171, 7122, 7124, 7450
Melville, Herman, 4924
Mercer, Charles, 3854, 4496-97
Mergandahl, T. E., 7083
Meriel-Bussy, Y., 4681
Merlen, Johanna, 5040
Merrett, John, 6800
Merrick, Helen, 3324-25
Merriman, Henry, 2340
Meyer, Howard, 1608
Meyer, Jerome, 3975-78
Mezey, Robert, 5879
Michelsohn, David, 6780
Middleton, Drew, 5509
Miers, Earl S., 1697, 2481, 3899, 6203, 6538, 7032-34
Milgrim, Shirley, 4603
Millard, Anne, 7357
Millard, Reed, 6781-83
Millender, D., 2141-43
Miller, Donald, 5809
Miller, Helen H., 7227
Miller Helen M., 1717-18, 6339
Miller, Jack, 2930
Miller, Luree, 2275
Miller, Natalie, 2495-2500
Miller, Richard, 3326
Miller, Shane, 4633-34
Milne, Lorus, 4091
Milne, Margery, 4091
Mindlin, Helen, 7164
Miner, Lewis, 5173-74
Miner, Roy, 6075
Mintoyne, Grace, 2519-25
Mirsky, Jeannette, 1951
Mirsky, Reba, 5425-29
Mitchell, Arthur, 6413
Mitchell, Barbara, 4498
Mitchell, Minnie, 2144
Mitchell, Robert, 3720
Modak, Manorama, 5931
Moffett, Martha, 3327
Moffett, Robert, 3327
Molesworth, Mrs., 2341-42, 4857
Monsell, Helen, 2145-52

Montgomery, Elizabeth, 1746-50, 2013, 2536-37, 2698, 3963-65, 4057-58, 7251-52
Montgomery, R., 3108-3109
Montross, Lynn, 5614-15
Moody, Ralph, 5616-17
Mooney, Booth, 4604-4608
Moore, Carmen, 7125
Moore, Clyde, 2153-55
Moore, James, 4591
Moore, John, 6914
Moore, Lamont, 3328
Moore, Lilian, 3547-49, 3587-88
Moore, Marian, 7295
Moore, Patrick, 3154, 3457, 4119, 4726
Moore, Ruth, 4647
Moore, William, 3974-95
Moos, Malcolm, 4290
Morenus, Richard, 4291
Moreton, John, 5678
Morey, Joan, 4528
Morgan, Ann, 6076
Morgan, Elizabeth, 5996
Morgan, Julie, 6561-64
Morris, Desmond, 5521-22
Morris, Loverne, 4818
Morris, Richard, 3329-32
Morrow, Betty, 3826
Morsbach, Mabel, 2610
Morse, Flo, 2611
Moscow, Henry, 1698, 3855
Moseley, E., 2699, 5252-54
Mudra, Marie, 5175
Muir, Jean, 6340
Muller-Guggenbuhl, F., 5445
Mulock, Dinah Maria, 6186
Munson, Amelia, 2585
Munz, Peter, 2931
Myers, Elisabeth, 2156-61, 2538-39, 5176-78
Myers, Hortense, 2162-65

Naamani, Israel, 2516
Naden, C., 3333-35, 3425-27
Nano, Frederic, 5932
Nathan, Adele, 4292-93
Nathan, Dorothy, 4294
Nathan, Raymond, 1995
National College of Education, 6353

237

AUTHOR INDEX

Pike, E. R., 5740, 7376-78
Pilkington, Roger, 1975
Pimlott, Douglas, 4794
Pine, Tillie, 1576-87, 6703-6708
Pinkerton, Robert, 4302
Pinna, Giovanni, 7307
Pinney, Roy, 7352
Pittenger, W. Norman, 4037-38
Place, Marian, 1699, 2177, 2612, 2708, 3343, 4303, 4500, 5716, 5866, 6449
Plamenatz, John, 4164
Platt, Rutherford, 1700
Plotz, Helen, 2587-88, 5880
Podendorf, Illa, 6357-58
Poe, Edgar Allan, 2346, 2583, 3509, 4926
Polatnick, Florence, 5219
Polgreen, Cathleen, 3589
Polgreen, John, 3589
Polking, Kirk, 1961-62, 4501-4503
Pond, Seymour, 4304
Poole, Frederick, 3344-46
Poole, Gray, 3590
Poole, Lynn, 2980-81, 3590
Poole, Peter, 7258
Popescu, Julian, 4594
Porter, George, 4790
Porter, Jane, 6473
Posell, Elsa, 1808
Pough, Frederick, 1563, 6662
Pounds, Norman, 5464
Powell, Brian, 7379
Powell, Lawrence, 2589
Powell, William, 3446, 3797
Power-Waters, A., 6917-18
Powers, David, 3347-48
Powers, Richard, 4635
Powers, Wm., 1727-28, 3797
Pownall, Eve, 7327
Pratt, Fletcher, 1564, 4305
Preston, Edna, 1829
Preston, Edward, 2783
Price, Christine, 6022-25
Price, Olive, 6543-44
Priddy, Frances, 2784
Priestley, J. B., 7150
Priolo, Joan, 4684
Proctor, George, 7380
Prodanovic, Nada, 5449

Prolman, Marilyn, 2501-2504
Proudfit, Isabel, 5220-22
Prytz, Ulla, 4694
Purcell, H. D., 5490
Purdy, Claire, 5223-27
Purdy, Ken, 7405
Purton, R. W., 3804-3805
Putnam, Peter, 1952
Pyle, Howard, 3510-11, 4862, 7114-15

Quennell, C. II. B., 2939-41
Quennell, Marjorie, 2939-41
Quigley, Lillian, 5510
Quilici, Folco, 4076
Quinn, Vernon, 5816-22

Raboff, Ernest, 1763-74
Rachlis, Eugene, 1701, 4306-4307
Radford, Ruby, 2490
Radlauer, Ruth, 1472-73
Ramsdell, Sheldon, 7083
Randal, Judith, 1565
Randall, Betty, 5359
Randall, Ruth, 6206-6210
Ransome-Wallis, P., 4121
Rappaport, Uriel, 6663
Raskin, Edith, 2982
Raspe, R. E., 2347
Rausen, Ruth, 2590
Rawlings, Marjorie K., 6474
Ray, E. Ray, 7085
Razzell, Arthur, 2989-94
Reader, W. J., 2908
Reck, Alma, 1474
Redford, Lora, 3648-49
Reed, H. Clay, 3447
Reeder, Red, 2638-39, 2709, 3538, 4308-4309
Rees, John, 4165
Reeve, Christopher, 5738
Reeves, James, 5450
Regli, Adolph, 5228
Reid, George K., 3711
Reid, Keith, 5542
Reidy, John, 5777-83, 6802
Reilly, Robert, 6919
Reines, Bernard, 5741
Reinfeld, Fred, 1609

Reisdorf, Patricia, 4504
Reit, Seymour, 1610
Renault, Mary, 1953
Renick, Marion, 6602
Rennert, Vincent, 1611
Reynolds, Quentin, 4310-15
Reynolds, Reginald, 6803
Reynolds, Robert, 1702
Rhodes, C. O., 4530
Rhodes, Frank, 3722
Rice, Alice, 6772
Rice, Tamara, 2942
Rich, Louise, 3349-53, 3428
Richards, K., 2505-2507, 5777-94
Richards, N., 2998
Richards, Norman, 2508-2512
Rickett, Harold, 6077
Riesenberg, Felix, 4316-17
Rikhoff, Jean, 1719
Rink, Paul, 1720, 5229, 5362-64
Ripley, Elizabeth, 6283-99
Ripley, Sheldon, 5867-68
Ritchie, Carson, 4685
Ritchie, P., 5511
Robbin, Irving, 3903-3908
Roberson, Paul, 3155-56, 7331
Roberts, Eric, 2613
Roberts, Hortense, 1475
Roberts, John, 3354, 5365
Robertson, Keith, 6603
Robins, Eric, 3650
Robinson, Bill, 1880
Robinson, Charles, 3355-58
Robinson, Emmett, 5663
Robinson, Jackie, 1954
Robinson, Louis, 2785
Robinson, M. Gregg, 6791
Robinson, Mabel, 4318
Robinson, Ray, 4703, 6147-51
Robinson, W. W., 4173
Robottom, John, 5435-36, 6090
Rockwell, Anne, 6330-32
Rogers, James, 5717
Roland, A., 5512
Roland, Albert, 1612
Rollins, C., 3056-57
Rollins, Frances, 3651-52
Romeika, William, 1866
Ronan, Colin, 3459, 5524, 5543

239

AUTHOR INDEX

AUTHOR INDEX

244

TITLE INDEX

TITLE INDEX

TITLE INDEX

TITLE INDEX

TITLE INDEX

TITLE INDEX

Lou Gehrig: boy of the sand lots, 2225
Lou Gehrig: iron man of baseball, 1743
Louis Armstrong, 5779
Louis Armstrong: young music maker, 2142
Louis XIV of France, 4044
Louis Pasteur, 5146
Louisa Alcott, 2232
Louisa May Alcott, 5624
Louisa May Alcott: author of "Little Women," 2529
Louisa May Alcott: her life, 5752
Louisiana, 2839
Louisiana Purchase, 4335
Love and marriage, 2594
Love for three oranges, 5678
Loving, 1852
Low countries, 7300
Lucretia Mott: foe of slavery, 2676
Lucretia Mott: girl of old Nantucket, 2076
Lumberjacks of the North Woods, 3966
Luna, 4878
Luther Burbank: boy wizard, 2081
Luther Burbank: partner of nature, 2677
Luther Burbank: plant magician, 5042
Lydia Longley, 6913
Lyndon Baines Johnson, 6501

Machines, 1837, 3976, 6254
Machines at work, 1784
Mackenzie, 6311
Macrame, 4683
Mad Anthony Wayne, 4749
Madame Secretary, 5177
Made in . . . ancient Egypt, 6022; ancient Greece, 6023; Canada, 4938; China, 4942; Iceland, 4939; India, 4943; Italy, 4945; Japan, 4944; Mexico, 4941; Poland, 4940; Thailand, 4937; the Middle Ages, 6024; the Renaissance, 6025
Magic flute, 5680, 7408
Magic mixtures, 5961
Magic of steel and oil, 7101
Magic of words, 5960
Magna Carta, 6643

Magna Charta, 4216
Magnets, 1838, 6255
Magnets and how to use them, 1581
Magnificent barb, 3091
Magnificent house of man alone, 1655
Mail riders, 3483
Maine, 2840
Majola, a Zulu boy, 5692
Major Andre, 6577
Major: the story of a black bear, 4879
Make your own elegant jewelry, 4660
Makima of the rain forest, 6014
Making of a rookie, 6056
Making of an Afro-American, 5798
Making . . . our government work, 2047; paper flowers, 4691; pictures move, 3777; shell flowers, 4665; things is fun, 6729; things that move, 6730; your own musical instruments, 6731
Malaysia, 5475
Malaysia and Singapore in pictures, 6981
Malcolm X, 2545
Male reproductive system, 4029
Mama Hattie's girl, 4444
Mammals, 3716, 4642
Mammals and how they live, 3582, 4897
Man . . . against storm, 2026; alive, 5563; and his body, 5540; and insects, 5541; and woman, 3002; earth and change, 5574; in space, 4108; in the making, 6436; nature and history, 5544; of steel, 5026; probes the universe, 5543; the thinker, 7133; who changed China, 4197; who transformed the world, 5065; who wouldn't give up; 5251; with a microscope, 5171; without mercy, 7310
Manners made easy, 7434
Man's impact on nature, 5539
Manuela lives in Portugal, 2269
Many islands of Polynesia, 7225
Many worlds of Benjamin Franklin, 1686
Many worlds of Herbert Hoover, 5244

Marc Chagall, 1767
Marco Polo, 5139, 7244
Marco Polo's adventures in China, 3857
Marconi, 5060
Marcus and Narcissa Whitman, 2708
Margaret Sanger, 7122
Marguerite Bourgeoys, 6895
Maria and Ramon, a girl and boy of Puerto Rico, 6348
Maria Mitchell: girl astronomer, 2140
Maria Mitchell: stargazer, 2712
Maria Tallchief, 2562
Maria Tallchief: American ballerina, 2530
Marian Anderson, 2563
Marie Antoinette, 4266, 5143
Marie Curie, 7319
Marie Curie: pioneer of the atomic age, 5737
Marie Curie: woman of genius, 2531
Mark Twain, 1605, 4045, 6488
Mark Twain and the river, 5620
Mark Twain: boy of old Missouri, 2135
Mark Twain: his life, 5753
Marquette and Joliet, 4602
Marquis de Lafayette, 4200
Marriage, 1853
Mars, 1810
Mars: planet No. 4, 2955
Martha Berry, 2559
Martha Washington, 2233
Martin Luther, 4231
Martin Luther: leader of the Reformation, 5733
Martin Luther King, 4722
Martin Luther King: fighter for freedom, 2783
Martin Luther King, Jr.: boy with a dream, 2143
Martin Luther King, Jr.: man of peace, 1751
Marvelous mammals, 5983
Mary McLeod Bethune, 2082
Mary Mapes Dodge, 2136
Mary, Queen of Scots, 4240
Mary Todd Lincoln, 2252
Maryland, 2841
Maryland Colony, 3444
Mary's star, 2478
Masai, herders of East Africa, 1913
Masers and lasers, 4086
Masks, 4654

TITLE INDEX

New Jersey colony, 3441
New Mexico, 2852, 6604
New sound, 5720
New ways in math, 5977
New world of . . . aluminum,
5587; banking, 5584; commu-
nications, 5585; computers,
5580; construction engineer-
ing, 5586; copper, 5588;
fabrics, 5576; food, 5581;
helicopters, 5575; iron and
steel, 5589; paper, 5577;
petroleum, 5582; plastics,
5583; rubber, 5578; the atom,
5590; wood, 5579
New Year's day, 3824
New York, 2853
New York colony, 3445
New York: the story of the
world's most exciting city,
4360
New Zealand, 5491, 5507
New Zealand in pictures, 6984
Nicaragua, 2895
Niger, 6324
Nigeria, 5487
Nigeria: republic of a hundred
kings, 4769
Night people, 2415
Nika Illahee, 4823
Nikolai lives in Moscow, 2271
Nile: lifeline of Egypt, 6327
Nile: the story of pharoahs,
farmers and explorers, 6305
Nine makes a team, 5839
Nine planets, 2959
1918: decision in the West,
5390; gamble for victory, 3734;
the German offensive, 5391
1914: the battles in the East,
5392; the battles in the West,
5393
1968, year of crisis, 5345
Nineteenth century art, 2646
No hablo ingles, 5668
No room for a dog, 3569
Noah Webster: boy of words,
2118
Noah Webster: father of the
dictionary, 5220
Noble experiment, 1920-33,
3405
Nobody promised me, 5659
Nobody stops Cushing, 4714
Non-flowering plants, 3724
Noriko, girl of Japan, 2285
Norman Conquest, 6644

North American Air Defense
Command, 2416
North American bighorn sheep,
6021
North Carolina, 2854, 6589
North Carolina colony, 3446
North Dakota, 2855
North Pole, 2791
North to liberty, 6786
Northmen, 4948
Norway in pictures, 6985
Numbers old and new, 6256
Numerals, 6257
Nuoolari and the Alfa Romeo,
2053
Nurse around the world, 5191
Nutcracker, 2625
Nutcracker and Swan Lake, 7406

O. Henry, 5207
Oak and ivy, 5796
Oceanographers in action, 6380
Oceanography lab, 6455
Oceans, 6258
Oceans and continents in
motion, 4087
Oceans in tomorrow's world,
6780
Octopus, 4626
Odysseus comes home from
the sea, 2569
Of beasts, birds, and man, 5458
Off-loom weaving, 4659
Ohio, 2856, 6602
Oil, 6282
Ojibway, 4814
Oklahoma, 2857
Old Ben Franklin's Philadelphia,
3963
Old-fashioned girl, 6172
Old Ironsides, the fighting
"Constitution," 4241
Old Rosie and the horse nobody
understood, 3548
Old Rough and Ready, 5258
Old Stormalong, 1640
Old World stories, 2736
Oliver Cromwell, 5156
Oliver Hazard Perry, 2130
Oliver Wendell Holmes, Jr.,
2101
Olympic games, 4069
Olympic thrills, 5303
Omar Nelson Bradley, 2639
On guard, 4773
On my own, 5644

On the banks of the . . . Delaware,
4964; Hudson, 4965
On the job training and where to
get it, 5282
On the mound, 3538
One day in . . . ancient Rome,
5638; Aztec Mexico, 5639;
Elizabethan England, 5640
101 science experiments, 6358
Opossum, 4880
Oregon, 2858, 6597
Organization of American
states, 2027
Oriental immigrants in
America, 7096
Origins of . . . language, 6440;
World War I, 6062; World
War II, 6063
Osceola: Seminole war chief,
4052
Osceola: young Seminole
Indian, 2085
Otto of the silver hand, 4862,
7114
Otus, 4881
Our earth, 6449
Our independence and the
Constitution, 4227
Our Lady came to Fatima, 6902
Our living world, 3149
Our national heritage, 5625
Our neighbors in . . . Africa,
7260; Australia and New
Zealand, 7261; Brazil, 7262;
Central America, 7263; India,
7264; Japan, 7265; Korea,
7266; Peru, 7267; Thailand,
7268; the Philippines, 7269
Our space age . . . army, 2417;
jets, 2418; navy, 2419
Our threatened wildlife, 5571
Our tiny servants, 5984
Our wonderful eyes, 2979
Our wonderful wayside, 2446
Our world: Bulgaria, 5700;
. . . France, 5702; Mexico,
5703; the taming of Israel's
Negev, 5701
Ouray the Arrow, 5055
Out of the sun, 5705
Outlaw Red, 3068
Over mountains, prairies, and
seas, 6788
Over the Mormon Trail, 3475
Overdrive, 5721

268

TITLE INDEX

TITLE INDEX

274

TITLE INDEX

276